RETRIEVAL &
Ressourc
IN CATHOLIC THOUGHT

MW00616209

The middle years of this century marked a particularly intense time of crisis and change in European society. During this period (1930-1950), a broad intellectual and spiritual movement arose within the European Catholic community, largely in response to the secularism that lay at the core of the crisis. The movement drew inspiration from earlier theologians and philosophers such as Möhler, Newman, Gardeil, Rousselot, and Blondel, as well as from men of letters like Charles Péguy and Paul Claudel.

The group of academic theologians included in the movement extended into Belgium and Germany, in the work of men like Emile Mersch, Dom Odo Casel, Romano Guardini, and Karl Adam. But above all the theological activity during this period centered in France. Led principally by the Jesuits at Fourviére and the Dominicans at Le Saulchoir, the French revival included many of the greatest names in twentieth-century Catholic thought: Henri de Lubac, Jean Daniélou, Yves Congar, Marie-Dominique Chenu, Louis Bouyer, and, in association, Hans Urs von Balthasar.

It is not true — as subsequent folklore has it — that those theologians represented any sort of self-conscious "school": indeed, the differences among them, for example, between Fourviére and Saulchoir, were important. At the same time, most of them were united in the double conviction that theology had to speak to the present situation, and that the condition for doing so faithfully lay in a recovery of the Church's past. In other words, they saw clearly that the first step in what later came to be known as *aggiornamento* had to be *ressourcement* — a rediscovery of the riches of the whole of the Church's two-thousand-year tradition. According to de Lubac, for example, all of his own works as well as the entire *Sources chrétiennes* collection are based on the presupposition that "the renewal of Christian vitality is linked at least partially to a renewed exploration of the periods and of the works where the Christian tradition is expressed with particular intensity."

In sum, for the *ressourcement* theologians theology involved a "return to the sources" of Christian faith, for the purpose of drawing out the meaning and significance of these sources for the critical questions of our time. What these theologians sought was a spiritual and intellectual communion with Christianity in its most vital moments as transmitted to us in its classic texts, a communion that would nourish, invigorate, and rejuvenate twentieth-century Catholicism.

The *ressourcement* movement bore great fruit in the documents of the Second Vatican Council and has deeply influenced the work of Pope John Paul II.

The present series is rooted in this twentieth-century renewal of theology. The series thus understands *ressourcement* as revitalization: a return to the sources, for the purpose of developing a theology that will truly meet the challenges of our time. Some of the features of the series, then, will be a return to classical (patristic-mediaeval) sources and a dialogue with twentieth-century Western culture, particularly in terms of problems associated with the Enlightenment, modernity, and liberalism.

The series will publish out-of-print or as yet untranslated studies by earlier authors associated with the *ressourcement* movement. The series also plans to publish works by contemporary authors sharing in the aim and spirit of this earlier movement. This will include any works in theology, philosophy, history, literature, and the arts that give renewed expression to Catholic sensibility.

The editor of the Ressourcement series, David L. Schindler, is Gagnon Professor of Fundamental Theology and dean at the John Paul II Institute in Washington, D.C., and editor of the North American edition of *Communio: International Catholic Review,* a federation of journals in thirteen countries founded in Europe in 1972 by Hans Urs von Balthasar, Jean Daniélou, Henri de Lubac, Joseph Ratzinger, and others.

RETRIEVAL & RENEWAL

IN CATHOLIC THOUGHT

Volumes available

Madeleine Delbrêl

WE, THE ORDINARY
PEOPLE OF THE STREETS

MADELEINE DELBRÊL

Translated by

David Louis Schindler, Jr.,
and Charles F. Mann

WILLIAM B. EERDMANS PUBLISHING COMPANY
GRAND RAPIDS, MICHIGAN / CAMBRIDGE, U.K.

First published 1966 in French under the title
Nous autres, gens des rues
by Editions du Seuil.

English translation © 2000 Wm. B. Eerdmans Publishing Co.
All rights reserved.
No part of this publication may be reproduced, stored in a retrieval system, or
transmitted, in any form or by any means, electronic, mechanical, photocopying,
recording or otherwise, without the prior permission of the publisher.

Published 2000 by
Wm. B. Eerdmans Publishing Co.
255 Jefferson Ave. S.E., Grand Rapids, Michigan 49503 /
P.O. Box 163, Cambridge CB3 9PU U.K.

Library of Congress Cataloging-in-Publication Data

ISBN 978-0-8028-4696-9

www.eerdmans.com

Contents

vii

CONTENTS

PREFACE TO THE ENGLISH EDITION OF
Nous autres, gens des rues

Fr. Jacques Loew's magnificent introduction to the life and work of Madeleine Delbrêl requires the addition of only a few words for an American audience. Born in southwestern France in 1904, Madeleine lived until after the beginning of the Second Vatican Council and through the pontificate of John XXIII (whom she greatly loved), dying at her desk on October 13, 1964. The American with whom Madeleine invites obvious comparison is her contemporary, Dorothy Day. Despite the inevitable differences of cultural-historical circumstance, these two remarkable women shared a radical life of witnessing to the Gospel at the heart of the world. The radical life they shared began for both in atheism, and was spent in missionary activity to and among those suffering injustice—or indeed suffering in any way. It was a life marked for both by the spirit of Thérèse of Lisieux.[1]

"*We, the Ordinary People of the Streets*": the words express the core of Madeleine's vision:

> These are the people who have an ordinary job, an ordinary household, or an ordinary celibacy. People with ordinary sicknesses, and ordinary

---

1. See Peter Casarella, "Sisters in Doing the Truth: Dorothy Day and St. Thérèse of Lisieux," *Communio* 24 (Fall 1997): 468-498; cf. also Jim Allaire, "Thérèse of Lisieux Inspired Dorothy Day," *Houston Catholic Worker,* May-June 1996, p. 6; Frederick Christian Bauerschmidt, "The Politics of the Little Way: Dorothy Day Reads Thérèse of Lisieux," in *American Catholic Traditions: Resources for Renewal,* ed. Sandra Yocum Mize (Maryknoll, NY: Orbis, 1997), pp. 77-95.

times of grieving. People with an ordinary house, and ordinary clothes. These are the people of ordinary life. The people we might meet on any street. . . .

We, the ordinary people of the streets, believe with all our might that this street, this world, where God has placed us, is our place of holiness. (p. 54)

Madeleine was twenty-nine in 1933 when she arrived in Ivry (just outside Paris), the first Communist city and more or less the capital of Communism in France. There she founded a house for her small group or *équipe,* whose purpose was to live a contemplative community life in the world. Together they affirmed a permanent vow of celibacy and a will to live a simple, rustic life in the thick of humanity, without borders or methods. Their home was a place of hospitality for people of the most varied backgrounds and philosophies. Madeleine spent her life working in private and public social service. She was a model for Christian engagement with the world: identifying herself with Communists in their dedication to the fight against injustice and living among them in profound friendship and community, she was exquisitely clear about the deficiencies of their ideological program. Madeleine explains her time in Ivry thus:

> We did not come [to Ivry] with many plans. What we sought was the freedom to live shoulder to shoulder with the men and women of every walk of life, with those who were our neighbors in time, with the same years on our calendars and the same hours on our clocks. . . . (*VM,* p. 40)[2]

> It was not the "proletariat" that I was joining, which was something I didn't know much about, nor was it "Marxism," which I wasn't well informed about either. It was just that I had been told that there were poor people and non-believers in Ivry. And I knew, from experience, the suffering caused by atheism; and the gospel had revealed to me what poverty was. If the encounter with Marxism turned out to be long-term, it was nevertheless not what I initially chose. (*VM,* p. 48)

2. Abbreviations for the titles of books cited are as follows: *VM:* Madeleine Delbrêl, *Ville marxiste* (Paris: Ed. Desclée de Brouwer, 1995); *RVCD:* Christine de Boismarmin, *Madeleine Delbrêl: Rue des villes, chemins de Dieu 1904-1964* (Paris: Ed. Nouvelle Cité, 1985). References to pages alone are to the present book.

As Loew points out, the life of Madeleine's youth was full of passion: for writing poetry, for playing the piano, for dancing. (This passion never left her: a year before her own death, Madeleine dropped her work and joined the multitude of mourners in the long funeral procession in Paris for singer Édith Piaf. Madeleine had always regarded Piaf, in her difficult childhood and her endless quest for an absolute anchor for love and freedom, as a kind of "kindred spirit.") Madeleine's greatest strength, finally, was her passion for God. The following lines written by Madeleine were found after her death:

> You were alive and I was completely unaware of it. You had fashioned my heart to your size, you had made my life to last as long as you and, because you were absent, the whole world seemed to me tiny and ridiculous, and the destiny of man stupid and cruel. When I realized that you were living, I thanked you for having given me life, I thanked you for the life of the whole world. (*RVCD*, p. 26)

We should note here the link Madeleine makes between a genuine passion for God and a passionate entering into the absurdity and darkness of a God who is dead. When we do so, we are enabled to see the preamble and spring of her missionary activity already in the extraordinary negation she pronounced at seventeen: "*God is dead . . . long live death*" (p. 47). Again as Loew points out, we find in this negation the first seed of the tender and compassionate understanding she would later show to unbelievers.

Indeed, it is God's absence that Madeleine identified as the greatest of the hardships suffered in contemporary society. She insisted that the struggle against injustice receives its proper form from within the struggle to recover true relation to the living God. Meaninglessness, and the suffering it generates, occurs when people "have no hope that God is alive, [are] without hope that he loves, without hope that God is God."

But Madeleine was always keenly aware that faith in God was a *gift*, and she insisted on awakening a sense of this gift not only in atheists but equally in those Christians who were too accustomed to their faith, who were "cloistered in their certainty about God, and unmoved by people who are . . . at home in the absence of God."

It is important in all of this to understand that, for Madeleine, God could never be separated from Christ nor Christ from the Church, from the body of Christ with its mystery of hierarchical office. As she once put it: "I would like to write the word 'Church' on every line, as often as I write the word 'God.'" Her profound sense of ecclesial obedience was not at all naive: she was acutely aware of the Church's abiding temptation to substitute mechanical and routinized procedures of power for the spirit of the Gospel, in its legitimate exercise of authority. The depth, subtlety, and clarity of Madeleine's spirit of obedience are well exemplified in the manner of her enduring collaboration with the Communists: she clarified her views on Catholic-Communist relations in *Ville marxiste, terre de mission* (1957);[3] and also of her involvement in the Worker Priest Mission from its beginning in the Mission of France in 1941: responding to Rome's efforts to regulate this movement, she helped all to have a better understanding of this new type of missionary life in the Church, to see why it was urgent and what sort of dangers could be anticipated by those who undertook it.

Let me conclude with two passages from Madeleine that aptly summarize the spirit and form of her engagement with the world:

> We have come to realize what dry bread justice is when it is not preceded by or completed with goodness. When public funds are distributed on the occasion of an accident, when they come to provide assistance with the burdens of having children, when they accompany old age, these subsidies, pensions, grants, and benefits correspond to a kind justice . . . but they do not in any way substitute for goodness. In such cases, it is not James or John himself who, in his misfortune or well being, finds help; instead, it is a condition or situation that is helped. General measures regulate collective categories. I resist criticizing the justice that society is able to achieve; criticism serves better to provoke progress in what remains to be achieved. What I am trying to say is that goodness is something else, it achieves something else.
>
> For a person to encounter the goodness of Christ in another person is in particular to encounter that person for what he really is. . . .

3. Charles F. Mann, in his short biography of Delbrêl, points out that the title of this book was chosen by the publishers, not by Madeleine. According to Mann, Madeleine balked at the choice, since it emphasized the need to convert the Communists, but without sufficiently emphasizing the need simply to befriend them. He says that "she preferred a title such as *Marxism: An Impetus for Christian Development,* which more accurately reflected the book's perspective based on the benefits she had derived from her association with the Communists of Ivry. These benefits described in her book included the stimulus to act more justly and the incentive to deepen Christian faith. Faced with the publisher's insistence, Madeleine was forced to give in" (*Madeleine Delbrêl: A Life Without Boundaries* [San Francisco: New World Press, 1996], pp. 138-39).

The goodness of Christ . . . teaches us that this "who we are," which has been so manhandled by the world, possesses a value that is absolutely independent of wealth, power, smarts, influence, strength, and success. The goodness of Christ works with us; even more, it hopes for something from us, from each one of us. The goodness of Christ is above all something else: an encounter which affirms for us that we exist, which makes us present to ourselves, which walks alongside us in a common life. . . .

This brings us to an example. . . .

I will most likely never know whether the woman about whom I'm going to speak was Christian or not.

I was in a big foreign city many years ago, coming to the last hours of the several days I had spent there. I was almost entirely out of money, completely exhausted, and was suffering the pain that shakes the animal in the rational animal that we are: the pain of loss brought about by death, by the several deaths of those who were of the same flesh as mine. I do not believe that I represented any social category. The clothes I was wearing had nothing particular about them.

I had been walking through the streets for several hours while I waited for my train. And why not say it? I was crying. But I didn't care anymore, and I waited for it to pass. A foreigner. A stranger. A sorrow that all people know, one that brings tears just as certain forms of work bring sweat.

It started to rain; I was hungry. The few coins remaining to me determined what I was permitted to eat. I went into a tiny café that also served food, and ordered what I could afford: some raw vegetables. I ate them slowly so that they would be more nourishing and also to give the rain a chance to stop. Every once in a while my eyes filled up with tears. Then, all of a sudden, a warm and comforting arm took me by the shoulders. A voice said to me: "You, coffee. Me, give." It was absolutely clear. I don't remember exactly what happened afterward, which is lucky for me because I don't much care for melodramatic scenes.

I have often spoken about this woman, thought about her, and prayed for her with inexhaustible gratitude. When I look today for an example of goodness in flesh and bones, she is the one who comes to mind.

What makes this woman a Christian sign, a distant but faithful image of the goodness of God, is that she was good because goodness dwelled within her, and not because I was "one of her own," familially, nationally, or religiously. I was a "stranger" without any identifying marks. I was in

xiii

need of goodness, and even that goodness that goes by the name of mercy. It was given me by that woman. Today she represents an absolute example of goodness because I was just "anybody," it didn't matter what or who I was, and because what she did for me she did simply because there was goodness in her. (pp. 141-43)

Perhaps Thérèse of Lisieux, patroness of all missions, was meant to live out a destiny in which her time was limited to the minimum, her actions were reduced to essentials, her heroism was indiscernible to those who looked for it, and the scope of her mission covered a mere few square meters, in order to teach us that the effectiveness of a mission is not always measurable by the hands of a clock, that actions are not always visible, that missions covering vast distances will be joined by missions that penetrate straight into the depth of the crowds of humanity. In that abyss, these missions will make contact with the human spirit that questions the world, and oscillates between the mystery of a God who wants it to be small and stripped bare, and the mystery of a world that wants it to be great and powerful. She alone is enough to show us that the best missionary approach to Marxism [and to all contemporary forms of atheism] is not shoring up artificial defenses, but gathering strength precisely where our faith is being undermined. (*VM*, p. 148)

DAVID L. SCHINDLER
Washington, D.C.
Monday of Holy Week, 2000

PREFACE TO THE GERMAN EDITION OF
Nous autres, gens des rues

Not wanting to anticipate Fr. Jacques Loew's excellent introduction, we will address only a few words to the German reader.

Uniting the highest reason with the most daring courage, shaping her activity out of the deepest obedience to God and Christ-Church: Madeleine Delbrêl is thus cut from the same wood as Joan of Arc. The style of battle has perhaps changed, but the total engagement of both body and soul has remained the same.

Madeleine started out writing verse; thus, even though she is thankfully far from being an aesthete, she cannot help, even in her private notes, writing a clear, sometimes slightly affected French, which is reminiscent of Péguy's litany style. . . .

The clear style is, however, only an expression of her relentlessly precise thought and Christian decisiveness, which over the years and through the course of her battles became increasingly sharp.

In the first place, it is about either God or nothing.

Then, the Gospel, the "good news" comes into view, with its beatitudes and the urgent calls for radicalism. Here, instead of the soul's exposure in the spiritual desert before God's "luminous darkness," there is the even more radical self-expropriation in the world's avowed Godlessness. And, in this world, the need to discern the line — which cuts through and now truly "divides soul from spirit, and bone from marrow" — between perfect love of her Communist brother (including common work in all human issues) and a decisive rejection of his ideological program.

Madeleine is able to make this hairline distinction so expertly, that, in hours of confusion, she is able to become the great advisor for the worker-priests who were being regulated by Rome. The accuracy of her diagnoses is unsurpassed — we must in this context always keep in mind that she had as partners the Communists of postwar France.

She finally goes beyond the mere I-Thou between Christians and Communists, and discovers the comprehensive phenomenon of atheism worldwide, and not just the Communist form. Next to this phenomenon, the Communist doctrine seems to her something "outdated."

Her Catholic single-mindedness is unprecedented: No God without Christ, and no Christ without his body, his bride: the Catholic, hierarchical Church, and the mystery of office. She understands that it is only here that the Christian receives the gift of the *concretissimum* of obedience in the following of Christ.

Madeleine's texts are of an unusual density. This is not the sort of book one could read on a train; one should allow these passages to take effect slowly, piece by piece. Doing so, one will discover in them an ascending spiral: the same themes are enriched and deepened; they become more sober, more concrete, until in the end all of the motifs converge into a multifaceted fugue. Such masculine hardness of spirit and motherly gentleness of heart, such tense attentiveness and relaxed surrender: who in our century has more convincingly embodied the paradox of the Catholic style of life and speech?

HANS URS VON BALTHASAR

PREFACE TO THE FRENCH EDITION OF
Nous autres, gens des rues

Madeleine Delbrêl had asked that her papers be entrusted to the care of Fr. Jean Gueguen, O.M.I., after her death. It is largely through his efforts that the texts she left have been collected and organized.

Fr. Gueguen assembled the texts we present here with the help of Fr. Loew and Madeleine Delbrêl's *équipe*.

These texts were not written with a view to publication. Rather, they are conference notes, jotted-down ideas, personal reflections, and attempts to respond to questions she was asked. Certain recurring thoughts may thus seem repetitive; however, they merely give us an idea of the themes that were essential to Madeleine Delbrêl.

At the head of each of the five sections of this book, after an epigraph recalling the dominant theme in Madeleine's thought and action during this period, we indicate by a brief chronology certain events in the life of the Church which may in particular have provoked her reflection, and we likewise note what she herself was experiencing at the same time.

Introduction

JACQUES LOEW

If the word "introduction" means "to lead someone inside," it enjoys its fullest meaning here, since these preliminary pages do not intend to present either a brief biography of Madeleine Delbrêl or a commentary on her writings. They are genuinely meant as an "introduction": they seek to facilitate and bring to life an encounter with Madeleine Delbrêl by marking out the human, spiritual, and apostolic itinerary of this woman, whom God chose and prepared over the course of thirty years to teach us how to live the post-conciliar Church.

Her very best friends are familiar with only fragments of her thought or certain aspects of her life. In fact, however, the logic of the development of her apostolic mission is profoundly connected to the internal development of her life. Illuminating each by means of the other will thus give us a better understanding of the relevance of her message, while at the same time, we will be inspired by contact with this new sort of mission.

Fr. Jacques Loew is himself a convert to Christianity. He was ordained a priest of the Dominican Order in 1939. Along with P. Lebret, in 1941 he founded the scholarly journal *Economie et Humanisme,* and in the same year he went to work as a dockhand in the Port of Marseille. In 1965 he founded The Worker Mission of Peter and Paul, a missionary movement made up of priests who hold ordinary jobs and live among the poor and working-class people. In 1969 he opened The School of Faith in Fribourg, Switzerland, for the formation of future leaders of small Christian communities. He is the author of numerous books on contemporary Christian life.

1

JACQUES LOEW

I. A Sketch of Her Life

Introducing a person would seem easy: one need only open the door, say a couple of words, and then draw back, leaving the reader face to face with the author. With Madeleine Delbrêl, however, it is not so easy.

She defies all ready-made images, all categories that would try to capture her: "Her vast originality, once it was put at the service of God's own creativity and nourished on it, made her an extraordinarily unique individual."[1] That is why, even though so many of us cherish more than twenty years of memories and experiences, it would be a betrayal of both God and Madeleine — of grace and friendship — not to quote some of the diverse and yet convergent testimonies of her friends. We do so not so much for the sake of accumulating praise, but simply to initiate an encounter.

The nearly impossible portrait of Madeleine Delbrêl is nevertheless painted with a remarkable fidelity, thanks to the perceptive insight of a Polish woman, Krystyna W.:

"From far off, you catch sight of a thin, nimble, and frail silhouette, but one whose gait and every gesture bore a trace of energy and decisiveness. You would think you were watching an old soldier whose instinct for being constantly ready to respond to orders left an indelible mark.

"Coming closer, you first notice her eyes — large, lucid, hazel eyes, fixed on you with vigilant attention. And then a gentle, sometimes timid, smile. Her presence on the whole created an atmosphere of serenity, strength, and cheerfulness.

"Even if you didn't feel like it before, a discussion or conversation, in the deep sense of the word, catches fire. If you are an intellectual who enjoys an exchange of ideas, you are delighted to find a wealth of profound and precise thinking emanating from a high forehead, with delicate, blue-veined skin. If you are unable to speak, or if you feel no need to, her handshake and deep look is enough.

"But if you let yourself be carried off by her expressiveness and take the great risk of letting her see a little of your joy or your pain, then her whole face becomes animated, like transparent water suddenly rippling under a gust of wind: her expressions of compassion, genuine understanding, and truly borne suffering, allow you to see, as through an open door, just how far she had traveled in order to come to this encounter.

1. A letter from N.C.

2

"If you are destitute, broken, wounded, or if you have suffered an injustice, her eyes widen and grow dark blue, almost black; her entire body stiffens, as if getting ready to make a move, to act, to defend.

"It's then you might see her hands swing into motion: small, delicate, sensitive, and intelligent, hands that know how to greet a friend or a coworker, but which can also reach out and caress your head with the tender gesture you would have thought was a secret only mothers knew.

"And no matter who you are, child or adult, man or woman, you find yourself in her tiny shelter, close to her heart, for a brief second of the eternity in which 'there will be no more tears.' With Madeleine, you feel like a child, soothed and dazzled by the pure sun of a childhood innocence renewed.

"In leaving her — as eventually you one day must — you will perhaps realize, with a slight sense of humility, that there always remains, in every human being, the possibility of passing over such a vast wealth of humanity merely because it is found in the tiny, insignificant body of an aging woman.

"And when it comes to say good-bye — an act that serious people experience as so heavy because it wrenches one apart — you may be caught off guard once again by the unexpected charm of her face, aglow with happiness, and by the decisive gesture with which she turns from you to continue her next important activity.

"And you have to give your assent, because what she does is truly the most important activity in the world, and you yourself have already been its beneficiary: she is digging holes with a child's pail in the vast desert sands of human suffering, in order to bring forth springs that will never run dry. It is, indeed, the very work of Hope."

The last image of this portrait, wellsprings of hope bubbling up from holes dug in the dry desert sand, joins the waves of another testimony:

"My memories of Madeleine Delbrêl are facts which, taken by themselves, are no more or less significant than facts that might be used to describe other people. What is important about these facts is the wave they formed, a wave that has not yet ceased to swell. But how do you talk about that? What can you say about a wave?"[2]

2. Testimony of A.H.

Though Madeleine Delbrêl was so energetic, she was also deeply sensitive. Being unaffected was a quality opposed to her very being; but when she entered into the uncertainty of events or other people's insecurities, she was always able to create a sense of "peace, confidence, and courage." She was able to make eternity out of time.

"How often I think of that unique human being, Madeleine Delbrêl. In this desert of a world, people like her give their friends a missionary's strength to go on. I believe the predominant characteristic of such people is the *intelligence* of their love. I found in her that quality that you so rarely find in others: the ability to give to each person precisely the form of love that he needs, according to 'his hunger.' That is clearly a grace — and what a grace! — to have such insight into people's hearts."[3]

"Madeleine is the only person in the world who loved me in hope. She was able to discern my real self, distorted for others, unknown to myself, full of self-hate, unwittingly chained in various prisons, from which after ten years I have finally managed to escape thanks to her help. Because of her, I lived for one of my peers before I lived in my self, while everyone else could do nothing but ignore me. . . . If there is no greater love than to give your life for another, how do you praise the love of one who gives back a life that was lost, who gives it to a person who never even knew she had it?"[4]

Natural gifts, and a wealth of grace, to be sure, but also the humble honesty of a craftsman of the mind and heart.

"She always spoke in order to say something to someone. She brought to her writing and to her public interventions a meticulous preparation. She always worked 'as the situation requires,' as she would put it. She also loved 'as the situation required.' I would have to mention her imaginative heart, and the gift she had to build friendships. Madeleine knew how to give every person her attention, her time, and her love — to the richest as well as to the poorest. Some 'small personal matter' would mobilize her as much as an 'official, public matter.' People came from all

3. Letter from N.D.
4. Letter from a friend.

over to see her; she formed friendships internationally and maintained a wide correspondence."[5]

In addition to these reports from others, we have another portrait that Madeleine herself wrote about Thérèse of the Child Jesus, but which could equally be said about her. This passage describes the lively and careful attention she gave to the lowliest of things out of the highest of convictions:

> "Perhaps Thérèse of Lisieux, patroness of all missions, was meant to live out a destiny in which her time was limited to the minimum, her actions were reduced to essentials, her heroism was indiscernible to those who looked for it, and the scope of her mission covered a mere few square meters, in order to teach us that the effectiveness of a mission is not always measurable by the hands of a clock, that actions are not always visible, that missions covering vast distances will be joined by missions that penetrate straight into the depth of the crowds of humanity. In that abyss, these missions will make contact with the human spirit that questions the world, and oscillates between the mystery of a God who wants it to be small and stripped bare, and the mystery of a world that wants it to be great and powerful. She alone is enough to show us that the best missionary approach to Marxism is not shoring up artificial defenses, but gathering strength precisely where our faith is being undermined."[6]

Though Madeleine was an extraordinarily original individual, she was the complete opposite of eccentric. The frequent uprooting during her childhood, painful family circumstances, and a thirst for life "in which the soul, the spirit, the heart, the body, the emotions, and the imagination were intertwined with the challenges that all this can imply for our logic"[7] could certainly have disposed her to it. But everything in her was held in unity by two impulses, an impulse of nature that was too rich to allow the tiniest aspect of being to be lost, and an impulse of grace that also refused to let go of the smallest jot or tittle. Madeleine always wanted, and always knew how, to integrate everything. Here, too, just like Thérèse, she "chose all."

5. J. P. Guérend, in an article from the *Journal de la Paix, Pax Christi*, 1964.
6. *Ville marxiste*, p. 148.
7. Recollections of M.M.C.

Madeleine Delbrêl was born on October 24, 1904, in Mussidan, the Dordogne, a southwestern region of France, in her maternal grandparents' home. (She wore her "Gascon" origins like a button or banner, and liked to joke about it when she nervously faced a large audience.) Adjacent to this house was a factory that produced beeswax, candles, and lamp oil, which her grandfather had founded in 1869. In this respect, she enjoyed a traditional and affectionate environment: Madeleine often returned to visit her grandmother while she was young, and, as soon as she learned to write, kept up a correspondence with her. Her father was a railroad worker — another title she was glad to claim. Originally from Lot, his family line was diverse and colorful, "pieced together from all sorts." In addition to the one grandfather who was fairly conventional, Pierre Delbrêl (1764-1846), Madeleine had a grandfather who was a boiler maker, that is, someone who hammered copper, and a grandmother who, after a stint with Public Assistance in Paris, was hired as a midwife at the Hospice de Périgueux. This was somewhat unusual for the time.

Madeleine's father quickly earned a series of railroad promotions and was transferred from Lorient to Nantes, then to Bordeaux, Châteauroux, and finally in 1913 to the post of station master in Montluçon. These frequent transfers, along with Madeleine's frail health, did not favor a consistent education. From the age of four, she was privately tutored, "a bit anarchical," she liked to say. The same was true on the religious level: rather than receiving instruction from her parents, who were basically indifferent, she received private religious lessons as well. In Châteauroux, and then in Montluçon, she met certain priests who managed to awaken in her a simple and deep faith. They prepared her for her First Communion, which she received very devoutly when she was twelve years old.

But Madeleine was soon submitted to other influences, and did not hold on to her faith. In 1916, Monsieur Delbrêl was transferred to Paris. The friends who frequented the family apartment, and especially the professors M. Delbrêl chose as Madeleine's tutors, surrounded her with a new and very powerful intellectual environment.

M. Delbrêl himself was no ordinary man: as a passionate railroad worker, a man with great talent for organization, and an ardent patriot, he was moreover a lover of literature and wrote poetry as a hobby. Madeleine was quite attentive to the brilliant discussions that took place in this cultured and more or less agnostic milieu, and these adults welcomed and encouraged the young "prodigy" in her attempts at poetry, inviting her to recite them at their gatherings. It seems she was particularly influenced by a certain Doctor Armaingaud, a "disciple of Littré, a convinced atheist, and the self-proclaimed ambassador of Montaigne,"[8] who took pleasure in cultivating Madeleine's sharp intelligence.

"From the age of seven to twelve I received instruction in the faith at the hands of several remarkable individuals. In Paris, however, other remarkable individuals offered me a contradictory formation. By the time I was fifteen, I was a strict atheist, and the world grew for me more absurd by the day."[9]

A childhood friend, who eventually (and by quite a circuitous path!) became a nun, recalled these years:

"Madeleine was at that time a lyrical and serious adolescent, without the sense of humor she would later display.

"It was poetry that united us, and we loved to meet under the sign of art, whether it be for museum visits, discussions over books, or promenades in the Luxembourg. Neither she nor I (who was often sick) had a normal education, and so we had quite a lot of time to 'go exploring' together. Faith was absent from our lives.

"Around 1920, we took the philosophy courses that Léon Brunschvicg offered at the Sorbonne. One day after the lecture, our heads stuffed with theses and antitheses, we sauntered along the Boulevard Saint-Michel, sharing our impressions — and there were many indeed! Suddenly, as if in answer to the blooming of springtime in the Médici Plaza, we reached an important decision under a brilliant sun and amid the greening Luxembourg trees: we would *stay young forever,* whatever else may happen, whatever the years would bring. . . . *To be young* — we found our vocation! Madeleine kept to her word.

"Around 1922, it was ball season, with dances always being held for one reason or another. Other concerns and earthly tastes occupied our hearts. I remember a particularly festive soirée at the Delbrêl house to celebrate Madeleine's nineteenth birthday. She was dressed in Greek costume, which highlighted her cameo profile. And she was especially radiant with joy for having officially become engaged to a tall, dark, young

8. *La Vie intellectuelle,* August-September, 1956, p. 15.
9. "What Ivry taught me," p. 260.

man who looked like the philosopher Lacordaire — and the similarities didn't end there. While he danced with me, he asked me what I thought of Thomism. Being more interested in Asiatic religions and ignorant of scholastic philosophy, I thought he was referring to some Chinese philosophy. . . . Fortunately, the rhythm of the dance hid my confusion."[10]

But for Madeleine, these years held more than the ignorance of Thomism or the pleasures of dancing. She literally wrestled over two words in particular: "death" and "absurdity." When she later described youth as "the greatest capacity to unmask absurdity,"[11] she was exactly describing her struggles from the age of seventeen to twenty. On the one hand, "God was absurd in the twentieth century because he was incompatible with sound reason; intolerable because he cannot be categorized"[12] — God is dead. On the other hand, under the influence of her rationalistic milieu, Madeleine believed in "Intelligence with a capital 'I,'" and yet at the same time she saw that "the world and its history has revealed itself as the most sinister farce imaginable"[13] — the highest knowledge man is capable of is the knowledge that he will die. And at the heights of absurdity, Christ's saying carries the angst that arises from the absurd to the very end: "What does it avail man to win the whole universe, if he loses his soul?":

> "At the time, I would have given the whole world just to know why I was in it."[14]

But then, a significant event set her reflection in motion:

> "I met several Christians, neither older nor dumber nor more idealistic than I was; in other words, they lived the same life I did, they discussed as much as I did, they danced as much as I did. They even had a few things in their favor — they worked harder than I did, they had a technical and scientific formation that I didn't have, and they had political convictions that I didn't have and didn't practice."[15]

10. Recollections of M.M.C.
11. From an unpublished talk given to the students of the *Enseignement supérieur technique,* 1960.
12. *Ville marxiste,* p. 224.
13. *Ville marxiste,* p. 223.
14. From a talk to students, 1960.
15. *Ville marxiste,* p. 224.

Having met these people, Madeleine "was no longer able to leave God in the absurd":

> "At the age of twenty [that is, in 1924], my intellectual religious search ended in a radical conversion."[16]

We know very little about this search, but certain poems from this period — from 1922 to 1925 — give us an idea of her development by their very titles.

Ice
. . . My cheerfulness will scatter its words, rich and false,
Along the slow passage of solemn hours

. . . Then beneath the cloak of a phony joy,
And carrying a dead bouquet of withered garlands
And the heavy jewels of fountains run dry,
I will conceal my heart under a mask of ice.[17]

The Road
. . . The road is not the light,
It is the hope of a glimmer;
It is not the first blaze,
But the promise of truth

It is the object of the waiting
And an ever-renewed struggle:
The goal of the steep road
Is the passage through death.[18]

Resurrection
O Christ, the last doubt has finally pierced your side. . . .
. . . He said to me "I am the pastor of the flock
Who has no shepherd and who trembles in the open field.

---

16. "What Ivry taught me," p. 260.
17. *La Route,* p. 35.
18. *La Route,* p. 1.

". . . I will teach you the words that wound the void,
And you, tiny speck of the infinite, tossed by an ocean,
You will participate in the rising tide of Being."
. . . He came into my home, sat at my table,
And I recognized him in the breaking of the bread.[19]

To learn the itinerary of Madeleine's encounter with God, we ought to read in particular the final four pages of her book, *Ville marxiste, terre de mission:*

> "In order to be completely honest, I had to admit that if God were no longer strictly impossible, I couldn't treat him as necessarily non-existent. And so I chose what seemed to me the best way to express my change of heart: I decided to pray. . . . By reading and reflecting, I found God; but by praying, I *believed* that God found me and that he is living reality, and that we can love him in the same way we love a person."[20]

What Madeleine retained from this search was an existential sense of the *gift* of faith, the certitude of an extraordinary and absolutely gratuitous treasure. She was intent to awaken a sense of this gift, not only in atheists, but equally in those Christians who were too accustomed to their faith, who were "cloistered in their certainty about God, and unmoved by people who are completely at home in the absence of God." This awakening cannot happen, however, unless we realize that faith is not something we are owed, that God is not our property or our personal capital, and that he is not the "God of only certain people." Rather, faith is a "stupendous and staggering happiness" that we receive from the God who loved the world, who loved men first and gratuitously.

From the age of twenty to sixty, Madeleine never ceased to be a convert, someone "overwhelmed by God"; her "greatest strength [was] a passion for God, [which turns us] off of dangerous missionary trails without our even noticing it."[21] But, to love God's light with passion, one must no less passionately have entered deeply into the absurdity and darkness of a God who is truly dead. From this perspective, one of the poles of Madeleine's life, the preamble and the hidden spring of her missionary activity,

19. *La Route,* p. 133.
20. *Ville marxiste,* p. 225.
21. "Light and darkness," p. 195.

emerged out of the extraordinary negation she pronounced at seventeen: *God is dead, long live death.*[22]

The pious twelve-year-old child's transition from the light to the "nowhere" and the "total nothing" of God's absence four years later is already the first seed of the tender and compassionate understanding she would later show to unbelievers.

But there was another reality that deeply marked Madeleine's life. We hesitate to mention things concerning which she herself kept an absolute discretion, but an entire aspect of her inner life would remain inexplicable if certain lights were not provided to illuminate what amounted to thirty years of constant and boundless trials, with sudden new and unforeseen outbreaks.

Around 1924, at the age of fifty-four, M. Delbrêl lost his vision. This hardship served to aggravate his already difficult character. He began to lead an increasingly disordered life cut off from his wife and his daughter, and yet burdening them with the entire weight of his eccentricities. His exclusive love for Madeleine was mixed with a certain unhealthy hostility. Until the death of her parents, which took place within the space of a couple of months in 1955, Madeleine experienced the most complete wrenching of her heart and spirit: Krystyna was not wrong, with regard to Madeleine's ability to welcome people, to speak of "the immense road she had to travel to arrive at this meeting." Madeleine's capacity for compassion was truly the fruit of the Cross, and much more excruciating than we can speak of here and imagine.

When she converted, Madeleine at first thought of entering the Carmelites. However, she abandoned this idea because of her mother's sufferings, even though her mother had assented to this sacrifice. In 1927, after many days of reflection, prayer, and trials, Madeleine became certain that she was doing God's will by remaining in the world and working there for him. She thus turned herself toward a completely lay life. Around this same time, Madeleine participated in the French scout movement, and organized meetings with other scoutmasters, and with Abbé Lorenzo, their priest, around the Gospel. At the death of Fr. Lorenzo, Madeleine explained in her own words what she learned from him:

> "How many of us were shaken to the core by what he himself liked to call 'metanoia,' this turning back, this conversion, through the irruption

22. This text is printed below, pp. 47-49.

of the Lord's Word into our lives, a word addressed to us in particular, and addressed on that very day.

"The Lord Jesus was so alive that he could speak, speak to us, call each one of us, ask, demand, guide, and lead. Fr. Lorenzo didn't talk *about* the Lord; instead, he said, 'The Lord tells you such and such; he calls you as he has always called you.' And then: 'Look at the Lord in his words, he himself tells you what he's like; he himself tells you who he is. Look.'"[23]

Madeleine never ceased proclaiming the Gospel wherever she went. Though the Christian is free with respect to all things, he is not free with respect to the Gospel. In those hours in which she knew the temptation of Marxism, and likewise during the missionary events that took place between 1955 and 1960, Madeleine learned to accord the Lord's words their absolute status: Jesus' "But I tell you" is the bare minimum — any lower and you are no longer a Christian. And her unconditional love for neighbor has no other source.

"The Christian is a captive.

"*Captive* of a life: the life of Christ. He is not a propagandist of an idea, but the member of a body that lives and wants to grow.

"*Captive* of a thought: he is neither a free-thinker, nor one who propagates an idea, but the voice of another: 'the voice of his Master.'

"*Captive* of a spirit: of a desire as vast as God himself, which wants to save what is lost, heal what is sick, unite what is divided, always and everywhere.

"To be Christian is to be captive of an event; captive of dimensions which are in all things no longer our own; captive, so to speak, of a freedom which was chosen in advance for us.

"It is in this captivity that a missionary must proclaim the Christ that he lives, announce a message that he has received and which he is not permitted to modify, to pass on a salvation which does not come from him, and which is as vast as the world over. The Christ that he lives cannot be modified, for the Christian is his captive. This message cannot be corrected, for he is its captive. This salvation cannot be kept back, for he is its captive."[24]

---

23. "Le Père Lorenzo, Une voix qui criait l'Évangile."
24. "Mission et missions," an unpublished personal note.

The fundamental orientation of Madeleine's life grew out of this constant contact with the Gospel: "To live the Gospel freely and openly in the midst of the world."

From 1931, with the priestly support of Fr. Lorenzo, a true "man of the Gospel," Madeleine began to prepare in prayer for her departure for Ivry, which took place in October, 1933, with two companions. During this same period, she completed a degree in social work — "just in case." But, for her, social work was never the essential thing. It was only one element in a life dedicated to "follow Christ in an unconditional availability to do the very work of the Gospel."

A small group of people formed around her who sought, like her, to live the demands of the Gospel while remaining a layperson and practicing various professions: "a tiny cell of the Church, born in our time, making its home in our time."

Madeleine's great richness sprang out of her free obedience to this vocation. She lived the life of this *équipe* for thirty years, "without secrets or anything to hide," "with no other commandment than that of Love." The house they kept in Ivry was a genuine family home, wherein one could meet people of all stripes, belonging to the most varied of milieus and ideologies. Each person felt "at home" there, because he was accepted for who he was, and because he experienced in this house a spirit of generosity.

Madeleine was twenty-nine when she arrived in Ivry, the first Communist city and more or less the capital of Communism in France. For thirteen years, from 1933 to 1946, Madeleine was constantly engaged, first in private social service, and then in public.

It was, indeed, quite contrary to her desires that, from the very first months, she found herself monopolized primarily by the activity of parish work; and yet it was through this work that she began to embody in her own flesh the encounter between the Church and nonbelievers, between the Church and the City. Here she describes this crucial encounter in her own words:

> In 1933, the year of my arrival in Ivry, the Church and the City were completely and aggressively at odds with each other. Christians suffered genuine public oppression from city hall. In the streets, they were mocked by children, and priests even had stones thrown at them. At official functions, the organization called the "Godless" [*Sans Dieu*] engaged in boisterous propaganda. The Christians responded with a cold war: practical excommunication of certain businesses, the ostracism of

liberal professions, the self-isolation of people of the same faith. In the housing projects and in the schools, the children fought with each other.

In 1935, Maurice Thorez, the leader of the French Communist Party, started the "outreach" initiative. The first signs of the initiative in Ivry were huge posters on all the city walls, inviting every organization, regardless of ideology, to participate in a meeting to assist the unemployed. At the time, there were thousands without work.

Abbé Lorenzo, the newly appointed pastor of Ivry's main parish, decided to undertake an initiative, along with the other priests in Ivry, to invite to this meeting a representative from each Catholic organization, and to attend the meeting himself. There were about forty Christians there.

The committee did an enormous amount of practical work. It was only later that I was able to appreciate a far more significant fact about this event: it was an encounter between the Church and nonbelievers *within* the city.[25]

Madeleine undertook a large part of this work, even more so when, in September, 1939, with the declaration of war, she and her friends were drafted into official public service.

Since the time the hostilities began, the government had replaced the Communist city council members by delegations appointed by the Prefecture. However, within the city hall itself, the department heads and the employees remained the same. Despite the mistrust that such a situation might have entailed, Madeleine was able to create in the departments in which she worked an atmosphere of honest collaboration and mutual trust.

The government had appointed her as Minister of Social Services, which meant she had to coordinate all the public health and social programs for Ivry and the district. At the same time, she was named Minister of National Public Assistance and given the responsibility of creating nationwide wartime services such as emergency shelters, soup kitchens, clothing drives, and training programs for social workers and their assistants. For these workers, Madeleine wrote a pamphlet and a book, which remained a bedside book for many people.[26] Moreover, she was asked to bring aid to prisoners' families, and — what was more difficult — she helped arrange secret aid to be given to victims of the occupation; and fi-

---

25. Unpublished notes, 1935.
26. *La Femme et la Maison,* 1941, and *Veillée d'Armes,* 1942.

nally, she created such social works as the "Maison de la Mère," assistance to the elderly, and youth organizations.

After the liberation, Madeleine was asked to continue her activities at city hall, which was again run by the French Communist Party. After Ivry suffered through its second bombing on the 25th of August, 1944, another Committee was formed, similar to the previous one for the unemployed, which included a large number of Christian participants. As she explained, it was "a second 'free' encounter between the Church and the people *within* the city. It lasted several months. . . ."

In every circumstance, whether it was the soup kitchen, the clothing drive, a train-station welcome center, a social service project, or emergency aid during the bombings, it was always because of meticulous preparation or masterful improvisation, with firm authority and in consort with her leaders and often with a thrown-together staff, that everything came off as well as possible for the sad beneficiaries of all this work. For everyone, for each of the participants, at every meeting (and how diverse they were!), she had a friendliness and a human warmth that left a lasting impression on many people.

When, later, she insisted that a Christian needs to be "someone who is capable of doing something well, seeing it through to the end, a person who is spontaneously aware" of what is going on in the world,[27] she knew what she was talking about.

When she likewise described the appeal of Communism, its genuine attraction, the heroic dedication of the militants, and their sincere fight against injustice, it is because she had seen these things, had lived them daily with some of the "greatest folks" of the Party. And it is hardly surprising that these same men had honestly hoped to "convert" Madeleine; they were in such profound agreement "concerning the scandalous world we live in together, and the decisive action necessary to put an end to the scandal." It was for Madeleine "a temptation for Marxism at a time when it would have been somewhat unusual to fall to it."

Around 1944, during these experiences, Madeleine had what might be called a second conversion. To be sure, she would never for a minute have considered "leaving God by the wayside, or slipping away from Christ by even a hair's breadth,"[28] but couldn't she nevertheless, leaving her

---

27. "Atheism and evangelization," p. 243.
28. Unpublished talk given to students, 1960.

friends to their atheism and keeping her God to herself, fully participate in the same battle for the same human justice?

Madeleine never lived anything superficially: she did not seek in any degree to attenuate the battle that occurred in the encounter between the Christian and the atheist world. She refused to accept that a Christian must be a stranger to this world or "out of the circle," or that a Christian could be a tacit accomplice to injustice. But on the other hand, "the absence of God is for man worse than all hardships put together." It is man's *characteristic* hardship: the absence of food is a hardship that can occur also at the animal level, but to exist without God is a hardship that touches man's very nature, and the world that he thus constructs will necessarily be "unnatural" or "inhuman." The violence of revolutions is not our biggest worry; the problem of atheism concerns the very human condition.

Madeleine herself will explain in this book how she resisted this final temptation, and how she "gave her references: the Words of Christ."

Henceforward, Madeleine lived and possessed the resources necessary to build a Christianity adequate to the needs of our time.

At this point, we discontinue the account of Madeleine's life, which was spent to the end in Ivry, and which was completely bound up with her missionary life. The significant events that punctuate her experiences there will be noted at the beginning of each chapter.

II. A Message for the Post-conciliar Age

The One Thing Necessary

The center of Madeleine's thought converges with the center of her life: as one who knows that God is a living person, that he loves, and that he is truly God, she encounters people "who have no hope that God is alive, without hope that he loves, without hope that God is God." When she came to Ivry in 1933, "what I sought was the freedom to live shoulder to shoulder with the men and women of the world, who are my neighbors in history, sharing the same years on our calendars and the same hours on our clocks."[29]

But, as a Christian who had discovered the inexpressibly extraordinary love that God bears her, and knowing that she had to imitate this love

29. *Ville marxiste*, p. 17.

vis-à-vis God himself and "every person that Jesus Christ said we should love as we love ourselves," this desire to live shoulder to shoulder with people acquired a finality, "a religious intention," that Madeleine proclaimed "to be the first and primary goal" of her life.

When she decided to publish her book, *Ville marxiste, terre de mission* — and here too "the intention that moved me to write is uniquely religious" — she inscribed under the title the remark "composed in Ivry, from 1933 to 1957," which indicates the internal unity of her life, her thought, and her action.

But to unify her life between God and the Church, on the one hand ("I would like to write the word 'Church' on every line, as often as I write the word 'God'"), and, on the other hand, the love for those who despised God and the Church, is a seemingly insurmountable contradiction. How can one join together an affirmation and a negation? To this seeming impossibility, Madeleine responds with a fact: "the presence of people who are uncompromisingly religious and apostolic, freely giving their lives to whatever the love of God requires."[30]

She never spoke of a double fidelity. For her, there was never any question of a double belonging, because she belonged solely to God. But this single belonging gave her such a strength of affection, such a capacity to love all people spontaneously and with clarity, that she truly became the neighbor of whomever she met, from the very moment she met them. One day, something happened that would have been insignificant for most of us but struck Madeleine very deeply — she always kept her eyes and ears open in case God should want to speak to her through events or people. A soldier who was an important member of the Party, ardent in his atheism — and moreover profoundly bound to Madeleine, who returned his deep respect — learned that his own sister had entered the convent. Everything thus separated them. Nevertheless, because of their previous sibling affection, there were never two more mutually understanding people: for him, this nun was first truly his sister and only then a nun, and, for her, this atheist was first truly her brother and only then an atheist. Madeleine knew how to translate the bond of flesh uniting these two human beings into a bond of grace, which unites us in Christ and through him to every person that comes into the world. And because the love that results from this is stronger and rooted more deeply than our differences, it does not try to blunt these differences through illusory compromises.

30. *Ville marxiste*, pp. 11-12.

For if there are Christian women whose husbands or children, whose brothers or sisters, are Communists, they love them with a love that God makes his own. To love them, they don't have to accept the Party card that declares their opposition to God. . . . But by refusing their card, these women aren't required to deny their flesh, their heart, their affection.

Year after year, I refused and I continue to refuse the card my friends carry; it is the key to enter into the living organization of Marxism and it is what would unite me locally with my friends, but it would fundamentally set me in opposition to God, through solidarity with the Party. But year after year, I have been and continue to be their friend, just as Christ and our Church teach us to be.[31]

From this unifying center, Madeleine's life and thought radiated outward — in tension — both to everything that was essential in Marxism, and to everything that was essential in faith. As she walked this path, she mercilessly pruned away everything secondary, everything accidental, all of the caricatures of the one or the other. This is one of the most fundamental features of her character and her work — the "Christian manifesto to the atheist world" is composed entirely around this theme:

If you criticize the mediocre Christians that we are, you can do so. However, we will not accept disputes over definitions that were never applicable to Christians, over figments of the imagination or caricatures. The Christian seeks to resemble Christ. Discuss Christ, and then we'll talk.[32]

And if the Christian's faith is often fragile, it is because it is encumbered, mixed up with additives and non-essentials that do not belong to the faith as such.

What is essential for the Christian is baptism: Madeleine took the three sentences of the dialogue between the Church and the person awaiting baptism as the illuminating and inflexible axis of her apostolic life:

- "What do you ask from God's Church?" — "Faith."
- "What will you gain through faith?" — "Eternal life."
- "If you thus wish to possess eternal life, observe the commandments: you will love the Lord your God with all your heart, with all your

31. *Ville marxiste*, p. 14.
32. "A Christian manifesto to the atheist world," p. 180.

soul, and with all your mind, and you will love your neighbor as yourself."

She will have in life no other sources of support than these: faith, the "nothing more and the nothing less" of the Gospel, the expectation of eternal life, and the two commandments. But she will follow the realism of these things to the end:

> To ask for and receive faith as on the day of baptism, the faith such as the Christian asked for and received, such as he continues to receive if he asks for it, the faith that he received from God through God's Church.
>
> To possess eternal life, from day to day, by living the two commandments.
>
> Being rooted deeply in the Church, having become Christ, being the son of a God who is father, a brother to all people, streaming forth for them the goodness by which God loves us — this is what faith must constantly mean for us; all of this is what we must obey without respite in faith, what ought to be as it were within our very eyes no matter what we are looking at, within our very mind prior to every reflection, within our very will before we make any decision.
>
> We should be obsessed and possessed by this, simultaneously fascinated and captivated.[33]

God, Jesus Christ, and the Church

As we saw from the beginning, Madeleine was a convert — the further she advances through life, the more aware she becomes of this fact; and she does not hesitate to express it publicly, as we see in the very last text she wrote, a month before her death:

> I was and still am someone bedazzled by God. It was and still is impossible for me to place God on one side of the balance and, on the other, all the goods of the world, whether they be for me or for the whole of humanity.[34]

---

33. "Goodness," pp. 136-37.
34. "What Ivry taught me," p. 263.

This stupendous and staggering happiness remains as precious to her thirty years after her conversion as it was the day it happened, because she became increasingly aware that faith is not "an idea," or a "piece of property," some "capital" that one has at one's disposal, but a constantly renewed gift, and, in the strictest possible sense, a gift that is continually given. Everything brought her daily back to this discovery, whether it be the unbelief of atheists or the dullness of Christians too "accustomed" to their faith.

"Dead" is the word she would use to describe a faith that has thus lost the sense of the divine:

> A world that once was Christian seems to be in the process of being emptied out from within. It first loses God, then the Son of God, and then everything divine that the Son would communicate to his Church. It is often the surface that is the last to collapse.[35]

This is how we can explain a lot of illusions — Christianity seems still to be holding up, while in fact the living reality worthy of the name God has long since disappeared.

What is tragic about Christians with a dead faith is that they have reduced belief in God to a natural fact, a "naturalization" that denatures the supernatural:

> In this mentality, the gratuitous gift God gives us — the gift of knowing who he is, the gift of acting according to his will, the gift of created life and eternal life, the gift of creation, and the gift of the saving Incarnation — have become a sort of innate property of the Christian stock, a sort of inherited good passed down through Christian families.[36]

How could such a Christian be a missionary? Once one has lost "a sense for 'God's gift,' the gift of his revelation, the gift of his life, we cannot have a sense for who the atheist is."[37]

If we take a second, this time positive, look at the text cited above concerning the process of the deadening of faith, we discover the triune source of Madeleine's joy and strength, the living reality inseparably

---

35. "Characteristics of a missionary parish," p. 164.
36. "Atheism and evangelization," p. 231.
37. "Atheism and evangelization," p. 233.

bound together in Madeleine's soul: God, Christ, and the Church together cast a transfiguring light on the whole of her existence.

God "is a Somebody." What Madeleine means by this is that he is not an idea, but a "living and efficacious presence": he acts, he lives, he loves. . . . She borrowed this expression from the popular language used in Ivry to describe an important person, and the word was never uttered without being accompanied by a comical facial expression.

The darkness of faith is but the logical consequence of our being literally dumbstruck by God. Blinded by so much light, we let ourselves be guided by faith.

> In the broad and real sense of the word, [our life becomes] a religious life, a life referred to, bound back to God.
>
> [It] is the overwhelming, penetrating presence of God. It is a call to encounter God, and God allows himself to be encountered only in solitude.[38]

One hesitates to comment on words such as these; and yet they should not be read too quickly. For, in this text Madeleine gives us the key to living a contemplative life in the heart of the world — solitude. Ever able to integrate all of the Kingdom's treasures, Madeleine desired, sought, and found the solitude, which generations of monks and nuns have declared essential for those who wish to find God, right in the heart of the world:

> It would seem that this solitude is something that those who live among the people of the world have to forego.
>
> But this would be to believe that we precede God in solitude, while, on the contrary, it is he who waits there for us; to find God is to find solitude, because true solitude is spirit, and all of our human solitudes are merely relative approaches toward the perfect solitude that is faith.
>
> True solitude is not the absence of people, but the presence of God.[39]

There is no higher solitary peak. To encounter God is to encounter Christ.

The intuition Madeleine had of God's being all, and of the relativity of all things human, reveals to her the extraordinary fortune brought by Jesus Christ: "If we want to be saved, we have to know that we are lost."

38. "Whoever follows me . . . ," p. 64.
39. "Whoever follows me . . . ," p. 64.

Christ is man, he is God, he is risen: this is not a dusty old legend, but *facts*, however unintelligible they would remain for reason were it not fulfilled by faith. Madeleine explains all of this in her *Christian Manifesto to the atheist world*.[40]

Madeleine chose Christ, and chose to be his captive:

> Through his baptism, the Christian exchanged his freedom for the freedom of Christ.
>
> He is free because Christ is supremely free, but he no longer has the right to choose a state of life other than that of Christ, an action other than that of Christ, or a thinking other than that of Christ.[41]

Both by temperament, and because of the Marxist critique of idealism, Madeleine was a realist: the realism of faith is living like someone who is aware that "*God is the one leading* [us]," that God compels us to become a different person so that we can go further.[42]

"CHRIST IS WHO HE IS," she writes, in capital letters; we cannot change him, "we cannot correct his message." To do so would be blasphemy and an absurdity; we would be putting ourselves in God's place.

> For if Christ establishes for us an absolute minimum in the Gospel, on what grounds could we claim to live if we did not make use of what he told us was necessary for life?
>
> In the Gospel, Christ in no way leaves it to us to establish the absolute minimum; he is the one who fixes it.
>
> To accept it is to live; if we do not accept it, we do not live, and there are dozens of passages in the Gospel, wherein the Lord takes it upon himself to say: "But I tell you . . . ," "True, that is what you have been told; but I tell you. . . ."[43]

Madeleine does not lose herself in the labyrinth of academic discussions: "When it comes to what Christ thought, we are not free thinkers." And: "The Cross is not something optional, either for the world or for us. To accept the Cross and to take it up is the lion's share of our work."[44] She makes

---

40. Cf., above, pp. 179-87.
41. "Church and mission," p. 96.
42. "The risk of submission," pp. 127-28.
43. From an unpublished conference in Toulouse, 1962.
44. "Church and mission," *passim*.

us God's children in Christ. "The Gospel is made for disciples who want to obey."

But such obedience is what gives Madeleine her realism and strength, as well as the joy and agility of the dancer in the dance of obedience.[45]

Having a living faith means being a child of God in Christ, with all of our brothers and sisters who are with us in Christ — the whole Christ, Christ-Church. The Jesus who saves, as he is for us now and as a whole, is not only Jesus the God-man from Palestine, but "the Jesus of today, the Church."

Here we touch the point at which Madeleine's "unretouched and un-altered" faith emerges in full force: without the slightest trace of artificial piety, but without the tiniest rift slipping in between Jesus Christ and the Church. "Jesus Christ and the Church are one," said Joan of Arc, and Madeleine would fully agree. In fact, there are many similarities between Madeleine and the fifteenth-century heroine. With her involvement with the origin of various missions in France, from Lisieux to Marseille, her listening to and discussions with groups of all sorts, with orientations of all sorts, receiving wounds in her own heart and flesh, watching the death of what she most dearly loved, no one was more tried by the Church than she; and yet no one was more unflinchingly loyal than she. On the contrary, faithful to her most fundamental grace, she recognized "the necessary trial, hidden within temptation":

> On the earth, the Church is made for fighting; by vocation, she wages war against evil; by mission, she stands on the front lines of evil; by office, she delivers from evil. . . .
>
> A realistic love for the Church necessarily entails taking your blows and living with bruises. . . . We open up space for God's life to pass through. Nothing can carry us more deeply into the inner reality of the Church.[46]

When the Council was first beginning, before anyone else thought in these terms, Madeleine championed "People of God" over "Church-institution" as the definition of the Church, but, taking the image as far as it could go, she brought it to life through the vital influx of grace.

Two brief texts from 1953, *The love of the Church*, and from 1960,

---

45. "The dance of obedience," pp. 71-74.
46. "Communist hope and Christian hope," pp. 227 and 228.

The Church: a single life in a single body, are so to speak two unshakable testimonies of Madeleine's message, offered at the threshold and at the end of the storm.

> Even when we think of the Church as a society, it is not about being citizens: the most unknown baptized person *is* our brother in a mysterious life. The most hidden priest has received the power to carry out certain functions belonging to Christ himself; he is a miracle of fruitfulness. The bishops and the Holy Father bear for us the crushing burden of preserving and transmitting the faith of Jesus Christ, and it is only because of them that we can participate in the most invigorating of tasks: the revelation of God, the communication of the Gospel.[47]

Madeleine encounters her neighbor, she enters into her mission, in and through the Church.

> Two thousand years of the Church's life have taught us that only the Church is capable, in the strict sense of the term, of living the Gospel.
> We cannot live the concrete life of the Gospel in an abstract Church.[48]

> ... The work of the Church is the salvation of the world; the world cannot be saved except by the Church. The Church is not the Church unless she saves. . . . We are not bringers of salvation unless we are the Church. And we are not Church unless we are the *whole* Church.[49]

However great the sin of Christians may be ("Having allowed the proletariat to emerge and to grow as a separate class"), and regardless of the differences we may have among ourselves, to damage unity among Christians is to betray our most fundamental task:

> To be pleasing to the world, to be loved by the world, even if it is the world of our unbelieving neighbors, can never outweigh the importance of unity among Christians. It is not for us to choose, we are not free with our own freedom. The arm cannot choose to be a branch of the tree

47. "The Church: a single life in a single body," pp. 189-90.
48. An unpublished letter.
49. "Church and mission," p. 97.

24

from which it gathers the fruit; it belongs to the body, even if the body is standing too far from the tree.

If we damage the unity of Christians when we speak to nonbelievers about Christ, we are in effect choosing to give them a mere echo of what Christ is instead of giving them Christ himself in his sacrament *par excellence* — Christians united among themselves.[50]

Madeleine, who was ever faithful to herself and to the logic of her faith, never sought to evade the burdens of the "established" Church. She lived for thirty years intrinsically bound to her parish. If this occasionally caused her to suffer, she nevertheless never compromised the importance of the parish, because she understood the link between this "tiny cell of the Church" and the universal Church. Far from setting parish life and mission in opposition to each other, she wrote:

> Mission ought not to weaken but rather should require and encourage the strengthening of everything essential to a living parish.[51]

To live its twofold vocation, as something that is both "rooted and sent," the missionary parish "will not make its missionary activity into a sort of specialized novelty," which would only weaken it. But by returning to what it is by nature, "indissolubly both filial and fraternal, because the living God is our father, and because being his children makes us all brothers," the parish will strive to renew its life-giving energies, its supernatural strength, and divine dimensions. "Striving for such a life is *impossible for human beings*," and yet all Christians are called to it.

Faith: An Event and a Teaching

Faithful to her conversion and to her baptismal catechesis, Madeleine joins with St. John of the Cross in viewing light and darkness as one in the reality of the faith. It is worthwhile citing these two passages, for Madeleine's own method, as well as the fruit of her personal experience, led her always to seek out the essential and to make her home there. It is not by chance that she brings together the tradition and the Church's experience in the world. We are familiar with the rich text from the great Spanish mystic:

---

50. "Church and mission," p. 98.
51. "Characteristics of a missionary parish," p. 169.

Whence it happens that the over-bright light of the faith, which is given to the soul, is an obscure darkness for the soul, because the greater overshadows the lesser and deprives us of it. In the same way that the light of the sun eclipses all other lights. . . . Indeed, this light blinds the soul, and takes away its vision, insofar as its light is so disproportionate to, and so far exceeds, the soul's capacity to see.[52]

Madeleine follows this same path. For her, faith is an encounter with God in which he becomes so sovereignly important that we henceforward stand before his face in order that he can tell us what he thinks and what he wishes to do with our life:

But if this encounter means being totally bedazzled by God, in order for it to be totally true it has to be total darkness. To have a living faith means being so blinded by it that we can be led by it; it is hard for us to accept what has been called "the dark light."[53]

Despite its darkness, this light is also intelligibility; over the course of this book Madeleine will often repeat this fact, sometimes using the same words. Living in a world that is obsessed with science, and confronted by her Marxist friends who classify faith as an idealistic system, Madeleine believes that she cannot insist enough on the *realism* of faith: "To believe is to know." Like those who work in the field of scientific research, the Christian too is a technician, "a technician of mystery":

[*Faith is*] *the science of a reality that concerns us and yet transcends us.* A reality about which God himself has taught us. This reality is called eternal life. . . .
Faith is the science of our fundamental ignorance. . . .[54]

[It] is the science of mystery, of the true mystery, not of the mysteries concerning the origin of life, its laws, its evolution, and its development, which gradually receive elucidation.[55]

---

52. *The Ascent of Mount Carmel,* book 2, ch. 3.
53. "What Ivry taught me," p. 265.
54. "Now is the time for our faith," pp. 205 and 207.
55. "A Christian manifesto to the atheist world," p. 180.

The solidity of the knowledge that faith gives the Christian "is the Christian's great luck": just as biology opens up for us the laws of life, faith opens up for us the secrets of our destiny. And this knowledge, moreover, is completed in action: if faith is a "knowing" — that is, knowledge of what God has told us — it is just as much a *know-how;* it enables us to live out our time in this world in a particular way: "faith is the know-how for doing God's will."

But doesn't the actual state of affairs belie Madeleine's confidence? So many apostolic efforts have been in vain, so many attempts at catechesis have proved useless. But that is just the point: Have we in fact shown the mutual integration of practice and theory that brings life to both? On the contrary, instead of an organic whole, we tend to present merely fractured parts, disjoined from the great Mystical Body, like individual chapters in an anatomy textbook: first the skeleton, then the muscles, and later the larger systems. But all of that is dead.

For Madeleine, who was always faithful to the dynamic and comprehensive unity of the baptismal catechism, faith is that which brings life to each of these realities by linking them to one another, and thus integrating them within our life:

> Our missionary life is the actualization of the truths of faith. It is necessary for us to believe them, to know what they are and how they fit together.
>
> Since these truths were made to be lived, it is necessary that we understand what sort of education and formation they entail in the lives in which they are lived. For the Church never teaches us the truths of faith without educating us in them and without forming us in them.[56]

It is this daily apprenticeship in the faith that Madeleine teaches us, unselfconsciously, and without being pedantic. As far as she herself goes, she referred to the atheist milieu in which she lived as "Ivry, my school of applied faith." Madeleine here offers a crucial and liberating distinction: it is not the details about the particular contents of our faith, *what* we believe, that interests the nonbeliever; rather, it is the very *fact* that faith guides our lives, that provokes a reaction in them:

> *What* we believe is generally not what interests the people living around us. The people we run into in contemporary milieus usually do not start

56. "In the wake of a decision from Rome," p. 154.

out asking us about what we believe. What their questions — even the ones that remain unspoken — boil down to is this: "For you, what does it mean to believe?"[57]

But even if the questions remain unspoken, our response does not: for Madeleine, "to believe is to speak," "what else can you do if you're Christian?" But she speaks in order to explain a fact: in place of the all-too-common opinion that speaking out is something optional, she presents a life that remains with all the others, but that nevertheless shows its difference from them in the most trivial of daily choices:

> To the extent that the faith does not speak out loud and clear in this confrontation, the world can maintain a surface ambiguity. But the moment the faith shows itself to the world, the world can no longer remain ambiguous; the "world" that tries to hide within it is forced to come out and present itself as being *at odds* with the faith.[58]

This "world" (between quotation marks) within the world is everything that continues to resist conversion (first in us and then around us), everything that has not yet turned back to God. Now, since faith calls us to the continuous "Repent!", it is by that very fact God's witness:

> True Marxists are interested in facts. When faith presents a fact to them, even something uncommon in society, they don't joke about it — they study it, like a problem.[59]

Nevertheless, to be a genuine fact, the faith has to be lived according to its nature and the intensity proper to it:

> *To live* as Jesus Christ told us to live, and *to do* what Jesus Christ said to do; and to live it and to do it in *our* age.[60]

Madeleine spoke about such things only rarely at the beginning; but once she became aware of what she called the "absurd dilemma," or the "disconcerting paradox," she never stopped returning to this theme. Right where

---

57. "Now is the time for our faith," p. 204.
58. "In the wake of a decision from Rome," p. 161.
59. Unpublished text, 1954.
60. "Now is the time for our faith," p. 206.

faith is most necessary in terms of mission — namely, in atheistic milieus — it seems most often to break down. Rather than being a science of the real, it surrenders its unique perspective. Not only are vast strata of people becoming dechristianized, but even the priests and missionaries who came to these atheistic milieus in order to evangelize them are abandoning the Church, and even losing their faith.

Madeleine never ceased seeking out the causes and proposing the remedies for this conflict, for the seeming incapacity to evangelize atheistic milieus. In this respect, her significance can only increase, insofar as atheism, as the "most serious phenomenon of our time" (Paul VI), is more than just Marxism, which is only one of its forms.

The third and fourth parts of this book, the latter taken from a conference she gave one month before her death, distill "true faith, the faith that endures," from what Christians too often call faith, a faith confused with simple good sense, or a basic Christian outlook. Madeleine here teaches us to analyze the behavior of faith in good health, to diagnose which forms of faith are "truncated," "under-used," or "secularized," to connect these various defective forms with the loss of a living desire for the *gift* of God, to bring faith back to what is essential, and thereby to carry it into the whole movement of history, preventing it "from withdrawing into itself when it is frustrated, and pulling out of history." Thus, by standing the "disconcerting paradox" on its head, Madeleine makes "the atheistic milieu a privileged place for faith and for our own conversion."

A limitless faith, but one purified of all foreign additives; a faith that is a pure gift from God, but made to be lived by us right in the midst of everyday life; a faith that does not shy away from performing unusual actions, but one that thereby becomes a wake-up call for the nonbeliever; a faith that is constantly put to the test, but one that receives these trials as a cleansing agent, returning it to its purity; a faith that we cannot "give" to others, but that we are obliged to proclaim — in the end, "we are people who make a profession of faith like other people make a profession of baking or medicine."[61]

Madeleine's faith calls to mind those modern metals that are capable of bearing stress and use because they have been purged of every impurity: a refined, naked, unadulterated faith, which has become the perfect tool for the Christian living in the midst of the world. By its very nature, faith is missionary.

---

61. *Ville marxiste,* p. 172.

How can we keep from thinking once again of St. John of the Cross when we hear the words Madeleine chooses to depict faith in all of its attentive gentleness and its power:

> All of our other fidelities are tiny and relative whenever it is a question of fidelity to faith.[62]

Our Neighbor: "A Human Being"

Madeleine never hid from the world: she participated in massive campaigns, particularly for the release of political prisoners, and, in every case, sometimes completely on her own, she saw things through to the end. Always open to the goal she was assigned, but uncompromising in choosing the means — whether words or acts — to achieve them, she participated in the drawing up of pamphlets and countless posters, and collaborated in giving aid to people on strike, to those out of work, etc. In doing all of this work, she formed friendships with people of every class and every country.

To the end, she remained tied to the issue of the day, whether it was the most private or the most public issue. She experienced the alternating joys, sufferings, and risks that come from throwing oneself wholeheartedly into these issues, or becoming at turns discouraged by them. This is an area in which it is difficult to maintain a balance, in which partial truths are always the most dangerous. The salvation of the world and happiness; humankind and each individual human being; collective works and direct contacts; material aid and the proclamation of the Gospel; bodily suffering and spiritual suffering — Madeleine tirelessly sought out the correct vantage point from which the whole could be seen. For her, that point always was and only ever could be the theological perspective. In every case:

> to avoid risks and to give an apostolic response, we always need exactly the same thing: *to find every impetus for missionary activity in faith itself; that is to say, in Christ's two commandments, which are inseparable and like each other, though the second of them is as great as it is only because it is the consequence of the first.*[63]

---

62. "Atheism and evangelization," p. 237.
63. *Ville marxiste,* p. 57.

By instinct, Madeleine distrusted anything abstract; moved by charity, she went directly to human beings, on earth as they are in heaven.

> The only activity that holds any interest for us is being able to love the Lord more than anything else, and to love each person we meet as if he were our brother.[64]

Among the faces of all the people she met, it was unthinkable for her to leave someone out: a rich or powerful man is welcomed as a brother; but the "poor," as it says in the Gospel, have a privileged place. She listened with as much attention to a ten-year-old boy explaining his ideas about politics as to a soldier holding national responsibilities.

Madeleine was aware of the absolute necessity of public works, of social organization, health, etc., as she herself admitted, and yet she added immediately that there are nevertheless more important things:

> These measures genuinely fight against suffering and help to alleviate it. But for all of that they do not replace goodness. Otherwise, the person becomes number 99 of category Z, promised aid by paragraph A of form 7.[65]

As she explains, society "necessarily tends to line us up in series." However, the moment we take God as our starting point, the reverse movement occurs:

> It is impossible to love God without loving humanity; it is impossible to love humanity without loving all people; and it is impossible to love all people, without loving the people he knows, with a concrete and active love.[66]

If, already on the level of social structures, each human being *has a right* to a concrete and personal love, how much more is this the case when we speak of the Kingdom of God:

> The Kingdom of God is the encounter between God and a humanity composed of one person, plus another, plus another. It does not emerge from an anonymous mass, but is received by Peter, James, and John.

64. Unpublished text, Toulouse, 1962.
65. "Atheism and evangelization," p. 246.
66. "A Christian manifesto to the atheist world," p. 184.

> The Kingdom of God is not love of the world but love of people. . . .
> The Good News of the Kingdom tells us that the world is insignificant. It
> is people who are important. . . .[67]

This passage was written in 1951. Again in 1960, Madeleine spoke to future missionaries in Toulouse about "the trap we fall in when we believe in general ideas, all the while forgetting that *each* human being is a human being."

"A man," says the parable of the Good Samaritan; Madeleine emphasizes, "it doesn't matter which one." And when, at the end of the parable, Jesus asks "Which one was neighbor to this man?", Madeleine continually repeats: "we must become the true neighbor of our neighbor." A suggestion, she loved to say, that always leads to the most unexpected of adventures!

The first characteristic of these neighbors is that we do not have to chase them down: they are "the people we did not choose to meet, but whom God willed or allowed to enter into our lives." Neighbors are not only those people who want to get to know us. While Madeleine believed that in certain circumstances it is necessary to take part in joint efforts and collective activities, she was scandalized by the fact that some Christians fail to grasp "the most important thing: the Gospel relation that a Christian is called to have with the Communists living right next door, or in the same building, or in the same profession or office or family." According to Madeleine, the situation that stands right before our eyes is the best place to carry out the Lord's "Go!", which "consists in transforming our immediate indifferent relations into true intimacies with true neighbors, making use of the paths the Lord has prepared for us before inventing our own."

Whether this "immediate" neighbor is a Communist, an atheist, a Catholic, or a believer of whatever stripe, it makes no difference: he *has a right,* because of the Sermon on the Mount, to be treated like our genuine brother. He has a right (especially if he does not share my ideas) to find before him a contemporary and a genuine human being.

Madeleine often described the qualities that someone who desired to be a neighbor to his brother would have: he must be alert to the facts; he must be intensely capable of doing something well and thoroughly; he does not keep silent about who he is and what he thinks; he does not give in to fear, particularly when it is a question of confronting others' beliefs

---

67. "Church and mission," pp. 101-2.

with what he himself believes. His brother will become a true neighbor to him only if he seeks to understand his brother's perspective (otherwise they will speak a mutually incomprehensible language).

But that is not all: my neighbor, ultimately, has the right to find before him a man who refers to God, who says what God says, who does what God asks him to do. For if my neighbor has the right to be treated like a brother, he has the right to be evangelized:

> What we have to dare to tell them, *if we have truly become their brothers,* is that happiness is not distributive justice, but poverty; that no tomorrow will ever hit the right note, but that eternity will sing; that the world looks tiny in light of death.[68]

Madeleine never changed what she meant by "evangelization"; her definition is clean and simple:

> [To tell] people, who don't know, who Christ is, what he said, and what he did — so that they do know it . . . in order that they may know what we believe and what we are sure of.[69]

Is such an attitude indiscreet? No, because "evangelizing is not converting; proclaiming the faith is not giving faith." This last phrase, which respects God's primacy as much as it does our neighbor's freedom, should be inscribed above our every endeavor: it brings a complete inner freedom.

On the basis of this approach, Madeleine delivered a symphony of reflections that help to free the modern apostle from the various anxieties that might assail him. One of these reflections echoes St. Paul's phrase, "We do not preach ourselves, but Jesus Christ." Madeleine writes:

> Jesus did not ask us to be ourselves stellar examples of his teaching; the example of his doctrine that we're meant to furnish is Jesus himself, an account of his life.[70]

Two things are required of the apostle:

---

68. An unpublished letter to a priest.
69. "Atheism and evangelization," p. 240.
70. Unpublished text, 1960.

The only witness he (Jesus) demands is that we love one another and that our lives exhibit acts that presuppose someone who is invisible but alive, unable to be grasped but at work.[71]

A third aspect follows from the fact that we have become a "neighbor" to our brother: we have to become what she calls "a reporter," someone who transmits what's new, a "current event," as they say in the movies or on television — a living fact, a living reality, concerning which we ourselves are "students." The transmission of something "which is just now going on," of "an ongoing event," requires a living language, one that is capable of adapting itself to its hearer. In this respect, too, we must be able to find a vocabulary that is accessible to our neighbor. But, far more significant than an up-to-date vocabulary, Madeleine presents us a discovery as ancient and new as the Gospel itself:

> To proclaim the Gospel in the language of the people with whom we are speaking is not enough. We have to proclaim the Gospel in the language of the Gospel, in the language of Jesus Christ. . . . And Christ's language is that of a good and brotherly heart.[72]

For Madeleine, "the goodness of a heart that comes from Christ gives the nonbeliever a presentiment of God himself." The final years of her life were a hymn to goodness: she did not miss a single opportunity to talk about it; the people around her were struck by the care with which she lived it. She rehabilitated this devalued word ("he's a good kid," "she's a good girl," etc.) by referring it back to love: "goodness is the ABC of love; where there is no goodness, there is no love."

With a genuine passion, she herself discovered, and brought many others — from Paris to Toulouse to Lyons — to discover, a living model of this humble and miraculous goodness, whom she described with a sense of humor full of affection: John XXIII. The last lines that Madeleine wrote, a month before her death, end with a reference to him:

> John XXIII showed us that, even for a pope, it is possible to live a Christian life in our world and in our age.[73]

71. "Atheism and evangelization," p. 243.
72. "Now is the time for our faith," p. 211; "Atheism and evangelization," p. 245.
73. "What Ivry taught me," p. 270.

Introduction

A Lesson We Never Learned

In Madeleine's understanding, the missionary life is not an expertise re-served for those who write the word on their identity papers in the space marked "Profession." For her, it is neither "optional nor out of the ordi-nary"; "a missionary is a Christian before all else," and mission is just "the fullness of Christian life." A "missionary without a boat" is "an apostle be-cause she is a Christian, insofar as she is Christian"; "it is the unbelief of her neighbor that calls her to her mission":

> From a sand dune, dressed in white, the missionary overlooks an ex-panse of lands filled with unbaptized peoples. From the top of a long subway staircase, dressed in an ordinary suit or raincoat, we overlook, on each step, during this busy rush-hour time, an expanse of heads, of bustling heads, waiting for the door to open. Caps, berets, hats, and hair of every color. Hundreds of heads — hundreds of souls. And there we stand, above.
> And above us, and everywhere, is God.
> God is everywhere — and how many souls even take notice![74]

No doubt more than anyone else, Madeleine participated in the im-mense twentieth-century Christian rediscovery that we become mission-aries precisely in the places we live, by the very act of becoming the neigh-bor of those around us. Madeleine's missionary impulse is one of the very first (1933), and few of these new impulses were as genuine. In any event, she was the first to discover and point out an unsuspected similarity be-tween the missionaries of old, who sailed to distant lands, and those "ordi-nary people of the streets [who] believe with all of our might that this street, this world, where God has placed us, is our place of holiness."[75]

To be sure, the missionary in foreign lands knew that he would en-counter great dangers and perhaps even death, but what the missionary of the suburbs and of the great crowds does not know is that he too is in dan-ger: in him, and around him, the Kingdom of God is suffering violence: "*What we have never learned* is that the supernatural, constitutive state for the missionary is as a matter of course a state of violence."

As we will see, Madeleine never yielded to the temptation to play

74. "Missionaries without a boat," p. 59.
75. "We, the ordinary people of the street," p. 54.

down real antagonisms; for the "world" and the Gospel are at odds with each other, and faith represents "the choice between the world and the Kingdom of Heaven, a choice that Jesus Christ won for us, and for which he has given us the strength."

Despite the clear differences that exist between them, Madeleine borrowed an image from John of the Cross's *Reform of Carmel* to characterize the situation of the Christian living in the midst of the world: it is a sharp peak that "traced out at every moment within us and in front of us," the juncture of two slopes that seem "to mount an attack upon each other" and that "come together in us": one has its foundation in the promise of the God who saves, the other descends to the point of rejecting God: "I will not serve."[76]

When Madeleine says that Christians have never learned this lesson, she is not wrong, even if it can be found in dusty books or piety manuals for ascetical practices! For this violence and this battle are typically presented in abstract or disincarnate forms, or, better, as an exercise to be practiced in the barracks; while the reality is that the Christian is thrown into battle, without even knowing that war has been declared and is raging. But this image, which Madeleine employs on occasion, is not strong enough. What is at stake is something greater, something in the throes of birth: one day, in the heart of the crisis of 1954, she writes to a missionary:

> I'm worried that, like a woman who doesn't realize that we give birth only in pain, and who doesn't understand a thing about what it means to be torn apart, and who has stifled within herself both what is tearing her apart and what is coming to birth, you are *keeping* your Mission within you. While the little child is inside the mother, he has an adult body; but to be born into the world, he must necessarily become tiny, and limited, . . . and yet he has to pass through infancy in order to become a man. What people are waiting for is precisely this little man, and not the adult that you yourself are. If this Mission is not able to pass through your suffering, it would perhaps remain in the working class, but like a dead child that a woman carries inside herself in the street.
>
> It seems to me that it is just like this that the Church is always born, which is at once one and many. It is always the same contractions that have always caused the saints such pain. They were called to fruitfulness; when they accepted the fact that everything "grown up" they now pos-

76. Cf., "In the wake of a decision from Rome," p. 163.

sess first had to emerge from them impoverished and shrunken through the cruel and bloody, yet organic, tremors of obedience, the Christ-Church has continued to be born into the world. Others who were called to this very same fruitfulness could not come to grips with the laws of this life, they confused these laws with the sufferings of a sick body, and so Christ was not able to emerge from them in order to go further.

Every true Christian who lives in an atheistic environment is called to undergo the same trial. If he is not prepared for it, like a mother for childbirth, he will fail the trial. Wanting to be faithful to his vocation as a witness, he will be tempted to make an expertise out of the dimension that strikes him as the most missionary, and he will thus lose a view of the whole:

> This area starts to become feverish, extremely sensitive, and congested; it throbs in echo of the heartbeat; and by drawing all attention to itself, it gets special treatment to the detriment of the rest.[77]

To a priest who was responsible for the formation of missions to the working class, she wrote:

> We often get the impression that those who have been prepared for missions have been well nourished for everything concerning their particular task, but undernourished for everything concerning the common lot of all Christians and all priests.

Here we touch upon a point in which Madeleine showed herself to be an extremely bold guide (she didn't turn away from any encounter, any appropriate task regardless of what it was, regardless of whom it involved), but a no less extremely trustworthy one: she analyzes the risks the adventure entails, the false trails. And, considering these in light of what is essential — "the difficult challenge of joining together our immediate circumstances with the vision of the faith" — she provides the means for following the task through to the end.

In the months following her conversion, Madeleine had to live with her father in the country. While there, she studied the texts of St. Thomas Aquinas that appeared in regular installments in the *Revue des Jeunes*, and

---

77. "In the wake of a decision from Rome," p. 153.

she read Fr. Garrigou-Lagrange. Was it from these readings that she drew the conviction that truth (and energy) is a summit standing between two exaggerations? In any event, this conviction became the core of her being, her most fundamental characteristic. Her whole life could be interpreted as a discourse on the method for ascending the narrow peak of antagonisms, with decisive (but no less arduous) steps. But the secret of how she kept her balance and held off vertigo can be found in the fact that she accepted the mystery of God in its fullness and entrusted herself to this supernatural fullness in order to penetrate into the heart of earthly realities incomparably more deeply than any earlier method.

She did not alter a fraction of the divine truth, she did not bother accommodating it to popular tastes, to whatever might be pleasing (of course, presenting this truth in a way that is accessible is something else entirely); rather, the truth that Madeleine received from God is something she took in its totality, willingly expanded it as far as possible, and thereby resolved every antagonism and transformed whatever seemed to stand in contradiction.

Examples abound, and the reader will have no trouble finding them. Here are just a few.

When a Christian becomes deeply conscious of the suffering and misery of the world and, at the same time, is continually immersed in an environment in which God is absent, it is hard for him to strike a balance between the earthly happiness he feels compelled to give his brothers, and salvation, that is, the entrance into the life of God that comes from God: to serve the one without neglecting the other shows itself in practice to be a continuous source of conflict. For her part, Madeleine took a decisive stand in the absoluteness of God, and refused to be pushed elsewhere. The only "stupendous and staggering happiness" that man has is God, earthly joys being merely "ever-changing superfluities next to him who stays the same." In this, we find the pure echo of the Gospel: seek first the Kingdom of Heaven.

Madeleine did not confuse the order:

> Saving the world does not mean making it happy; it means showing the world the meaning of its suffering and giving it a joy that "nothing can take away." If we must fight against the misery and misfortune which Christ took so seriously as to speak of judging us in the end solely by what we did for others in this regard, we must keep in mind that what is at stake is ultimately not solving these problems and constructing a second earthly paradise; rather, what is at stake is eternal life.

But, if the Kingdom of heaven is not of the world, it is nevertheless in the world.[78]

The Christian who thus takes God seriously, without rivalry, hears God say to him: "I have made you a *covenant* for the people." Being "made a covenant" and given the task of mediating, the Christian ceases "being distracted from the world by God, or distracted from God by the world," because in the most heated battles for human justice, the Christian, whose eyes are fixed on the glory of God, sees the God who has loved men first and gratuitously.

To be sure, the happiness and the salvation of men continue to come into conflict in the most inward point of his being:

> But this confrontation will not create confusion or sterile tensions. The service of human happiness, which [the Christian] pursues in the likeness of the heavenly Father, is ordered, hierarchized, and brought to completion within the vast horizon of salvation.[79]

In reality, the desire for earthly happiness and the desire for salvation take concrete shape *in the hope of the Communist and the hope of the Christian,* two contradictory hopes that confront each other through two permanent and universal bodies: the Party and the Church. Madeleine does not underestimate this Communist hope; she accords it the breadth and the dimensions that she experienced of it in the people she knew: a response to the hopes of the poor, a hope for a better tomorrow, a love that translates into action, and perseverance in expectant waiting.

But, in practice, this earthly hope puts our divine hope to the test and tempts us to doubt the urgency, the importance, or the usefulness of a perspective or a praxis founded on what is invisible. In this case, either we slip toward the realizations of the sole earthly hope because we have lost sight of the treasure that is ours, or, worse still, we withdraw into our hope as into a fortified front, acting as if those who do not share our hope were incapable of receiving the salvation brought by Jesus Christ. In either case, we sin against Hope and we make God less. If we have hope only in times of peace, says Madeleine, we will pass from failure to failure. But if, by contrast, "we discern in every contradiction a provocation to expand our

---

78. "Church and mission," pp. 99-100.
79. "Light and darkness," p. 196.

Hope — to hope more and better — our Christian life will recover, in the struggle for which it was made, the normal condition of its strength and growth." Through being "knocked backwards," she arrives at a "living degree of certainty."

From this higher altitude, the Communist is no longer considered only according to the human weight of his earthly qualities, which might be legitimately impressive, but also as the victim of the most terrible misfortune possible, the systematic negation of God, which is connected with these very qualities. Thus, precisely because the Communist is my neighbor, I cannot hide my Hope from him; nor can I water it down; nor can I cease to consider him as my brother.

The same can be said about faith. Its significance lies in its ordering everything toward eternal life, and Madeleine so to speak surrenders herself to it unreservedly. But, precisely for this reason, like cosmic rays close to their source, her faith was able to penetrate the densest shadows of our age. Organized according to "eternal laws, faith is embodied in time. It is given to us so that we, with human souls, can choose God above all other things." Moreover, when she "examines her faith," it is not so much to look for "building blocks, which are often merely remnants of God which have become foolish or else simply rational," but, looking first and above all else at God himself, she discerns what meaning to give her human endeavors in light of what God said to do.

What Madeleine teaches us once and for all is that the truth of our love for the world, the quality of our witness (incidentally, this is a word she rarely uses), the precision of our response, and the effectiveness of our action, can in a Christian sense come only from Christ and from God, understood as absolutes, as unfailing rocks. And by the same token, the answer we seek in God, which satisfies so fully and finally, reveals itself moreover to be the missionary fact that poses the true question to the nonbeliever.

> We have to realize that sharing the way of thinking and the sensibilities of the working class, sharing their loves and their hatreds, even if we correct and purify them, if it is our sole witness, constitutes a counterwitness to our actual mission. We must never allow there to be any ambiguity about the fact that God is for us the only absolute good, and that he thus relativizes all other goods because they are so only insofar as they come from him.
>
> But this God of ours, this good that we call absolute, would strike

people as a reasonable possibility only if we took seriously, as things that come from God, all the real goods that man desires, and the real evil that the lack of these goods represents for people.[80]

What is at issue here is much more than recognizing a rare magnanimity in Madeleine. Instead, we must see that she holds the key that we have been given for our confrontation with the world. Madeleine never describes the Christian's engagement in the world as a sentimental or facile idyll. The Christian's love can tolerate no compromise the moment God is at issue; this love will be invincible precisely to the extent that it entrusts itself to nothing other than God. But, once it does so it will no longer be foreign to anything else existing in the world.

> Love knows that she is stronger than everything else.
> She loves to fight. And when she fights, she makes a game of watching the proportions reverse themselves between the greatest obstacles in the world which constantly try to bolster their own strength, and love herself, who constantly surrenders everything so that the only thing that remains in the end is herself.[81]

One day — here we are in the midst of the crisis of 1954 — Madeleine felt an obligation to disclose her thoughts to her priest friends, and on one point in particular, her differences. What she asked them — and God knows with what fraternal affection and how much agreement over the necessities of mission — was not to let the injuries they received make them shortsighted.

> To sacrifice the continuity of a presence because of the fractured possibilities that are offered to her would not be for the Church a waiting, but a step backwards.
> Catastrophes are what allow us to see how life can be sustained through the tiniest possibilities. When man's instinct thus tells him "you can make it," he automatically comes up with a "how to make it."
> It is the same question of life that is being posed here, albeit in different terms.[82]

---

80. "Goodness," pp. 138-39.
81. Excerpt from a letter.
82. Unpublished text, 7 February 1954.

Among the antagonisms, the chasms, the arguments, and the oppositions that swallow up or sterilize missionaries — that is to say, every Christian today who is confronted by atheism — Madeleine in a few brief lines explains the secret of her deep confidence:

> If our greatest strength is our passion for God, we will turn off of dangerous missionary trails without our even noticing it. The path left open to us will scale dizzying heights, but it will not be dangerous. Or more precisely, its danger will be no match for our strength.
>
> This passion for God will reveal to us that our Christian life is a pathway between two abysses. One is the measurable abyss of the world's rejections of God. The other is the unfathomable abyss of the mysteries of God.
>
> We will come to see that we are walking along the adjoining line where these two abysses intersect. And we will thus understand how we are mediators, and why we are mediators.[83]

Madeleine was always very attentive to the signs given by Providence; I myself see a sign in the name she bore and in her patron saint. On Easter morning, the Holy Women saw that the tomb was empty: the apostles who were alerted arrive at the tomb and then leave. But Mary Magdalen will not accept this emptiness, this disappearance of her Lord; she stays close to the tomb, she leans into it. She looks in, remains unbiased, and is finally the first to see Christ again.

Similarly, Madeleine, confronted with the negations of atheism, seeks more profoundly, trusts in the word of Christ, and, until finally the infinitely more beautiful response is given to her, refuses to leave what appears to be an empty tomb.

The more official apostles around her — the priests and the missionaries of every denomination — often return from their pilgrimage to the vacant tomb like the apostles and the pilgrims of Emmaus, with "a sad face," and saying "we were hoping. . . ."

Both Madeleines teach us the same thing: a love stronger than death, a faith that grows in times of trial, and a hope that is not Péguy's little girl, but "a hope grown into womanhood,"[84] by which we inscribe in salvation history the events we were destined to inscribe.

83. "Light and darkness," p. 195.
84. "Communist hope and Christian hope," p. 215.

But all of this has a single source, a spring that gushes forth like the river of Revelation, irrigating the heavenly Jerusalem: namely, the fact that "God is a Somebody."

Madeleine's lesson is that we have to be theological: she teaches an unconditional trust in God, a fidelity to his mystery, a patient waiting upon his gift and seeking strength solely in the one Word and in divine generosity. The lesson God teaches through Madeleine is that, to those who set nothing in competition with his glory, he gives a remarkable attentiveness to others, a clarity that is focused, and an effectiveness in history that transcends all human measure.

It is an urgent message addressed to the Christian who is present in the world, but who sees this world from heights unknown to men, like the astronauts of our day who can take in a whole continent at a glance.

PRELUDE

God is dead . . . long live death!
1922

Madeleine is seventeen years old.
She is an atheist.
If one day God would be her All,
it is because at this point she experienced
the extremities of Nothingness.
Our love for God will be small-hearted to the extent
that our turning away from him was mediocre.

God Is Dead . . . Long Live Death!

It's been said that "God is dead."

Because this is true, we need to have the honesty to live as if God does not exist. Since we have settled the question for him, now we have to settle it for us.

So now we can be sure where we stand: if we do not know the exact length of our life, at least we know it will be short, a tiny little life. For some people, unhappiness will take up all the space. For others, happiness will take up more or less of the space. But it will never be an immense unhappiness or happiness because it all has to fit into a tiny life.

The great, indisputable, and reasonable unhappiness is death. Faced with death, we have to become realistic, honest, and practical. I say, "*become.*" Even though I am only seventeen and there are still many people left to meet, I am amazed at people's general lack of common sense.

Revolutionaries interest me, but somehow they have missed the point. They may be able to change the world, but all the same one day we will still have to leave it. The scientists are smart, but somewhat naive. They think they will be able to conquer death just because they have overcome some of the causes of death such as rabies or smallpox. But death does just fine.

I sympathize a lot with the pacifists, but they are weak in their calculations. Even if they had managed to muzzle the war of 1914, those whose lives would have been spared will still be laid out in their graves by 1998.

I'm shocked by the confidence of the do-gooders — they have no modesty. They are so sure they are contributing to other people's happiness. At best, it is doubtful. The better life is, the harder it is to die. The proof? When their meaning of life is killed off, people take their lives by their own hands.

Lovers are totally illogical and hard to reason with: "I love you forever!" They won't face the fact that they will be unfaithful whether they like it or not; their infidelity gets closer day by day . . . not to mention old age, which is the death of one's constitution and health. As for me, I don't plan on sticking too close or too long to a man I might one day love, because then he would have to watch my teeth fall out, my chin droop, and my body shrivel like a prune or swell like a balloon. If I do love, it will be for the moment, on the quick, like someone with a deadline to meet.

Mothers, the poor things, seem unable to keep themselves from saying or doing such ridiculous things: "Oh, how I want my little one to be happy." If they could, they would just create happiness and give it to their kid. But of course, mothers don't want to think for a second that their children could become cannon-fodder — and just try to tell them that whatever they do their children will end up fodder for death. I do not want to have children. It is enough each day to have to imagine burying my parents.

Perhaps the most logical people are the bricklayers, the carpenters, the photographers, the artists, and the poets. They make things that last, and consequently they make something of themselves last. Kings die, but their thrones remain in museums. Having your picture up somewhere is a way of existing. Monuments hold out for a long while. Mona Lisa would have stopped smiling long ago if someone had not made a portrait. In class, when a student recites a poem by LaFontaine, LaFontaine's thoughts are still alive in a way.

Then there are people who just have fun, who kill time waiting for time to kill them. I am one of these. Serious people scoff at us in the name of their serious occupations.

The legacy of God's death has yet to be settled. He left everywhere bonds of eternity, power, and spirit. So who's the beneficiary? Death! God was everlasting; now only death lasts forever. God was all powerful; now death dominates everyone and everything. God was spirit — I'm not even too sure what that is — but death is everywhere, invisible, and effective. It gives a little tap, and boom! — love stops loving, thought stops thinking, babies stop smiling, and then there is . . . Nothing.

Long ago, people used to say "we're dancing on a volcano." Yes, I am dancing, and if it's on top of a volcano, then I would rather know. Near volcanoes there are mansions and shacks, young people and old, geniuses and imbeciles, sports champions and lame people, some well loved and some loved not at all. When the volcano spills over, however, nothing is left but fire. As they say, it all goes down in flames.

We are all so close to the one true unhappiness, but do we have the guts to say so? Say so?! But with what? — God has even wiped out our words. . . . Is there any way to say tactfully to a dying person, "Have a good day," or "have a good evening"? . . . And so we say, "Farewell, until we meet again," . . . because we haven't yet learned how to say: "Until nowhere," "Until nothing at all," . . .

PART ONE

THE MISSIONARY

1933-1949

Because God is Everything, we have to carry him everywhere; the only thing that should distinguish us from others is our faith.

"To be people immersed as deeply as possible in the midst of the world, with no rules, no vows, no habits, and no convents separating us from the world; to be poor, but just like people you find everywhere; to be chaste, but like people from every social stratum; to be obedient, but just like people of every nationality."

(Missionaries without a boat, unpublished text)

To be a missionary — with or without a boat — that's the point; but that's simply what it means to be Christian.

September 1940. Emile Cardinal Suhard, Archbishop of Paris, announces at the Carmelite convent in Lisieux his plan to begin a seminary for the formation of priests who would hold manual labor jobs and live among the working-class people. This project was to be called *The Mission of France.*

June 1941. P. Lebret and Jacques Loew found the magazine *Economie et Humanisme,* a Catholic periodical calling attention to the economic inequalities and injustices of modern society.

July 1941. The Conference of French Bishops approves the foundation of *The Mission of France.* Louis Agros is named as the first rector of the seminary, to be located in Lisieux. Madeleine Delbrêl is appointed as lay advisor.

December 1941. Jacques Loew, a Dominican priest, becomes a dockyard worker at the Port of Marseille and lives in a poor neighborhood among the people.

October 1942. The opening of the worker-priest seminary in Lisieux. Abbé Lorenzo, pastor of Ivry, is named as director of students.

April 1943. Henri Godin and Yvan Daniel present their book *France: A Missionary Country?* to Cardinal Suhard. The work is an in-depth study of the phenomenon of "dechristianization" in France, and attributes it to a division that exists between the Church and the modern, working-class world. Among other suggestions, the study calls for change and renewal in the Church and the creation of new forms of basic Christian communities among the people.

July 1943. Cardinal Suhard begins *The Mission of Paris,* a movement of both laity and clergy who would live and work in small groups and share the problems of the urban working class.

October 1943. Bishop Delay allows several priests of Marseille to hold ordinary jobs and live in the working neighborhoods.

January 1944. Henri Godin, co-author of *France: A Missionary Country?,* is killed in a car accident.

January 1945. The first group of worker-priests leaves from Lisieux for Paris and cities throughout France.

Easter 1947. Cardinal Suhard issues a pastoral letter: *The Rise or the Decline of the Church?*

July 1949. The Holy Office issues a decree prohibiting all collaboration with the Communists.

From the moment God first took hold of her, Madeleine Delbrêl's sole concern was to root herself in the Church, at "the crossroads of love."

For her, "God touches the horizon at every point; simply by the fact that he exists, he is to be preferred above all other things."[1] But love for Jesus Christ requires that we respond to him, and leads us to love all our brothers; Jesus fuses together the two ends of love: the love of God, who must be loved for his own sake, and the love of man "which brings us close to our neighbors and inclines us to a 'preferential option' for whomever we encounter."

For the sake of this love, Madeleine "consciously set up a genuine family life with any human being she happened to meet, and this family life is the necessary sign of the other family life that is continually deepened with all the people on the planet."[2]

This love made her reject all the barriers that social conventions and tradition — even pious tradition — impose on human relations. It set her on equal footing with the "people of the street," believers and nonbelievers alike. With them, both for her sake and for theirs, she discovers in their life new pathways to prayer, to contemplation, and to the proclamation of the Gospel.

In and with the small missionary *équipes* that she inspired, Madeleine herself lives this new life; during this time, she writes very little. Nevertheless, a few manuscripts were published, which quickly reached a wide circulation, passing from hand to hand. Most notably among these was, *We, the ordinary people of the streets,* a text that changed the way a lot of people understood and lived mission.

---

1. *Pourquoi nous aimons le Père Foucauld,* p. 539.
2. *Pourquoi nous aimons le Père Foucauld,* p. 542.

We, the Ordinary People of the Streets

There are many places where the Spirit blows,
but there is one Spirit that blows in all places.

There are some people whom God takes and sets apart.

There are others he leaves among the crowds, people he does not "withdraw from the world."

These are the people who have an ordinary job, an ordinary household, or an ordinary celibacy. People with ordinary sicknesses, and ordinary times of grieving. People with an ordinary house, and ordinary clothes. These are the people of ordinary life. The people we might meet on any street.

They love the door that opens onto the street, just as their brothers who are hidden from the world love the door that shuts behind them forever.

We, the ordinary people of the streets, believe with all our might that this street, this world, where God has placed us, is our place of holiness.

We believe that we lack nothing here that we need. If we needed something else, God would already have given it to us.

Silence

We do not need to find silence; we already have it. The day we lack silence is the day we have not learned how to keep it.

54

All the noises around us cause much less disturbance than we ourselves do.

The real noise is the echo things make within us. It is not necessarily talking that breaks silence. Silence is the place where the Word of God dwells; if we limit ourselves to repeating this word, then we can speak without ceasing to be silent.

Monasteries appear to be the place of praise and the place of the silence that praise requires.

In the street, crushed by the crowd, we make our souls into so many caves of silence wherein the Word of God can dwell and resound.

In those crowds marked by the sins of hatred, lust, and drunkenness, we find a desert of silence, and we recollect ourselves here with great ease, so that God can ring out his name: *"Vox clamans in deserto."*

Solitude

We, the ordinary people of the streets, do not see solitude as the absence of the world but as the presence of God.

Encountering him in all places is what creates our solitude.

For us, being truly alone means participating in God's solitude.

God is so great that nothing can find room anywhere else but within him.

For us, the whole world is like a face-to-face meeting with the one whom we cannot escape.

We encounter his living causality right there on the busy street corners.

We encounter his imprint on the earth.

We encounter his Providence in the laws of science.

We encounter Christ in all these "little ones who are his own": the ones who suffer in body, the ones who are bored, the ones who are troubled, the ones who are in need.

We encounter Christ rejected, in the sin that wears a thousand faces.

How could we possibly have the heart to mock these people or to hate them, this multitude of sinners with whom we rub shoulders?

The solitude of God in fraternal charity; it is Christ serving Christ, Christ in the one who is serving and Christ in the one being served.

How could apostolate be a waste of energy or a distraction?

Obedience

We, the ordinary people of the streets, know very well that as long as our own will is alive, we will not be able to love Christ definitively.

We know that only obedience can root us in his death.

We would envy our religious brothers and sisters if we too could not "die to ourselves" a little more each day.

However, for us the tiny circumstances of life are faithful "superiors." They do not leave us alone for a moment; and the "yeses" we have to say to them follow continuously, one after the other.

When we surrender to them without resistance we find ourselves wonderfully liberated from ourselves. We float in Providence like a cork on the ocean waters.

But let's not act like heroes: God trusts nothing to chance; the rhythms of our life are vast because he has willed it so.

From the moment we wake up these circumstances take hold of us. It is the telephone that rings; it is the key that won't work, the bus that doesn't arrive or arrives full, or doesn't wait for us. It is the person sitting next to us who takes up the whole seat; or the vibration of the loose window pane that drives us crazy.

It's the daily routine, one chore that leads to another, some job we wouldn't have chosen. It's the weather and its changes — which is exquisite precisely because it is completely untainted by human doing. It's being cold, or being hot; it's the headache or the toothache. It's the people we meet and the conversations they choose to start. It's the rude man who nearly knocks us off the sidewalk. It's the people who need to kill some time, and so they corner us.

For us, the ordinary people of the streets, obedience means bending to the ways of our times whenever they are not harmful. It means wearing the same clothes as everyone else, taking on the same routines as everyone else, and speaking the same language as everyone else.

When we live with others, obedience also means we set aside our own tastes and leave things in the place others have put them. In this way, life becomes an epic film in slow motion. It does not make our head spin. It does not take our breath away. Little by little, thread by thread, it eats away at the old man's frame, which cannot be mended and must be made new from the ground up. When we thus become accustomed to giving up our will to so many tiny things, we will no longer find it hard, when the occasion presents itself, to do the will of our boss, our husband, or our parents.

And our hope is that death, too, will be easy. It will not be a big ordeal, but rather the outcome of small ordinary sufferings, to which we have given our assent as they passed, one after the other.

Love

We, the ordinary people of the streets, are certain we can love God as much as he might desire to be loved by us.

We don't regard love as something extraordinary but as something that consumes. We believe that doing little things for God is as much a way of loving him as doing great deeds. Besides, we're not very well informed about the greatness of our acts. There are nevertheless two things we know for sure: first, whatever we do can't help but be small; and second, whatever God does is great.

And so we go about our activities with a sense of great peace.

We know that all our work consists in not shifting about under grace; in not choosing what we would do; and that it is God who acts through us.

There is nothing difficult for God; the one who grows anxious at difficulties is the one who counts on his own capacity for action.

Because we find that love is work enough for us, we don't take the time to categorize what we are doing as either "contemplation" or "action."

We find that prayer is action and that action is prayer. It seems to us that truly loving action is filled with light.

It seems to us that a soul standing before such action is like a night that is full of expectation for the coming dawn. And when the light breaks, when God's will is clearly understood, she lives it out gently, with poise, peacefully watching her God inspiring her and at work within her. It seems to us that action is also an imploring prayer. It does not at all seem to us that action nails us down to our field of work, our apostolate, or our life.

Quite the contrary, we believe that an action perfectly carried out at the time and place it is required of us binds us to the whole Church, sends us out throughout her body, making us *disponible* in her.

Our feet march upon a street, but our heartbeat reverberates through the whole world.

That is why our small acts, which we can't decide whether they're action or contemplation, perfectly join together the love of God and the love of our neighbor.

Giving ourselves over to his will at the same time gives us over to the

Church, whom the same will continuously makes our saving mother of grace.

Each docile act makes us receive God totally and give God totally, in a great freedom of spirit.

And thus life becomes a celebration.

Each tiny act is an extraordinary event, in which heaven is given to us, in which we are able to give heaven to others.

It makes no difference what we do, whether we take in hand a broom or a pen. Whether we speak or keep silent. Whether we are sewing or holding a meeting, caring for a sick person or tapping away at the typewriter.

Whatever it is, it's just the outer shell of an amazing inner reality: the soul's encounter, renewed at each moment, in which, at each moment, the soul grows in grace and becomes ever more beautiful for her God.

Is the doorbell ringing? Quick, open the door! It's God coming to love us. Is someone asking us to do something? Here you are! . . . it's God coming to love us. Is it time to sit down for lunch? Let's go — it's God coming to love us.

Let's let him.

Missionaries Without a Boat[3]

A Voice Praying in the Desert

There has been a lot said about "the desert of love." Love seeks the desert because the desert is where man is handed over to God, stripped bare of his country, his friends, his fields, his home. In the desert, a person neither possesses what he loves, nor is he possessed by those who love him; he is totally submitted to God in an immense and intimate encounter.

That is why in every age the Holy Spirit has compelled all lovers to seek the desert.

We, missionaries without a boat, are seized by the same love and led by the same Spirit into new deserts.

From a sand dune, dressed in white, the missionary overlooks an expanse of lands filled with unbaptized peoples. From the top of a long subway staircase, dressed in an ordinary suit or raincoat, we overlook, on each step, during this busy rush-hour time, an expanse of heads, of bustling heads, waiting for the door to open. Caps, berets, hats, and hair of every color. Hundreds of heads — hundreds of souls. And there we stand, above.

And above us, and everywhere, is God.

God is everywhere — and how many souls even take notice?

In a moment, when the subway doors open, we'll climb aboard. We'll see faces, foreheads, eyes, and mouths. Mouths of lonely people, in their natural state: some greedy, some impure, some malicious; some mouths

3. Excerpts from an unpublished text, 1943.

that hunger, some filled with every earthly sustenance, but few — very few — that bear the form of the Gospel.

Once we arrive at our station, we will surface into the dark, breathe the night air, and go down the street that leads home.

In the fog, the rain, or the moonlight, we will pass by other people. We will overhear them talking about their purchases, about butter, about money, about promotions, about fear, about quarrels — but hardly ever about the one we love.

To the right, to the left, stand darkened houses with tiny cracks of light, announcing that there are people alive in all this blackness.

We can well imagine what they are doing. They are constructing their fragile joys, bearing their long suffering, doing some good, doing much that is sinful.

We cannot help wonder how little light there would be if a light shined only for each person in prayer.

Yes, we have our deserts — and love leads us into them.

The same Spirit that leads our white-robed brothers and sisters into their deserts, also leads our beating heart down the turbulent stairways, into the subways, and up again to the darkened streets.

We do not envy our religious brothers and sisters.

In this crowd, heart against heart, crushed between so many bodies, on the seat we share with these three strangers, in the darkened street, our heart beats like a fist closed upon a bird.

The Holy Spirit, the whole Holy Spirit in our tiny heart, a love great as God is beating within us, like a moiling sea struggling to break out, to spread out, to penetrate into all these closed-up creatures, into all these impermeable souls.

To be able to pace every street, to sit in every metro, climb up every staircase, carry the Lord God to all places: we are certain to find a soul here or there that has preserved her human fragility before the grace of God, a soul that has forgotten to armor herself in gold or concrete.

And we can pray, pray just as they pray in all the other deserts, pray for all these people so close to us, so close to God.

A desert of people. We can plunge into the crowd as if plunging into the white desert sands.

A crowded desert, a desert of love.

The nakedness of real love.

And we do not miss the countryside, or the friend who would understand what we have on our hearts, or the quiet hour in the corner of a church, or the favorite book left at home.

The desert is where we become love's prey.

Won't this love that dwells in us, that explodes in us, also transform us?

Lord, Lord, let the thick skin that covers me not be a hindrance to you. Pass through it.

My eyes, my hands, my mouth are yours.

This sad lady in front of me: here is my mouth for you to smile at her.

This child so pale he's almost gray: here are my eyes for you to gaze at him.

This man so tired, so weary: here is my body so that you may give him my seat, here is my voice so that you may say softly to him, "Please sit down."

This smug young man, so dull, so hard: here is my heart, that you may love him, more strongly than he has ever been loved before.

Missions to the desert, unfailing missions, sure missions, missions in which we sow God in the midst of the world, certain that, somewhere, he will take root, for: "There where love is lacking, put love, and you will reap love."

Witnesses

The Word of God is not brought to the ends of the world in a suitcase. We carry it in ourselves.

We don't set it off in a corner of ourselves, arranged in our memory as if on a cupboard shelf. We must let it go to the very core of ourselves, to the very center around which our whole being revolves.

We cannot be missionaries if we have not sincerely, generously, and warmly welcomed the Word of God, the Gospel, within ourselves.

The vital dynamic of this word is to take on flesh, to become flesh in us.

And when this word comes to dwell within us, we become capable of being missionaries.

But let's not misunderstand ourselves. We know how difficult it is to take in this message intact. That is why so many of us tend to touch it up, twist it out of shape, and smooth it over.

We feel the need to bring the message in line with the custom of the day, as if God weren't in line with the custom of all days, as if we could improve on God.

If the missionary priest is the spokesman of God's Word, we, missionaries without holy orders, are a sort of sacrament of God's Word.

Once we have heard God's Word, we no longer have the right not to accept it; once we have accepted it, we no longer have the right not to let it become flesh in us; once it has become flesh in us, we no longer have the right to keep it for ourselves alone. Henceforward, we belong to all those who are waiting for the Word.

The time of martyrs comes and goes, but the time of witnesses continues without end — and being witnesses means being martyrs.

This incarnation of God's Word in us, this allowing ourselves to be molded by it, is what we call witnessing.

To take the Word of God seriously, we need all the strength of the Holy Spirit.

If our witness is often mediocre, it is because we have not realized that the same kind of heroism is needed to be a witness as to be a martyr.

Charles de Foucauld said, "I must live today as if tonight I were going to die as a martyr."

At the beginning of each hour of the long day, we could say, "I must begin this hour as if I were going to be a martyr, and a witness" — because there is not one second that we have the right to let God's Word lie dormant in us. And this entails awakening a fervor in our very being in the presence of the grace of each moment, a wildly passionate expectation for that strength, without which we would turn traitor.

Whoever Follows Me
Does Not Walk in Darkness

We have to become aware of the two great expanses of darkness between which our life unfolds, the unfathomable darkness of God and the darkness of man. We must do so if we are to abandon ourselves passionately to the Gospel, if we are to discover the Gospel by means of our dual nothingness of being both creatures and sinners.

We have to be totally immersed in the walking death that constitutes our love for man: the ravages of time, universal weakness, the periods of mourning, the decay of age, of all values, of ourselves.

At the other pole, we have to grasp tangibly the impenetrable universe of the security of God in order to acquire such a vivid sense of the horror of the night that we cling more fervently to the Gospel light than to our very bread.

Only thus will we cling to it like a cable stretched over a double abyss.

In order to desire to be saved, we must know we are lost.

Unless you take this little book of the Gospel in your hands with the determination of a person who is holding onto his very last hope, you will neither be able to figure it out, nor receive its message.

If you are fortunate enough to be in such despair, to be so bereft of all human hope, it matters little whether you pick up the book from the shelves of a vast library, from the pocket of your workman's vest, or from your school backpack; whether during a retreat, or just any old day; whether in a church or in your kitchen, out in the field or in your office — just as you take hold of the book, so will it take hold of you. Its words, which are spirit, will penetrate into you like seeds in the earth, like leaven in bread, like trees in the sky. And if you yield yourself up to these words, you yourself will become simply a new expression of them.

Every book is already a mystery, a human mystery. In every book there is an interweaving of matter and spirit, of signs and the invisible realities they indicate. Every book bears witness that the soul's boundaries lie beyond the flesh and out of hands' reach.

But the Gospel is not just one book among others. It is not just one human word among others. It is the spoken Word of God. It is the Word of God spoken in Christ, whose life we contemplate and recount.

The Gospel has the power to enlighten and transform; it is a permanent and powerful gift from God. And like all of God's gifts, it is poured out only into the hands of faith; it can be received only in the vertiginous depths of hope.

For the Gospel to reveal its mystery, no special setting, no advanced education, no particular technique is required. All it needs is a soul bowed down in adoration and a heart stripped of all trust in things human.

"He who does the truth comes into the light . . ."
　"I have given you an example so that as I have done, you also will do . . ."
　"If you love me, you will keep my word . . ."

The Gospel's secret does not open itself to curiosity; it is not an intellectual initiation. Rather, the Gospel's secret is essentially a life-giving mystery.

The light of the Gospel does not remain an extrinsic illumination — rather, it is a fire that demands entry into us so that it may ravage and transform us.

A person who allows one word of the Lord to penetrate him and to be carried out in his life comes to know the Gospel more than the person who restricts his efforts to abstract reflections or historical considerations. The Gospel is not for minds seeking ideas, but for disciples who wish to obey.

The obedience demanded of the disciple of Christ on his knees before the word and example of his master is not an obedience that analyzes, thinks through, and interprets. Instead, it is the obedience of a child who has returned to the radical ignorance of being a creature, the universal blindness of being a sinner.

It is not given to us to meet the Gospel's simple and ruthless commands with a "perhaps" or an "almost." No, the only alternatives are the "yes, yes" that opens us to life, or the "no, no" that locks us in death. The Gospel words are meant to reach into the very roots of our corruption, the depths of which we cannot fathom insofar as we do not know the great heights at which our holiness lies. We should thus not be surprised at the sad, interminable journeys, the deep upheavals that each of these words initiates within us. We shouldn't try to hold back this sort of free-fall of the word into our depths. We need the passive courage that allows it to act within us — "Let it be done to me according to your Word."

And when once a single one of these words has stolen into us, we need to know how to desire communion with all the others, even if this little books seems vast, and our life tiny, narrow, and incapable of bearing it.

"My words are spirit and life . . ."
"It is the spirit who gives life, the letter is useless . . ."

The revelation of the Gospel is spirit and life. Whoever wishes to receive this revelation must listen with his spirit and his life. Often, we offer it only the "letter" of our lifetime, physical solitude, attempts to evade. When our way of life becomes an obstacle to the Gospel, we readily believe it is not meant for us, or that only a distorted and falsified version is for us.

We readily leave to those who have chosen the desert the fullness of a message that was lived and preached right in the very thick of the world.

Now, everyone of us has in fact been called to be "evangelized," each of us has the vocation to receive the whole word of Jesus Christ. But we can receive it only if we give ourselves as we are, if we give our lives as they are. We can receive it only if we hand ourselves over with all of our interior energies, with all that moves us, with all of our spirit.

From morning to night, every day of our lives, between the shores of our home, of our streets, of our encounters, flows the word in which God seeks to dwell.

The phrase from the Lord that we picked up from the Gospel at Mass in the morning, or during a ride on the metro, or between two chores, or at night in our bed, should no more depart from us than we would depart from our life or our spirit.

It seeks to fructify, to transform, to renew the handshake we offer, the effort we apply to our task, the look we give to those we meet, the way we react to fatigue, the way we wince at pain, the way we blossom in joy.

It wants to be at home wherever we are at home.

It wants to be us wherever we are who we are.

The Word of the Lord demands our respect; if during our workday we happen to have times for a break, it wants to take either a few or a lot of these moments, it demands that we be exclusively occupied with it, it wants us to give up all those things that are worth less. It wants us to pray over it, forgetting all those things that count for so little next to it.

If our day is so crammed with obligations that we have no time to take a break, if our children, our husband, the house, our work, takes up just about everything, it wants us to believe sufficiently in it that we respect it enough to know that its divine force will always be able to make space for itself. And so we will see it flash as we walk down the street, as we carry out our work, as we peel our vegetables, as we wait for the phone to ring, as we sweep the floor; we will see it flash between two words spoken by our neighbor, between the two letters waiting to be written, at the moment we wake up, and at the moment we go to sleep.

And that will mean that it has found its place, a human heart poor and warm enough to receive it.

"I am going to my father and your father,
to my God and your God."

Allowing the Gospel message into our life means letting our life become, in the broad and real sense of the word, a religious life, a life referred to, bound back to, God.

The basic revelation of the Gospel is the overwhelming, penetrating presence of God. It is a call to encounter God, and God allows himself to be encountered only in solitude.

It would seem that this solitude is something that those who live among the people of the world have to forego.

But this would be to believe that we precede God in solitude, while, on the contrary, it is he who waits there for us; to find God is to find solitude, because true solitude is spirit, and all of our human solitudes are merely relative approaches toward the perfect solitude that is faith.

True solitude is not the absence of people, but the presence of God.

To place our lives before the face of God, to surrender our lives to the movements of God, is to roam free in a space in which we have been given solitude.

It is the height of mountains that makes them solitary, and not the place where their bases happen to lie.

If the eruption of God's presence in us occurs in silence and solitude, it allows us to remain thrown among, mixed up with, radically joined to all of the people who are made of the same clay as we are.

To the one who consents to this solitary encounter with God, God gives human solitude in addition. He allows us to understand that, if we were to abstract from his gifts, his impulses, his wills, all that would be left would be a sort of common dough comprised of the same nothingness and the same sin, in which a person sees in other human beings only a sad and monotonous extension of himself.

In the midst of this formless mass, the only distinguishable differences are God's redeeming and creative wills; these are what call upon our enthusiasm and our love. But we know that they flow immediately from him. They do not distract us from God; they spread his solitude throughout the whole world.

Solitude

Like a person leaving Paris for the desert, and smiling at it from a solitary distance; like a traveler waiting with deep sighs for long days spent at sea; like a monk whose eyes caress the walls of his monastery, let us open our souls to the small solitudes of the day, from the first moment we wake up in the morning.

For our tiny solitudes are as immense, as exultant, as holy, as all the world's deserts, because they are filled with the same God, the God who makes solitude holy. The solitude of the darkened street separating the house from the metro; the solitude of a bench next to others who are carrying their part of the world; the solitude of long corridors streaming with souls on their way to the new day's tasks. The solitude of the few moments crouching to light the stove; the solitude of the kitchen, spent before the tub of beans. The solitude on our knees scrubbing the floor, in the entrance to the garden where we hunt for lettuce for the salad. The brief solitude of going up and down the stairs, a hundred times a day. The solitude of the long hours with the laundry, washing, mending, and ironing.

Solitudes that might be painful for us but which deepen our hearts: loved ones who have to leave though we'd like them to stay; friends that we wait for but who never show up; things that we want to say, but no one is listening; the strangeness of our heart while we're among people.

Taking leave is the first step into solitude. A person gains the desert — in both senses of the word — by taking a train, a boat, or a plane. We haven't learned to discern the various tiny departures that are scattered throughout the day, and that is why we do not manage to reach those solitudes that belong to us, the ones that have been prepared for us.

Because a new connection with solitude stands apart from us by the distance of the breadth of a door or the space of a quarter hour, we do not grant its eternal value, we do not take it seriously, we do not enter it like a fascinating countryside that stands constantly ready with essential revelations.

The reason the wells of solitude scattered throughout our day do not give us the living water overflowing in them is that our hearts lack expectation.

We cling to time superstitiously.

Though our love may require time, hours are nothing to the love of God, and a willing soul can be overwhelmed by him in a mere instant.

"I will lead you into solitude and there I will speak to your heart."

If our solitudes are for us poor transmitters of the Word, it is because our heart is absent.

"Happy is the person who hears the Word of God and keeps it."

There is no solitude without silence. Silence can sometimes mean not talking, but silence always means listening.

An absence of noise that was not at the same time an attentive listening to the Word of God would not be silence.

A workday full of noises and voices can yet be a day of silence if this noise becomes for us an echo of God's presence.

When we talk about ourselves or with ourselves, we have broken silence.

When we repeat with our lips the inner suggestions of the Word of God in the core of our being, we leave silence intact.

Silence cannot suffer a deluge of words.

We are good at talking or keeping quiet, but we are not very good at contenting ourselves with just the words that are necessary. We constantly vacillate between a dull silence that spoils love and an explosion of words that overflows the limits of truth.

Silence is love and truth.

It responds to the person who asks it a question, but it does so only with words full of life. Silence, like all the things life calls for, leads us to make a gift of self rather than a selfishness that has been gift-wrapped. But it keeps us recollected so that we can make this gift. It is impossible to give ourselves if we have squandered ourselves. The superfluous words in which we clothe our thoughts are a constant wasting of ourselves.

"You will be held accountable for all of your words."

For all of those that we should have said but that our selfishness held back.

For all of those that we should have kept quiet but that our immodesty cast to the four winds of our whimsical fancies and moods.

Silences

Why should the wind through the pines, the sand storm, and the squall upon the sea, all count as silence, and not the pounding of the factory machines, the rumbling of the trains at the station, and the clamor of the engines at the intersection?

In each case, it is just the humming of the great laws of the world around us at play.

Why should the song of the lark in the wheat fields, the buzzing of the insects in the night, and the droning of the bees among the thyme, nourish our silence, and not the crowds in the street, the voices of the women in the market, the yells of the men at work, the laughter of the children in the garden, and the songs coming from the bars? All of these are the noises of creatures advancing toward their destiny, all of this is the echo of the house of God in order or in shambles, all of this is the sign of life encountering our life.

Silence does not mean running away, but rather recollecting ourselves in the open space of God.

Silence is not a tiny grass snake that darts off at the slightest noise; it is an eagle with mighty wings that can soar above the commotion of the earth, of the people, of the wind.

"Say: Our Father, who art in heaven . . ."

Whoever says "Our Father, who art in heaven" while living like a child of this world is a liar.

To stop being a liar, we have to convert.

Our roots are in the earth.

We have to put them in heaven.

In order for the tree of our life to spread out its branches over the earth and for the birds to be able to make their nests there, we have to plant the top of the tree below.

The cross upon which Peter was crucified upside-down is the image of every Gospel life.

The life we seek with our Father introduces us into a continuously renewed youth.

The strength we ask from earthly food and the energy we hope to win from all human medicines, may provide for our weakness, but they leave it incurably weak.

When our weakness itself cries out to God, it becomes the dwelling-place of the mighty God.

The lights that we need to light up the world leave our eyes short-sighted and their field of vision narrow.

When we close them under God's touch, they themselves are changed and they learn to see even at night.

The love that we try to live by throwing ourselves into the lives of others leaves our heart incredibly fickle — sometimes ardent, sometimes cold, sometimes tender, and sometimes hard as a rock.

When we turn our heart toward God, he gives us "a heart of flesh" that sets everything it touches ablaze with the same fire.

To say "Our Father" in truth means to renounce death's inroad into us in order to allow ourselves to be born into eternal life.

The Dance of Obedience

"We played the flute but you did not dance."

It's the 14th of July.
And everyone's going to dance.
Everywhere, for months, for years, the world has been dancing.
The more we die, the more we dance.
Waves of wars, waves of dancing.

There's quite a lot of commotion.
The serious people have gone to bed.
Monks and nuns are reciting the matins of St. Henry, the king.
But I am pondering
Over that other king,
King David, who danced before the Ark of the Covenant.

For, if there are a lot of holy men and women who don't like to dance,
There are a lot of saints who felt compelled to dance,
They were so happy to be alive:
St. Theresa with her castanets,
St. John of the Cross with the Child Jesus in his arms,
And St. Francis, before the pope.
If we were happy with you, Lord,
We would be unable to resist
This urge to dance that spreads over the world,

71

And we would be able to discern
How it is you would like us to dance,
By following the steps of your Providence.

I think that maybe you're getting tired
Of the sort of people who talk about serving with the air of an
Army sergeant.
Who talk about knowing you with the air of a professor.
Who talk about reaching you with the rules of a game.
Who talk about loving you like people love each other in a tired old
marriage.

One day, when you felt the need for a change,
You created a St. Francis,
And you made him your juggler.
So now we have to let you recreate us
To be glad-hearted people who dance their lives with you.

To be a good dancer, with you as with anyone else, it's not necessary
That we know where it will lead.
We only need to follow,
To be cheerful,
To be light,
And above all not to be stiff.
We don't have to ask you for explanations
About the steps that you choose to take.
We need to be like an extension of yourself,
Quick and alive,
And pick up the rhythm of the music through you.
We must not desire to push ahead at all costs,
But allow ourselves to be spun, to be moved to the side.
We have to know how to pause and slide, and not walk.
And the steps would be rather clumsy
If they were not in harmony with the music.

But we tend to forget the music of your spirit,
And we turn our life into a gymnastic exercise;
We forget that, in your arms, life is something to be danced,
That your Holy Will

The Dance of Obedience

Is inconceivably creative,
And all monotony and boredom
Is left to the old souls
Who play the wallflower
In the joyful ball of your love.

Lord, come ask us to dance.
We're ready to dance this errand for you,
These accounts to do, this dinner to prepare, this vigil to keep
When we would prefer to sleep.
We're ready to dance for you the dance of work,
The dance of heat, and later the dance of cold.
If certain melodies are often played in the minor key, we won't tell you
That they're sad;
If others leave us a little breathless, we won't tell you
That they knock the wind out of us.
And if other people bump into us, we'll take it with a good laugh,
Knowing well that that's the sort of thing that happens when you're
dancing.

Lord, teach us precisely where,
In this endless novel
Which has begun to unfold between you and us,
The peculiar ball of our obedience takes place.

Strike up the great orchestra of your designs
Wherein everything you allow
Sends its strange music
Into the peace of your will.
Teach us every day to dress
Our human condition
In the dancing gown you love to have us wear
Adorned with all its details, like so many priceless jewels.

Make us live our life
Not like a game of chess, where every move is calculated,
Not like a contest, where everything is difficult,
Not like a math problem, which makes our head hurt,
But like an endless celebration, where our meeting with you is

constantly new,
Like a ball,
Like a dance,
In the arms of your grace,
In the universal music of love.

Lord, ask us to dance.

PART TWO

THE CHURCH

1950-1954

To live a mission means to discover the Church who sends us.

"Only the Church is strong enough to carry the Gospel without stumbling."

The Church is Jesus — now, the whole Christ.
The Christian is not free with respect to Christ and the Church: rather, he is "in a state of living faith."

"We could not live this love, which takes its measure from the Christ-Church and not from us, except by intensifying our intimate, internal, and living belonging to Christ in the Church."
(Love for the Church, p. 126).

Hence, the Christian's call to prayer and to personal conversion for the sake of Mission.

May 1949. The death of Cardinal Suhard, Archbishop of Paris.

July 1953. Vatican directives prohibiting French seminarians and religious from training to work in factories.

September 1953. Msgr. Marella, the Apostolic Nuncio to Paris, announces Rome's decision to forbid French priests from working in the factories.

May 1954. With the consent of their bishops, several French priests begin to work part-time in small factories.

August 1954. After a year of restrictions, the Vatican issues an Apostolic Constitution, *Omnium Ecclesiarum,* which sets up *The Mission of France* inside the Pontigny prelature.

The Church, 1950-1954

Beginning in 1941, Madeleine became deeply involved with the major events in the life of the Church of France: the birth of the seminary for *The Mission of France* in Lisieux, and the birth of the *Mission of Marseille*. She was likewise present during the crises and decisions: people would come to pour their hearts out to her, and she herself would hesitate just as little to write to a priest experiencing difficulties as to those in authority.

She was at once a person of extraordinary discretion, without the slightest urge to interfere, and yet present like a sister, a mother, or a nurse.

Such a precise and helpful attitude arose from the fact that she had always already, usually several years or several months in advance, lived through the paradoxes, dramas, and dilemmas of the age in such a way as to bring them together in a fruitful unity.

Madeleine always prayed before she spoke. It was this need to pray for Mission that, in 1952, led her into a somewhat comical adventure. She made known her conviction that the worker-priest movement was not getting the prayer support from every Christian, as it needed. Thus, she said, a pilgrimage had to be undertaken to request this prayer, which was so essential to their apostolate.

Always worried about the dangers her brothers engaged in the "blind confusion" of the workers' struggle underwent, always concerned for unity, for mutual understanding among all Christians, Madeleine one day confides to her somewhat skeptical *équipe* her desire to spend a full day in Rome in prayer at Peter's tomb.

She concedes a willingness to give up this idea when someone explained that it would be "an expensive hour of prayer," but she says she will do so only if a sum of money equal to the trip's expenses fell from the sky somehow unexpectedly. Now, that very week, one of Madeleine's friends, a nonbeliever, brought a distant relation from South America to Madeleine. This woman was a Catholic who wanted to learn something about the Church in France. After her visit, "Aunt Rosa" left the *équipe* with a national lottery ticket, which no one paid any attention to until someone noticed it was in fact a winning ticket — with a prize big enough to cover the expenses of a trip to Rome.

And so, Madeleine went "on a pilgrimage." Before leaving, she paid a visit to all those Catholics in Ivry with whom she had experienced some tensions in order to make peace with them. After her voyage, which took two days and two nights, she spent the twelve hours at the tomb of St. Peter as she had planned. When she returned, she communicated to those around her the report published here in this section.

This gift of the winning lottery ticket and the ensuing brief solitary journey was the beginning of nearly all of the relationships Madeleine subsequently had with Rome and the hierarchical Church.

The People of Paris Attend
the Funeral of a Father[1]

When a father dies, the children attend the funeral; they are the first to follow behind the coffin.

The people of Paris lost their father: and so they came to Notre Dame. The people with faith but also the people who had no faith.

They came with prayers, or with condolences, or to pay their respects, or out of curiosity. They came to the church, and the church was closed. At eight o'clock, the church was closed. At nine, it was still closed. At ten it was still closed.

The people thought that they did not want to let anyone in before the father himself, so that all of his children could follow, and enter the church with him. But the church was open for the priests and the religious, for public officials, and for those who carried cards of invitation.

The people of Paris thought that perhaps it was more convenient this way, and so they waited their turn, waited to take their place, with their families, behind the corpse.

The square was full of people, full of joined hands, full of puzzled looks. The crowd was buzzing with questions.

The sound system was hardly working, which was a shame.

When the procession entered, the people of Paris wanted to follow, but the barricades remained in place.

Out of luck or out of kindness, a handful of people managed to get through or to enter. I was one of them. The others had to stay outside.

1. This brief piece was published in *Témoignage chrétien*, on the occasion of the funeral of Cardinal Suhard, 1949.

If the church had been packed, it already would have been painful to have to leave the people of Paris at the door.

But the church was not packed.

Notre Dame was built to receive the people of Paris. It's used to it. If the people were left outside, it is not because Notre Dame was full. There were plenty of seats in the rear of the side aisles. The side chapels were empty. So were the enormous galleries at each side of the nave.

When the ceremony was over, the people of Paris wanted to come sit by their father.

But that's not what was wanted from the people.

They were asked to wait an hour and a half outside of an empty church. They could scarcely afford the time, and it was raining.

Those who believed lifted their hearts to their father, who would have been able to understand them and their doubly broken hearts.

Those who did not believe no doubt ended up believing even less.

In all of this cold pomp and bureaucracy, they did not have the chance to encounter the divine and maternal tenderness that may have been there waiting for them behind the stones.

The Many Faces
of the One Working Class[2]

Let's start with something concrete: we'll take Pierre, Jacques, and Jean, who live near me.

They will never leave behind the characteristics they inherited from their place of origins. They will remain Bretons whether they live in Brittany or in Puteaux; they will remain Gascons whether in Toulouse or in Briey; they will remain Lorrains whether in Nancy or in Clermont-Ferrand. If a speaker at a meeting were to begin, "we, Parisians" in a thick provincial accent, the whole room would break into laughter. The small old peasant with the red cheeks might unforeseeably pick up physical or psychological weaknesses from the city air, or he might develop new and stronger defenses. The little girl from the suburbs may grow into a woman without rest and without weakness, immune to all contaminations and failures. Now, if "each one" is concrete, then so are the working classes. I say "classes" and not "class." Pierre, Jacques, or Jean may become Jacques the carpenter, Pierre the metal worker, and Jean the miner, or else Pierre the dockworker — Jacques with his Paulette, and Jean with his Claudine.

2. Madeleine Delbrêl's missionary reflections are supported by a precise and concrete familiarity with the working classes. Though she herself never worked in a factory, she developed an understanding of and love for the men and women of the working class through twenty years of living in common with them in Ivry.

To give proof of her knowledge of the society she speaks about — if such a thing is necessary — we add this study on the working-class world, which originally appeared in the review *Esprit* (July-August 1951), to the various texts about mission. This is followed by an unpublished conclusion and poem in which Madeleine reveals in addition her own personal background.

Once they become part of a particular human community, they will bring scarcely perceptible influences to it, just as they themselves will be influenced by it. It is within this diverse and diversifying environment that Pierre, Jacques, and Jean will all be affected by the common modalities of the working condition. And the general human destiny will touch them only through what is specific to the working-class world.

On the outskirts of Paris: the enormous pocket of Renault, with its thirty thousand workers. A whole neighborhood depends on it. Lives on it. At specific hours, the streets are drained of people, who are later once again flushed back into the streets toward their low-income housing, their dilapidated boarding houses, stinking hotels, snug lodgings, and slums.

In the North: the great plains and the great skies. Sprawled flat over the ground are geometrically shaped cities, black walls and white curtains. Coal is king. Its subterranean presence and its dark radiance, painting things and people black.

Marseille: The rhythms of the port setting the work pace, the dockhands, their sundry disconnected tasks, the rumbling of their uncertain futures. At the water's edge, "boulevards" and shabby houses. Passageways leading behind, yards below, steep staircases running through and leading to other dead ends. A mishmash of nationalities: Spaniards, Italians, Algerians. Life on equal footing; sun for all and everyone knows each other.

Then flowing streets, mournful canals, patriarchal sailor folk, by trade or for hire, torn apart by a life constantly fluctuating between mooring points, the place where the children go to school, the place where relatives are hospitalized. Families enclosed within their own floating universe.

Longwy: steel-working plants. Ore and coke come together in a single village. A factory is born; the village swallowed up. Pink buildings spring up as if newly born from the slag heaps. Houses, the church, schools, hotels all more or less belong to the factory: to quit a factory is to quit everything. All the people are arranged in their boxes. The houses are built to fit their function and not to fit the family. Time is set by the factory; there are no more days and nights; the nights are lit up by explosions and glowing fountains; shifts are rotated three times every eight hours.

Itinerant and well-organized: the railroad workers. They feel at home wherever there are train tracks and wherever a train whistle blows; while on the coasts, professional fishermen undergo the constant ebb and flow of fishing seasons.

The Vosges: weaving, the monotony of a work without the possibility of making comparisons, which would wake people up and provoke indignation. A people who apply their strengths to surviving.

Paris, with its spectrum of industries, the churning and seething of discontent, the meeting point for the militant, the criss-cross of economic and political movements.

Each particular industry either reinforces or dismantles any given physical milieu. Steelworkers, railroad workers, miners, and a few others make up the professional aristocracy. The building is completely stamped with the character of intermittence, risk, and displacement. For road construction that needs to be done, a city of barracks goes up far from home to welcome the influx of a cosmopolitan workforce. Then the barracks disappear and everyone goes their own way. Food or chemical processing plants are the permanent refuge of the "unskilled." Few militants can be found there. The unions stagnate. A single militant from a stronger industry is able to bring unions to a company. I'm thinking, for example, of a food processing plant that, after remaining untouched by any of the various movements, boasts 100 percent union membership only four months later.

But inside the various professional branches, further differentiation occurs. The business itself entails its own particular environment. A factory with 1,500 workers is different from one with 200. A factory with a fast turnover is different from one in which the fathers are succeeded by their sons. Order and method foster ambiance; indifference and disorganization sap all ambiance. In a single factory, work areas that stand only a few meters apart are autonomous milieus: in this one, there's solidarity, over there, they're individualists; here, there's basic motivation, over there, there's timid prudence.

Moreover, different locations will have a different impact on the same industry. A sawmill in the city will not be the same as one in the Southwest: in one, the worker will earn a decent wage; in the other, he will be paid in the sawmill the same wage he earns in his evening or weekend job, in the fields or vineyards.

If, from one end of the world to the other, we witness the common features that characterize life in the working class, we must never forget the great diversity that likewise exists.

There is a suffering attendant upon the working class that bears the same names wherever it is found. Whether this suffering affects Jacques or Jean, the dockhand or the miner, the black man, the white man, or the yellow man, it is a patiently borne violence, a slavery, a poverty, the weight of contempt. To reduce the harm done merely to crimes of the economic order is to misunderstand the problem. To delimit it in time is to trivialize it; to treat it as a curable ill is to harbor cruel delusions. To consider it inevitable is to believe that an established social order is inevitable, which it is not. But doing away with it is not the same thing as making people happy. A person can be happy in suffering, and the lack of suffering is not always the same thing as happiness. Among the most oppressed of human beings, one can find lovers who are happy; one can find peaceful families, groups of people who laugh, crowds that sing. But the fact that some of them may be happy is no reason to defend their suffering.

Enslavement

If we tend to associate a certain *violence* with social revolutions, this should not lead us to forget the accumulated violence, the aimless and organic violence that daily grinds away at multitudes of human lives. To take up in one's hands a dozen new flashlights, a ready-made smock, or a coal bucket is to stain those hands — always with sweat, often with tears, and sometimes even with blood. Advertisements and packaging labels camouflage the grotesqueness of the food on which we live. Conscientious objectors come out against international wars. But conscientious objectors of another sort do not take their stand against the war of human labor. The violence of this war is so omnipresent, so well organized that it has become invisible. Here are a few simple facts:

We would find it unusual to have to spend an entire seven- or eight-hour train trip on our feet, and it would leave us with long memories of aches and pains. There are thousands of men and women who work in front of the same machine on their feet for years on end, and since they're supposed to be used to it, we get used to thinking they are.

The staunchest defenders of private property will nevertheless agree that the sun and the sky belong to everyone. But the fact that some people spend a third of their life in the shadow of a mine, in the basement of a factory, or in the sewer system, does not strike them as a transgression of this universal property right. The ones least subjected to work complain loudest that you have to work if you want to eat. They forget that work often earns only death. Certain jobs, which are fully available to any Algerian or Annamite, after a determined number of months, will lead the one who works them to the sanatorium.

If these examples, which I could multiply, seem like a number of isolated cases peculiar to France, we must not forget that they are basically the visible aspects of a worldwide reality. We must become aware of these constant battles, battles that send home mutilated bodies and ruined health. Certain forms of labor kill violently, others slowly. There are ovens that explode, machines that amputate, and presses that crush. Some industries eat away at the lungs, others weaken the blood. Living creatures languish in the desert climes of certain workshops, in the basements where it's always winter, in the hallways where a full gale is constantly blowing. Death is given the right in certain entire neighborhoods to kill more often and more quickly. Businesses never give their employees enough to eat. Weavers quit their jobs to go for a cure in a sanatorium after they have already become incurable. There are workers whose hands get burnt simply because it is not yet economical to replace these workers with machines.

Like the suffering it produces, the enslavement of man by man evolves with material progress. Each stage has its tyrant and engenders its revolt. My grandfather as a little boy hammered away on the anvil for sixteen hours at a stretch, and used to eat dishwater. They liberated him. Or at least they thought they liberated him. They show in the *History of French Labor* the sections of bulky chains that once bloodied his wrists. They proudly flaunt the schools that our children have to attend until they're old enough to wear long pants; they flaunt their medical consultation privileges, and their vacation colonies. They tell us these people are liberated. Should we believe them?

A youth from the middle class who is figuring out his future plans, has the *possibility* of doing so in terms of the skills he wants to develop or the risks he is willing to take. If he is prevented from following his plans, it is because of personal failure or because of social constraints merely at the level of the family. The one who is never given the chance to choose is the exception. In the working classes, this initial freedom of choice is drastically reduced. If a high school student wants to become a craftsman or a factory worker, practically speaking there is nothing stopping him. If, on the other hand, a child from the working class wants to become an architect, almost everything stands in his way. Manual labor is almost forced on such children. If there exist certain lawyers, doctors, or engineers who have come from working-class families, they are a minuscule minority, because, in order to get where they are, they had to have a constant string of "good luck." And how many people carry within themselves a potential doctor, lawyer, or engineer who will never see the light of day because they won't have been given the same chances?

A more substantial minority of children will be able to choose from among the various technical, manual jobs one that corresponds to their abilities. But even here there is a limitation of possibilities. The career counselors they'll be sent to for direction will have to take the job market into consideration: if the market is not favorable, the apprenticeship positions in the chosen area will be limited, and talents will be sacrificed to the current state of the market. Physical defects will greatly hinder a person's appeal. For manual labor, you need a proper body. The law student is never asked about his blood pressure, or whether he needs glasses to write. But these are the sorts of questions that are commonly put to students in a trade school.

For another fraction of young people, the area of expertise will be somewhat dictated by circumstances. In a mining region, it is quite difficult to find a job that doesn't in some way involve the mines; in a steel-working town, a job that doesn't involve steel. There are more than a few regions that are both highly overpopulated and industrially specialized. In these cases, a person's life will forever be occupied here with cars, there with fabrics, here with coal, and there with oil.

For a still larger portion of the youth, the career one ends up in is largely a game of chance. You become a carpenter because there is a carpenter shop down the street; you become a metalworker because a friend of yours has a job in the metalworks factory; you become a construction worker because you happened to read a want ad.

And thus emerges an essential observation: people don't seek *to get paid for the work they do, but to work in order to get paid.* And this is soon the dominant state of affairs for a whole population who "take a job" wherever "they need somebody," wherever they can make money right away. For these people, the paycheck quickly becomes the first matter of concern: it doesn't matter what you do, as long as you get paid. And the successive whittling away, the constantly narrowing limitations, entail a loss of freedom. You no longer choose where to live. The "it doesn't matter what" quickly becomes "it doesn't matter where." You go wherever they will take you in. The war of work also has its refugees. You abandon "home," which in some parts of the country means your family as much as it does your house. You become deported — willingly, legally speaking, but practically speaking, under constraint. The war of work is destroying families. The father goes off on his own. He will camp here or there in a collective apartment or a cramped room. He will remember or he will forget. If he manages before too long to find the means to send for his family, they will often be able to afford only a furnished room, keeping nothing from the old house. They will come to know the insecurities of anonymity. They won't have to worry about what the neighbors are saying anymore, but neither will they have their old chain fence. Parents, brothers, and sisters will grow apart from each other, just barely connected by letters that don't say much anymore. They will no longer hope for help, nor will they sustain interest in their obligations.

Uncertainty

The very freedom to live will soon become optional. The place that's hiring is often the place where you take your chances, the place that's avoided by those who have a choice.

You take your chances with your lungs, with your eyes, and with your nerves. You won't take the risk of bringing children into the world, or else you do so for some compelling reason.

But the right to earn a salary, a right that's paid for through such slavery, is itself endangered; unemployment may strike here or there; a man might be cruelly paralyzed by some extrinsic constraint, for causes unrelated to his will or his body. I've seen men weep as they looked at their useless hands. On the other hand, the right that French law accords the worker to reject a job if his labor is too cheaply bought seems a farce. It gives the worker the right to have absolutely nothing to eat the moment he stops his work precisely to protest that he doesn't have enough to eat.

And, at the end of the vicious circle, the old soldier-worker will watch his loss of freedom be pushed to the end. If his family did not put up a fight against the separations, the battles over work hours, and the displacements, then he will grow old alone. If you are not "retired" with "a pension," if you are simply "old," if you can no longer work, if you have no children to work for you, you are condemned either to die slowly from lack of necessities, or to check into an old folks' home. And there you surrender your last freedom, that of being someone who lives at house number x on street y. You yourself become merely the number over a door to a room in which nothing is yours. I once knew an elderly man whose sole ambition — which was an impossible dream in the place he was living — was to have his own drawer. If the war of work does not kill its old soldiers, it has a peculiar way of helping them die.

Poverty

The working man's poverty is not solely an economic issue. In fact, nothing is easier than demonstrating how similar the budget of a working-class family and the budget of a semi-bourgeois family are. Nothing is easier than comparing the strictly financial resources of certain paid professions favorably to so-called liberal professions.

The world is split in two: those who believe there will come a time when there will be no more poor people, and those who believe that we will always have the poor among us. The former group envisions a sort of ready-made happiness. The latter group bows yet again to the fatality of a social order that isn't fated. But both groups often err in their own particular directions by recognizing poverty in only one of its forms.

What counts as poverty for a docker in France, in terms of sheer buying power, would represent a small fortune for a Hindu farmer. But simply lining up the respective buying capacities would be deceptive insofar as we did not take into account the essential and different needs of the two different people. Money itself is something relative; it is multiplied and divided by the sort of person using it. If we took two families living on the same apartment floor with the same income, one could be struggling to get by while the other was almost comfortable. The fact that one manages to live makes the other seem that they don't know how to live. Here we touch on another kind of poverty: poverty in knowing how to do things. The woman who was never taught by her mother how to run a household is twice poor.

For someone who is able to read, exchange ideas, or even just reflect, having a radio might be a secondary matter. Does it then follow that for a man who doesn't read, who doesn't speak, who doesn't reflect, a radio is not something necessary? A person whose window opens onto a forest, who can leave the furniture where it is and perform in his house all the normal activities of daily life, would place movies in the category of leisure. Those whose window opens onto a wall, who must shift their room's furniture three times a day in order to eat, to work, and to sleep, might consider movies a necessity that keeps them from falling into insanity. . . . Being poor, no doubt, means not having what you need to live, but it also means not having what you need to lead a human life.

The poverty of other social strata in France, the poverty of other countries, is the lack of the means to live. The poverty that was born in the industrial age, and which continues to grow in this age, is the lack of the means to live like a human being. It is the wasting away of fundamental capacities, a wasting away that might lead to a total disappearance.

We can find only a minority of the people in the working world who are able to make complete use of their minds and wills. There are countless people, no doubt, for whom work is a return to primitive natural movements: manual laborers who load and unload trucks carrying steel, rock, and wood. But there are even more people who are riveted to a particular task, the monotony of which is as excessive as the pace. Thousands of metal plates that need the same tiny hole drilled into them; thousands of boxes of tissues that need the same label attached to the same place, etc. In these mind-deadening tasks, the will often has absolutely nothing to contribute, and so gets replaced by a mechanical will: namely, the assembly line, which commands, carries out, and confirms. Consciousness is replaced by a timing system, which accepts the work or speeds it up. The worker finds himself sharing a "common lot" with the fragmented materials he works with. Like them, he is the instrument of a plan that he doesn't know. He is tied to them through productivity levels, and each moment of his work is automatically tallied for its value in dollars. Because a person hypertrophies whatever he uses too much, the worker's physique goes through changes. His muscles and his nervous system become tyrants. The needs of a man thus reduced to his material aspect are themselves reduced to their material aspects and demand compensation for the individual's overworked areas: strong, stimulating foods become a necessity for him. His sexual life is given over to immediate encounters and reflexes. On the other hand, the unemployed faculties atrophy. Shriveled as they thus become, they can no longer have the spiritual riches that lie too high to be reached.

In the places of fundamental suffering — concentration camps, prisons, in the room of a starving student, on the street lined with homeless people — we catch a brutally clear glimpse of what constitutes the drama of modern poverty. In these examples of dizzyingly extreme suffering, human beings are more human than they are anywhere else. A man remains a man as long as we only take from him what he owns; he ceases to be a man when we steal from him what he is. It is clear that the multitudes of working classes and workers have not been afflicted with this incapacitating poverty. But those who do undergo it or who are threatened by it are already numerous and do not necessarily coincide with the lower working classes.

A new fact can easily pass unnoticed if it is not classified within a category. Such facts are often merely the first hint of what is to come. We occasionally become appalled when we compare the wage of a worker with the salary of the director of the factory, the lodgings of the one with the pavilion of the other. . . . But do we register any shock at all when we compare the fact that the mind of one is filled with the factory as a whole, while the mind of the other, day after day, month after month, is filled with the tiny task of punching the same hole in the same metal plate?

Disrespect and Misunderstanding

Another form of suffering that to a certain extent weighs on workers is *disrespect*. Its primary cause is a lack of awareness and understanding. In the factory, a worker feels less important to other people than the machines. In his home, if he lives in a workers' housing development, the sort of lodging he is given is determined not according to what sort of people he has in his family, but according to the function he performs. Rich neighborhoods obey the law of proportion between population density and surface area, which is not the same law obeyed in working-class neighborhoods, as if two-thirds of the inhabitants didn't count.

To identify this multitude, we do not have to appeal to an understanding of the people themselves, but an understanding of what already exists. They are treated like mentally handicapped adults, and not for what they represent: a social childhood, which does not entrust itself to the old masters who want to be teachers but who do not have what it takes to educate.

This multitude has the strength of every childhood: a mobility and a capacity to develop. As with every child, we find in this people a brutal sense of justice, and this sense of justice has recently crashed headlong with all of its spontaneous energy against the old systems that codify, explicate, and legitimize a chronic social injustice. As with every child, we find in it an intrinsic connection between action and instinct; hence the success of those worker movements that tap into wounded instincts. When hunger has turned into a genuine hunger, when a threat to life turns into a genuine threat, a worker movement is irrepressible. As with every child, we find in the working-class condition merely a sketch of the true face of those who together constitute it.

We measure a working-class family against an ideal bourgeois family or one from the country; we measure their morality against the morality of the middle classes; we measure their attempts at education against an educational program formed for others.

Even those among the workers who have willingly become workers participate in this lack of understanding. An adult cannot become a child again, even if that child is fed up with his adult mediocrity. I insist that we take account of the full meaning of the word, "child." What I am asking is that in the face of this vast world of work, those who are not themselves part of it at least become aware of its mystery. There is always something incommunicable between two people. Between the mass of people who earn their bread by their hands and those who earn it some other way, there is a second mystery that distinguishes them for life.

Understanding and Action[3]

Understanding the working-class world within the limits we have discussed and within its clearly demarcated areas is something that no person in the modern world can forego.

You have to understand clearly in order to act. But to be alive is already to act, and to be alive in 1950 is necessarily to take action with respect to the condition of the working class. We would like to believe that this sort of action is a concern only to the workers themselves or perhaps to those whose profession or vocation has a social character: doctors, administrators, welfare workers, etc. But that is not the truth.

Whatever place we might have in this vast world, we are all part of a huge machine in which everything is related to everything else, and the way we live says either "yes" or "no" to the way things presently are. We are free to say "yes," but we have to do so with a full awareness of what we are saying, and not simply in function of conventional opinion or mere habit. So who conveys the information about the working-class world?

The workers themselves? Yes, in part. But they are too much inside things and there is a great disproportion between the strength of their feelings and their ability to communicate them.

Those who run the businesses? Once again, yes, but they stand apart, and they measure the working classes with weights and measures that are not made for them.

The intellectuals? Yes, especially if they are poets they will be able to

---

3. Previously unpublished text.

contribute a few insights, either through their intelligence or through their intuitions.

The non-working-class people who have chosen for various ideological reasons to live a working-class life? Yes, but these are not yet the genuine article, because this is a life they have chosen, whereas the real working life is something one undergoes.

All these people can act as our informers provided they are joined by our principal informer — ourselves, but an "ourselves" that we have given fresh eyes and an impartial heart.

An "ourselves" whom we have ordered one fine day to adventure into society as if we were seeing it for the first time, as if we were seeing this street for the first time, and the people passing through it, the neighborhoods in Paris, the metro at seven o'clock in the evening, the escalators and service elevators, the children who have everything and the children who have nothing.

If this brand-new encounter between ourselves and the social machine leaves us satisfied and at peace, let us continue our lives exactly as they were before.

But if we come out disturbed and ashamed, let us have the courage to take stock of all those things in our life, like so many other lives, that contribute in passive complicity to the chronic violence mankind suffers from — a mankind made up of millions of human beings just like us. Perhaps the little cell of society that we represent can be cleansed of this violence.

And if many people have a change of conscience about this human race divided in two, the worn trunk of our old world will be able to bear the young and heavy branch of the working class, without perishing from it.

If not, the branch will have to sprout somewhere else: old trees no longer capable of spring are good only for the furnace.

A New Cry[4]

A cry rises up from the world: a new cry among all the old human cries.

It awakens alarm, unrest, and compassion.

We cover it up with paper wrappings.
We broadcast it with loudspeakers.
We say it is a cry of death or a cry of birth.
It is translated into every language.
It is passed on through impassioned songs.
It is accompanied by hearty laughter.
It is mixed up with sentimental romanticism.

From within their social boundaries, within their universal fatherland
The people of the working world cry out.
It would be a misunderstanding to try to translate the aspect of the cry that remains untranslatable.
It would be a misunderstanding if we failed to translate the aspect of the cry that can be translated.
It emerges from the depths of a dark abyss, it shoots through the shadows, and explodes into the sunlight.

Who is crying?

4. Previously unpublished.

A New Cry

They tell us it is the "working class," the "proletariat," the "masses."
We are looking for the person who is crying.
And they point to a universal idea.
Ideas don't cry.

These notes are on a quest for this person.
They want to shatter universal ideas, and find the breasts and the mouths at the source of this cry.
They want to penetrate through that which can be seen and that which can be touched in order to reach that which can be understood or grasped.
They want to have the humility to come to a stop before that which remains unknowable.

They aim to provoke a response to this cry, a response from hearts uprooted from their peaceful habits;
We are aware that mankind will never be able to live without crying; cries as old as humanity itself accompany what is eternal in humanity as well as what is sprouting, coming to be, and passing away.

The cry of death and the cry of love will never come to an end. But we know too that there exist cries that can be cured, cries for which our actions and omissions are responsible.

Is this new cry one of those that can be healed?
Someone is crying in the night — how can we go on sleeping?

Church and Mission[5]

The following reflections attempt to explain the attitude of those who are missionaries because they are Christian and who, if they feel the need in their life for an engagement [engagement], per- ceive to the same extent a need for detachment [dégagement]. They do not require every vocation to be just like theirs. Instead, they want to situate their own path, which they feel compelled to follow, within the place where the Church meets the world today.

Through his baptism, the Christian exchanged his freedom for the free- dom of Christ.

He is free because Christ is supremely free, but he no longer has the right to choose a state of life other than that of Christ, an action other than that of Christ, or a thinking other than that of Christ.

This is the state of living faith. Faith is for him a fact, and all he can do is accept it.

This state of life means being a child of God in Christ along with all his brothers and sisters who are with him in Christ. Standing before God and before the world, in God and in the world, it is together with all the others that the Christian is Christ. He is the whole Christ, the Christ- Church. This is a fact over which he has no control.

---

5. In this study dated 1951, Madeleine Delbrêl takes up and completes the text of a letter she addressed to Fr. Loew in 1950 that was published by *Nova et Vetera* in the January-March 1966 issue.

His action is not some small personal matter. It is bound, fused to the very act of God, to the "unceasing action," the action that is salvation history, the history of the Church, the history of the City of God. He has his own gesture to contribute, but this gesture is merely a flutter in the perpetual and universal movement of the Holy Spirit. His gesture is bounded on all sides by those of others, by gestures that prepare, complete, and continue his.

This thinking is designed by the Truth, which is Christ. What it brings to this design is like the information the senses bring to the brain — it is inserted into the brain's general data, and the brain evaluates it and makes use of it.

This state of life, this action, and this thinking exist for the sake of Christ and his work, which is the salvation of the world.

The work of the Church is the salvation of the world; the world cannot be saved except by the Church. The Church is not the Church unless she saves. We are not the Christ-Church unless we are bringers of salvation. We are not bringers of salvation unless we are the Church. And we are not the Church unless we are the *whole* Church: each member belongs to the whole body. And we are not the whole Church unless we are in precisely the place meant for us in the Church, which is the same as saying that we are precisely in our place in the world, where the Church is made present through us.

Mission means doing the very work of Christ wherever we happen to be. We will not be the Church and salvation will not reach the ends of the earth unless we help save the people in the very situations in which we live. And we will not be working toward salvation, we will not let it pass through us, unless in their very midst, we remain purely and unchangeably the Church.

We live in a world that seems completely impervious to salvation. Some other piece of the world "unjustly hordes the very lifeblood and nourishment of Christ's body." This is something we must suffer to the point of death. But we ought not to bring life to some people today while preparing mortal pains for others tomorrow.

It is not necessary that Peter or John work to save a small or large flock of people. What is necessary is that it be the Church who, through Peter and John, wins back this flock of people, because it is only the Church who can truly win them back.

97

A State of Life

Thus, mission has to be Church. It must be first "the Body of Christ," and only then is it free to take its own direction. Its state is the total Christ, "that they may be one as you, Father, are in me and I in you."

"If you were of the world, the world would love you, but you are not and so it hates you, just as it hated me before you." To be pleasing to the world, to be loved by the world, even if it is the world of our unbelieving neighbors, can never outweigh the importance of unity among Christians. It is not for us to choose; we are not free with our own freedom. The arm cannot choose to be a branch of the tree from which it gathers the fruit; it belongs to the body, even if the body is standing too far from the tree.

If we damage the unity of Christians when we speak to nonbelievers about Christ, we are in effect choosing to give them a mere echo of what Christ is instead of giving them Christ himself in his sacrament *par excellence* — Christians united among themselves.

Israel was called to be God's people among the nations, and everything had to be sacrificed to this end. We are called to be the visible body of Christ in the midst of the human body of society. For this, we too must sacrifice everything.

If this unity is an integration, it is also a living dynamism. Obedience in Christ's body is a fact of life. The blood flows in a particular direction. It does not reach the fingertips unless it has first flowed elsewhere. We cannot alter the course of this living movement. Church authority can sometimes be burdensome or hard to understand, but we obey because it is our very life. Besides, it would be rather silly for a living organism to prefer some *thing* to life itself.

Likewise, it is not up to us to rearrange a body's organs. We cannot attach our eyeballs to our fingertips or transplant our heart into our head. Just so, a mystic or a missionary cannot replace the *hierarchy*. Here we might fall into the trap of words. *Hierarchy* tends for us to become an idea. And yet it signifies the overall communication of Christ with each member of his body: Christ teaching, guiding, enlightening, and sanctifying us.

This gift remains intact even when it comes in forms that are weak or even corrupt. Because Israel dreamed of a triumphant Messiah, it could not recognize him crowned with thorns and spat upon.

Because we dream of a Christ-Church triumphant in the eyes of men, we do not always recognize that the mystery of Christ is the mystery of the Church. Until the end of time, Christ will be the humiliated Savior, concealed under people who have limitations and are sinful. Yet it is in these very people that we must recognize him. Reevaluating our dignity as baptized and confirmed Christians, our coming of age as laypeople "must not lead us to believe that we are invested with all of Christ's 'functions.'" Just because baptism makes us Christ does not mean it gives us all his functions.

The "greatest" of laypeople nevertheless remain less than the "least" of the priests according to a certain order of grace: The priest participates in a certain communication from Christ that the layman does not. But this does not mean that the layman must be passive. There will always remain a "become what you are" that infinitely surpasses what he manages to be.

The layman must tirelessly claim from priests and bishops what he may rightfully expect from them and what, when lacking, would constitute a state of spiritual poverty. But it is *they,* the priests and bishops, who are the ones to provide it.

Just as a Christian cannot be a "loner," so too he cannot occupy just any place in the Church. Here again, it is not a matter of choice but a consequence of the nature of the faith.

The Work of the Christ-Church

The work of the Christ-Church is that "the world be saved" — through the cross, which makes us children of God in Christ, and through the Gospel, which teaches us how to live as children of God in Christ.

The Cross is not something optional, neither for the world, nor for us. Accepting the Cross and taking it up is the lion's share of our work.

"You were crucified with Christ." The Cross is our most basic task; the rest comes afterward. "Those who want to be my disciples must take up their cross and" — only after that — "follow me." The world is saved, in potential, by the crucified Christ. And it is to a still-suffering world that we must impart the joy of Christ.

Saving the world does not mean making it happy; it means showing the world the meaning of its suffering and giving it a joy that "nothing can take away." If we must fight against the misery and misfortune that Christ took so seriously as to speak of judging us in the end solely by what we did for others in this regard, we must keep in mind that what is at stake is ultimately not solving these problems and constructing a second earthly paradise; rather, what is at stake is eternal life.

But, if the kingdom of heaven is not of the world, it is nevertheless in the world.

Though perfect in principle, in actuality the kingdom exists like a seed in the earth, like leaven in dough, like salt in food, or like a lamp in the night. This demands vital contact among Christians who have a duty to unity, but also a vital contact with unbelievers for the sake of spreading God's kingdom. Thus, Christians must remain in the midst of the world.

Christ does not provide his followers with a set of wings to flee into heaven, but with a weight to drag them into the deepest corners of the earth. What may seem to be the specifically missionary vocation is in fact simply what it means to be embraced by Christ.

Despite any apparent contradiction, we diminish and falsify our love for Christ and the Church wherever we diminish that which draws us to the world and enables us to plunge ourselves into it. This is what the love of the world means, a love that is not an identification with the world, but a gift to it.

The Gospel

It must be proclaimed: here stand all the walls that prevent the evangelists from being heard or from penetrating. Here is the place where all the openings have to be made, all the bridges need to be erected. But if it were the case that these openings were made, these bridges were erected, and our voices were heard, we would still not be satisfied. It is not a question of merely penetrating, of merely speaking, of being listened to or of "pleasing" — the message we speak must remain intact. At the crossroads at which we stand, there are a number of points that draw our attention.

The Gospel is the proclamation to people that they have the possibility of being justified in Christ. It is not the proclamation of the establishment of human justice. Christ came to justify and not to render justice.

"The poor have been evangelized." The Good News has been brought to them. It doesn't say: "Their poverty has been taken away." Quite the contrary: "You will always have the poor among you," and "Blessed are the poor."

Because of this beatitude, the Christian has a preference for poverty. Why would he be inclined through love to take this poverty away from others or to suggest that the elimination of this poverty is a condition for salvation?

Evangelizing the poor does not mean making them wealthy or thinking that evangelization is possible only after the poor have been made wealthy. That would run counter to the whole history of Christ in the world. The Gospel has never been rejected because of poverty or destitution, from the slaves in Rome, the "dockhands" in Corinth, to the camps in Germany.

What can prevent the spreading of the Gospel, on the other hand, is the wealth of those whose task it is to preach it; it is the wealth of Christians, in whatever sense they may be rich. To announce the Gospel, you have to become poor. It is not the poverty of the world that is an obstacle to the expansion of the Gospel, but the wealth of certain sectors of the Church.

Preach the Gospel — the Good News of the Kingdom of God and not that of a better world. We cannot let ourselves forget that salvation is a *"one way"* street: it can only come from God through Christ.

We cannot allow ourselves to mix up the Good News of salvation with the various recipes for happiness bandied about by the world. We cannot allow ourselves to give credit to the world for certain key notions that are in fact segments of the Gospel that have been taken out of their context and taken over by certain sectors of society. We cannot allow ourselves to let Christ's message be welded to other messages, making it a moment in man's salvation of man, putting the Gospel at the service of causes that are not purely and simply those of salvation.

The Gospel cries out from one end to the other that God alone is, that the world on its own is incapable of producing life, truth, or love. The kingdom of heaven is the personal love of God, through Christ, for *each one* of us, and the love of each one of us for *each one* of the others. It is through loving *each one* in particular that we are able to love humanity. *Each one* of us is meant to receive the Gospel. Salvation is not a collective abstraction.

For its part, the world oscillates between two poles, in which "each one" is sacrificed to an abstraction: on the one hand, in practice, self-centered capitalism, for the sake of the well-being of the few, casts out all the others into a collective destitution; on the other hand, Marxism, for the sake of a collective well-being, casts out those who oppose it into another kind of destitution. In either case, then, we risk losing from view all that the evangelization and salvation have to do with the individual.

The kingdom of God is the encounter between God and a humanity composed of one person, plus another, plus another. It does not emerge from an anonymous mass, but is received by Peter, James, and John.

The kingdom of God is not love of the world but love of people. The world is not an absolute reality: it is something relative, a realm of possibility that is constantly modified by the interplay of good and evil in the hearts of all people.

The Good News of the Kingdom tells us that the world is insignificant. It is people who are important, because what they are, the world is. The world is made and unmade every day by the people who live in it. Working on the world will not make the world better: the world will become better when each person becomes better. A world that would be built by our own hands, that would operate on accumulated energies, and then produce salvation at the end, is an abstraction.

It is not our task to try to balance the accounts between the "Kingdom of God" and the world. It is not the sum of just cities that will make up the heavenly Jerusalem, but the sum of all the love, in a Church that is great or small, composed of countless or only a few saints, extended to include people known or unknown, that will bring about the redemption of the multitude. Kingdom of God and world do not necessarily coincide. Periods of chaos and violence can awaken passions and an intensity of faith that brings about salvation. The pathway of the Kingdom of God in the world has its ends in eternity; the means ought to interest us only insofar as the end interests us; but we have to keep the perspective in mind.

If the confusion of the two orders, the world and the Kingdom of heaven, has led certain members of the Church into impure alliances with capitalism, we must not, under the pretext of breaking with capitalism, fall to the temptation of binding the Church to other systems that, because they are temporal and of the world, would burden her tomorrow with chains analogous to the ones we want to free her from today.

It is precisely through the labyrinth of possible pitfalls that the narrow but positive way of the Gospel leads, the Gospel that we have been given the task of passing on. *"That they may be one . . . so that the world may know that you have sent me."*

And this brings us back to unity and its promises of saving effectiveness. To work relentlessly at unity among Christians does not mean to cease being missionary; it is the very condition for evangelization.

The Truth Will Set You Free

Instead of the various forms of "economic" liberation that the world preaches, which, looked at more closely, are nothing but the granting of a certain comfort within the bonds of human needs, Christ proclaims liberation from evil.

Now, though many Christians accept this liberation from evil in their personal life, most of them accept the tyranny of evil in its social manifestations.

Some of them, on the one hand, divide their life in two and insert a sincere Christian life into a framework that has been constructed by the world, a framework they believe they are powerless to change: employers, careers once considered liberal, businesses. Some, on the other hand, believing all of these sectors of society to be definitively "possessed" by the spirit of evil, flee in the name of poverty and love into the mass of the small and the poor. This is the withdrawal of countless bourgeois or intellectual elements into the proletariat.

If this stage seems necessary for a new springtime of the Gospel, it seems nevertheless to be merely a stage and perhaps the easiest one. There is no class in the Gospel that is "condemned by heaven." The social status of people seems irrelevant to Christ. In the Gospel, it is the small people that he requires to abandon their jobs. But he doesn't tell Lazarus or the centurion or Nicodemus to become fishermen: he requires something completely different: a renewal of heart, an essential conversion that "will make all things new" in each of their lives. St. Paul does not attack slavery itself; it's the hearts of the Christians who have been evangelized by him that are no longer able to tolerate owning slaves.

If the renewal of heart of certain people leads them to share the life of the workers, we have to understand, I think, that this is only a tiny aspect of the question, and that a majority of hearts are meant to "be converted" and to *explode* right where they are, cracking open the mask of the world, so that, right where they are, the true face of Christ may appear.

It seems clear that what we are lacking within this vast arena is in particular a certain genius, a spirit of invention . . . or perhaps simply spirit. Those who have made the attempt, apart from a few exceptions, have done so with an endless timidity.

Here again we encounter the "recipe" temptation in the face of the Spirit's demands. A blind belief in "public duties" might lead us to accept what is unacceptable. A blind belief in "structures" into which we lump not only Peter or James but a whole bourgeois or economic class, cramps and binds the sovereignly free and re-creative promptings of the Spirit.

Here too what we need is an explosion coming from each person. We

103

have to be aware from the beginning that we don't know what forms these explosions will take or how they will show themselves.

Take for example an employer who performs a "personal" and "revolutionary" gesture in conformity to Christ, by taking the family of one of his workers into his home, against all normal customs. A militant Christian worker might be tempted to say: "He's going to weaken the workers' fighting spirit, and thus the chances for a liberation of the working class." That would be seriously problematic. It would be the condemnation of a tiny manifestation of the Spirit of God in the name of a "worldly program." It would be a condemnation of the first beginnings of the Kingdom of God in the heart of a man, in the name of a possible improvement of general human well-being.

And yet it might very well be precisely these sorts of hesitating and fragmentary gestures, that, in "doing the good," the Christians who are just as much a part of the world as the small and the oppressed will "walk in the light" and no longer be "of the world."

Mission must not forget that it is "for all creatures." If those who suffer sometimes unheard-of human ills because of the dead weight of the world have a right to the proclamation of the Gospel, then those who, from the same dead weight, suffer enormous supernatural ills, who *cause* injustice as if by force, who oppress and who hate by the mere fact of the social level fate placed them in — these people have almost more right to hear the Gospel, for they are more than just poor people, they are sinners. To refuse them the love of compassion and salvation would be to cut ourselves off from the heart of Christ.

Blessed Are the Meek

Our sector is overrun with injustice. All of the responses the world offers to injustice are violence, whether it fights injustice or consents to it. To counter it with the meekness of Christ is a scandal.

Who can calculate the courage that would be required of those who accept to take on this scandal of meekness. But isn't it an even greater — and in this case real — scandal that Christians left it up to a Gandhi to raise up in the world a mass of people who entrusted themselves to the incoercible force of such meekness?

And yet, once again, we have no other option. The Christ who is "meek and humble of heart" is a fact. We can neither correct nor modify this fact.

The Thinking of Christ

We are not free-thinkers. In the sector of the world in which we find ourselves, we are not at liberty to adapt the thinking of Christ to the world's thinking; and this is not always easy to avoid. It is perhaps useful to recall certain aspects of Christ's thinking.

The love of Christ is universal. Any love of some people that takes us away from the love of others is not Christ's love.

Christian poverty does not necessarily mean a small income, it is the state of a person who does not save his wealth, and who does not save because of the needs of others. The poverty of the Gospel is not the poverty of a particular class or particular job — it transcends all such things. It is much more a matter of not looking ahead than of insecurity. "Do not be afraid. . . ." That is why it is not possible to bring into perfect harmony efforts for the Kingdom and efforts for an economic system.[6]

The work of the Gospel is not human work. "My Father is always at work. . . ." The "work ethic" does not have value in itself.

The only time Christ speaks of human work in the Gospel is in the parables about work for the Kingdom of heaven. If Christ's public life seethes with prodigious activity, this activity is not connected with money or a human sort of work.

And yet, in his life, like that of the Apostles, the "You will earn your bread by the sweat of your brow" is sovereignly respected. The notion of work, which is always connected with the notion of being effective, is here lived out on a transcendent level for an efficacity that surpasses human ca-

---

6. Madeleine wrote to Fr. L.:

"Let's be on our guard against the sorts of adventures the militants tend to fall into: a lot of them were at one point fascinated by Christ; it was through Christ that they came to understand the injustice concerning the proletariat — they wanted to share the burden and fight against it. Originally, this fight was an aspect of their love for Christ, but then a reversal of values took place: now it's the fight that has become the essential thing, and Christ is placed in its service.

"Let's also be on our guard against losing the sense of God's encounter with each person, through dealings with class or mass mystiques.

"If one aspect of our love is to bring ourselves into harmony with the common denominator of the milieu in which we live, this can only be in function of the other aspect of our love, which is to carry the Christ whom we love into the very heart of this milieu — to go to the very limits of possibility in our identification with Christ."

pacity. The work of the Gospel is a constant movement of going out to meet people in order to "sow among them" the Kingdom of God.

All great human activities function as signs. Just as marriage is the most perfect sign of the union of Christ and his Church, and voluntary celibacy makes us live more fully the reality to which this sign points, human work is the sign of the Church's toil over the world, a suffering and fruitful labor.

This labor belongs to us as well. It places us at an equal distance from work being made into an absolute as from sterile idleness. Here, as elsewhere, the sign has to remain in its place and not overshadow the reality.

Those Who Are Unhappy

We cannot let mercy dry up, as so often happens today. A greater awareness of the economic hardship of the masses cannot lead us to have scorn for other forms of suffering, or to lose interest in them.

Christ's mercy for the poor is one part of a mercy as vast as all the human griefs combined. It is a mercy for sinners, a mercy for the sick, a mercy for those lamenting their dead, a mercy for those in prison, a mercy for all the little ones.

Because of a reductively materialistic notion of poverty, we are often in danger of forgetting that there are people who are poor in other ways than merely economically; there are other little ones than the workers. There are those who are morally or psychologically weak. There are those who are poor in gifts, in appeal, in love. In addition to the oppressed classes are those who are "unclassifiable."

Those who are little, those who are poor, are not only in the working class. And the working class itself is not made up exhaustively of militants, militants who are already rich in hope, rich in heart, rich in intellectual formation.

It is not up to us to correct Christ's heart either — it belongs to all people and we have to give it to all people.

The personal love of Christ, "He calls each one by name" — he does not call a category. He knows each one of us "as the Father knows the Son."

It is up to us to rediscover this personal love "of one person for another." This love has been distorted through the "social" definitions that we pin to our brothers and tag each other with. We have lost the ability to

encounter each other as one human being meeting another in his individual simplicity. We no longer know how to call each other by name.

Finally, the ultimate infiltration possible: Christ's truth is *free from
success*. The number of those who live it does not change what it is.

On the other hand, if we admire the generosity and love of certain
people who have devoted themselves to a certain idea, this should not lead
us to transfer our admiration for the person to the idea itself. Or, to put it
another way: this view of Christian life, which is missionary because it is
Christian, makes no claim to be for everyone. We do not deny that the
Holy Spirit wills to place others in a different perspective. Everyone lives
what each one lives. But if the Church had always and everywhere to live
the forms that have been lived and written as signs of her, then we would
be happy to say that our place in her is on the journey of Exodus.

Just as it is the task of some to live the exile and slavery of every
Egypt, and of still others to gravitate toward the Promised Land, we believe
our task is to live the journey through the desert. You cannot leave Egypt
unless you are in it. And you cannot leave Egypt unless you separate from
it. In every age of the Church's history, she has borne along those eternal
nomads who have ceaselessly left this world, which they are in but not of,
to set off toward that Promised Land that, in Christ, they already possess.

Of these people, it is possible to say that we don't know "whence they
come nor where they are going." In a world in which they remain as much
a friend as a foreigner, they know that the path they walk is "the way," a way
without signposts and resting places, but full of manna and living waters.
For the Exodus is not merely an event of the past. The Church continually
travels the same pathways.

As long as not all the families of the earth have been gathered and
blessed within Abraham's inheritance, that is to say, in Christ, the people
of God will ceaselessly have to go out of idolatrous Egypt, to march ceaselessly through the austerity of the desert, to do ceaselessly what it takes to
achieve the Promised Land.

The Church will remain in the desert until the Parousia. She will
never stop lamenting the loss of the easy life in Egypt, and even murmur-
ing in her people and sinning in her leaders. But God, who for his part is
faithful, pushes her unfailingly ahead, through chastisement and pardon,
until she reaches the new heavens and the new earth that Jesus will bring
into being the day of his Parousia.

The Poverty of the Mind[7]

Two factors in the secularization of the masses have been in large part already brought to light:

- that many people do not have what they need in the sense of living conditions, budgets, housing, salary, and culture in order to live a normal human life.
- that the majority of Christians remain among themselves: priests and laypeople in privileged social sectors; the Gospel is not proclaimed by word and by life. The witnesses no longer bear witness, in the first place because they aren't there, but also because their life itself does not bear witness.

There seems to me to be *another factor* that has received a lot less attention, and that is the "poverty of the mind" that those who are responsible have allowed the "little ones" to fall into.

Poverty means lacking something that's necessary. An impoverished human intelligence is one that no longer possesses that for which it was made.

In the Acts of the Apostles, it is said somewhere: "We weren't aware that there was a Holy Spirit."

Are we missionaries not able to confess likewise: we weren't aware that there was such a thing as spirit?[8]

7. Personal notes.
8. [Translator's note: the French word *"l'esprit"* means both "spirit" and

108

The Poverty of the Mind

A state of "poverty of mind" has slowly overtaken whole masses of human beings, comparable to the social poverty that we tend to take to mean merely a failure to have physical and cultural needs met.

As the meaning of "social," under the pressure of certain social and historical factors, has broadened far beyond family or country, the intelligence has acquired new forms of vitality.

At the same time, however, this intelligence has in many cases found itself deprived of one of its most ancient and proper accesses to reality: the community of life with nature, what we have classically referred to as nature: countryside, earth, the laws that govern them and that human memory, if not personal reflection, has connected with an appropriate image of God.

With this countryside and the nature it possesses, man was from time immemorial in communion with destiny. Through it he was educated — in the sense of the knowable and in the sense of mystery — concerning the relativity of certain things in relation to him, and concerning his own relativity.

I don't mean to say that "rural life" is some kind of fortress within which faith has nothing to fear; you only have to take a look at the rural map of France. But I do mean that, if what the Curé of Ars said remains true: "Let a village go for ten years without priests and they'll end up worshiping animals . . . ," what also remains true in this saying is the fact that they'll still have a need for worship. The idea that man could be the cause and end of everything will always smell of absurdity.

Urban life already to a considerable extent cuts off our normal relations to reality, regardless of whether we are of the working class or not. We just have to recall what Paris was like during the war: the blackout suddenly gave us back a sense of the significance of the length of the days and the phases of the moon. The lack of fuel reminded us what winter and summer are really like. The shortage of commercial exchanges made us remember that there are seasons for peas, lettuce, and onions.

Nowadays, the great majority of working-class people live in the big cities. A lot of people no longer have any contact with the land. Others go "to the country" only because they plan to do something there: sports, swimming, camping, bike races, etc.

"mind." When Madeleine speaks of *"La misère de l'esprit"* in the title and throughout this section, the accent is clearly on "mind." In this sentence, however, we rendered *"l'esprit"* as "spirit" in order to preserve the pun.]

At the same time, the "prime matter" offered to man's mind becomes different: iron, chemical products, machines by which we *produce* things: acid, energy.

Man's intelligence is no longer ordered toward a world in which he participates, the value of which comes from beyond and goes toward the beyond. Instead, it exists within a world from which it has to liberate itself so that it can exploit the world for its profit: this human profit enslaves the spirit. Biological and physiological research interest him in relation to advances in medicine.

Even death itself loses a bit of its *imminent* mystery. "Human causality" tends even to take over death itself. In the past, a person died in part because of man and mostly directly because of death. Nowadays, a person dies mostly because of man. The battle for peace has come to present itself as a battle against death. The analysis of the social factors of death — the lack of hygiene, infectious diseases, the victories over tuberculosis, the victories of chemical treatment and specialized therapies — *mask* the *ineluctable* character of death. Because we are able to put it off, we forget that it always comes anyway.

What was once a mystery has evaporated into a thousand experimental discoveries; and it has not been replaced for the mind by a denser and more question-provoking mystery, in which these experiments end up: the laws cover over the mystery.

For the "little ones," thinking no longer means learning how to die and to live, but rather learning how to be as happy as possible, for as many years as possible, and according to the definition of happiness accepted by the milieu in which one lives.

Once again the "downward slide" of the spirit entails the downward slide of the concept of happiness. We get closer and closer to those sorts of happiness that can be calculated in terms of buying power. This becomes what we desire not only for ourselves but also for those we love.

This reductively *utilitarian* concept of the intelligence — and moreover utilitarian specifically in relation to a *limited understanding of happiness* — is precisely what I call "poverty of the mind."

We are right to be scandalized about the fact that the human activity of millions of human beings has been reduced to mechanical gestures. We recognize that there is a violence being done here.

But I believe that there is a comparable violence being done to millions of human minds, which have been "reduced" to knowing always the same tiny pieces of truth, limited by an incredibly restricted sense of reality.

110

We are scandalized, and rightly so, at the fact that inadequate salaries prevent millions of people from receiving enough food and appropriate education. We are scandalized about the degenerated and pathologically afflicted personalities that result from this malnourishment of the body and the practical intelligence.

But I believe that there is also such a thing as a degeneration, weakening, and distortion on the level of the mind that is just as scandalous and that results from the starving of minds, which have no longer been fed on the nourishing food they need.

We are scandalized, and even more so, and even more rightly so, at the fact that certain people claim the privilege of dividing up the human community in the name of a caste to which they attribute particular rights and needs.

But isn't it an even greater scandal to divide up the natural community between God and man by allowing man to be bereft of his right to intelligence?

Every human being has a foot on the ground and an antenna in the air. We've left people's feet on the ground, but the antennae have all deteriorated — people can no longer pick up the airwaves.

To work at rebuilding the natural community between man and God does not mean giving people faith — it's God who does that. It does not mean evangelizing, but rather proposing the faith.

But this "poverty of mind" turns people's backs to the horizon from which faith comes; it cuts out of the vocabulary half of the words that make up the Gospel message.

At the same time that we face the temptations of having a charity that divorces itself from faith, on the natural level we face the temptation of a love that foregoes truth. As heirs of an age in which "knowledge was not ordered toward love," we tend in reaction toward a love that dispenses with knowing.

Out of love, we will end up desiring for those whom we love on this same natural level only a "materialistic" happiness in the strictest sense of the term, which is the happiness they themselves seek.

I think that certain Christians need a profound internal revolution so that love could enlighten them about the various lacks of collective love suffered by "those who are hungry," "those who weep," "those without shelter," etc., and those for whom we have prevented the heart from beating that Christ has given us to love them.

But I also think that an analogous revolution is required so that faith can enlighten us about the "ones in darkness," a darkness to which we have not brought the mind Christ also gave us.

We have to become aware of the invasion of *shrunken truths* that saturate the eyes of our brothers and ourselves. These truths come from school, from the factory, from the newspaper, from stores, from the radio. They are rather like arrows that point in reverse: they lead man back to himself. It is up to us, then, to *convert* them, to give them back their true direction even while leaving them what they are.

We have to become aware of the gaps in the bridge between man and the mystery of all that is. The bridge between man and the earth has been sundered.

We have to become aware of the bridgeheads that exist, to point them out, to make them known.

The man of the earth knows how to manipulate the laws of agriculture. But, even if he is not Christian, these laws lead his mind to something greater than himself. The man of the sea understands the movements of his boat; but, even if he is not Christian, the forces of the sea lead his mind to something that transcends him.

It is the same sort of order that needs to be reestablished between each man and the mystery of the reality with which he is in contact. Of course, this doesn't mean giving faith. But where is the capacity to receive the faith in a person who thinks God is absurd? Should we, too, encourage this absurd assumption?

"How will they ever come to believe if no one preaches the Gospel to them?"

— Yes, but "how will they ever come to believe" if they "don't have ears to hear?"

I'm not saying that this fight against the poverty of the mind is the most *essential* part of the missionary task.

But if the economic poverty of the proletariat has an effect on the purposes of mission, on its goal and the forms it takes, the poverty of the mind should also have an effect.

In all of the various forms of life in the working class, the missionary is never able, for his brothers, to put up with the economic poverty *just as it is*, and thus he tries to reduce it through efforts ranging from fraternal aid to structural reform.

Does he then have the right to put up with the poverty of the mind such as he finds it, without trying either individually or collectively to remedy it?

If, in all of the "forms" of mission, the sharing of work and of life, the evangelization through a life, work on social conditions, liturgical and parochial activities, the "Word" figures only as one element among many and sometimes even as a marginal element, is it not because we have lost a sense of the mind?

The fact that, for laypeople, "speaking" is a friendly and occasional function, is normal.

But, we may ask the missionary priests, is the "Go forth and preach" still one of Christ's primary orders for the spreading of the Kingdom of God?

It is a paradox in practice: the "priests" seem insufficiently missionary, and the missionaries seem no longer to be preachers.

We often hear the words of John the Baptist cited: "Prepare the way of the Lord. . . ."

But the words preceding this passage are less often cited: "I am a voice crying out in the desert."

A Quick Dash to Rome[9]

I went to Rome with a very specific goal:

- to pray that we would not lose the grace of apostolate that was granted to France, but that we would maintain it in unity;
- to pray that this grace be recognized and strengthened by the Church.

This trip to Rome was impersonal precisely to the same degree that my first trip there in 1933 was personal. This is the way the Lord wanted it.

In 1933, I didn't feel the beauty of secular Rome, the wealth of modern Rome, or the earthliness of "Vatican" Rome.

I was at that time immersed in an enormous encounter with praying people, in crowds of believers.

I attended a papal Mass.

As a free gift, I was given a rootedness in the Church, in the foundation stone from which every root must spring.

This time, however, I went directly to St. Peter's. On the walls of the square were a flood of political posters, "*Democrazia Cristiana*" . . . waging battle like all battles are waged.

Each time I left St. Peter's I saw cars of an extraordinary luxury coming and going in the Vatican.

---

9. A report sent to a few friends upon her return from a twenty-four-hour trip to Rome in May, 1952. The circumstances surrounding this trip are described above, pp. 77-78.

Crossing Rome in both directions, I was deeply moved by its beauty: Paris seems like a "latecomer" next to it. I was also struck by the elegant wealth of the modern city. I felt strongly the danger for all of these prelates, these men of the Church, living among such cultural charm and wealth.

In St. Peter's, where I spent the whole day, I attended Mass. Very few people were praying. There was a little traffic before the throne of Pius X, but that was about it. Almost no one, a few scattered priests, hardly any.

By contrast, a continuous caravan of English and Americans, in the Thomas Cook style, with tour guides. Underneath, work was going on, worker's conversations and wheelbarrows hauling debris.

It was in this atmosphere that I did what I had to do. I attached myself to "my" pillar, which had the advantage of being in front of the pope's altar, and, on St. Peter's tomb, I prayed with all my heart . . . and at first lost heart.

I didn't reflect, I didn't ask for "light," because that's not why I came. And yet, a number of things imposed themselves on me and they remain with me.

First: Jesus said to Peter: "You are Peter and on this rock I will build my Church. . . ." He was meant to become a rock and the Church was meant to be built. Jesus, who so often spoke of the power of the Spirit, of his life-giving force, said in relation to the Church that he would build it upon this man who would become like a rock. It was Christ's intention that the Church be not only something living, but also something built.

The second thing: I discovered bishops.

On my list of parting visits was Mr. — , who sells *l'Homme nouveau,* and who is a temptation to anger for me every Sunday. Wanting to say something nice to him, I looked for something to buy from him at his stand. He had the magazine *Fêtes et Saisons* there, with an issue devoted to "Our Bishops." I bought it and leafed through it quickly before leaving. There I discovered the original truth that the bishop holds "the deposit of faith" and the responsibility for "apostolates."

During the journey and also in Rome, I discovered the immense importance of bishops for the faith and the life of the Church.

"I will make you fishers of men." It seemed to me, in relation to what we call authority, we tend to react either as liberals or as people with a fetish. We do not flow back to the bishops with everything we have encountered in or learned from the world.

Either we obey like a second-class soldier; or else at best we submit our requests for their signature. We do not bring back images, or sensations, etc., like eyes to the brain.

We're under the rule of authorizations rather than the rule of authority, which would mean to receive that which is "to be done," that of which we are meant to be "authors" in the work of God.

All of this is still undigested, but it seems to me extremely important. When we speak of the obedience of the saints, we fail to grasp, I think, how much, in the body of the Church, they are wedded to that internal struggling that constitutes a living organism, in which unity is composed of various activities in tension with each other.

And lastly,

I also thought a lot about the fact that, though St. John is the "disciple Jesus loved," it was Peter that Jesus asked: "Do you love me?" and it was after his affirmations of love that Jesus gave him the flock. He also explained what it means to love: "That which you've done to the least of my brothers, you have done unto me."

It became clear to me how essential it is that people, all people, come to know that the hierarchical Church loves them. Peter — a rock who has been asked to love. I understood that all the expressions of the Church have to be penetrated through and through with love.

Forming an Alliance,
or Working Toward Salvation[10]

There are two ways we can relate to Marxism: either working to form an alliance or working toward salvation.

What is a particularly pressing call in the Mission's vocation is working toward salvation.

What represents the specific danger in this vocation is the desire to form an alliance.

This coincidence in the Mission between goal and danger must be met with a great supernatural audacity, since the normal temptations will be either to reject the one or to deny the existence of the other.

Wanting to Form an Alliance

The desire to form an alliance arises out of our admiration for the Marxist, a survivor from a hopeless proletariat, the prototype and forger of a socially reconstructed tomorrow. What we think to baptize is no longer the proletariat in his grievous sub-civilization, but rather a civilization of the future, the civilization the Marxists are working to create. We forget that, if a civilization can be baptized, we cannot baptize a heresy and more than a heresy: we cannot baptize an atheism that is both theoretical and practical.

We would be unable to understand this desire for alliance if we were unaware of the power of seduction that a courageously Marxist milieu holds. For many Christians, generosity, camaraderie, sincerity, and self-

10. A note written at the request of a bishop, October 1953.

sacrifice acquire a whole new reality in this milieu. The allure is all the stronger when it is a case of a Marxist circle that has no interest in the intellectual systems that support it.

To resist it, we need above all a constantly nourished faith, a head that has been candidly enlightened about Marxist teachings, and finally an asceticism of the heart. We cannot insist enough on this asceticism; without it, we will not be able to maintain the critical sense needed to discern not only our proper line of action, but also to be able to remain clearsighted about the narrow-mindedness and the weeds that arise even within Marxism.

The first feature of the desire for alliance will be a certain admiring recognition that the Christian will feel for the Marxists who ask him to work with them. It is a difficult feature to discern, since it so closely resembles the joy a Christian experiences who has been "cut off" from nonbelievers, and who finds himself reunited with them. . . .

It is quite clear that, within the Marxist milieu, within the city, the factory, or the administration, a human friendship will lead us to work together in common human activities, even outside of the political or professional arena.

I am certain that many of these activities do not entail any cooperation with Marxism, but that *almost always,* at the center of or alongside these activities, either an intervention or the taking of a stand will arise that, for its part, will touch the central nervous system of Marxism.

That is why we have to keep a clear head and our heart in check.

For this *cooperation* is something doubly to be avoided, because it hooks us up with an enormous dechristianizing force, and because it dechristianizes us ourselves.

Even the great Marxist teachers were probably unaware to what extent their two fundamental options were logically connected: the death of God and class struggle; atheism and hatred for certain human beings.

In the measure that this hatred is legally "practiced" somewhere, the Kingdom of God loses ground.

What is true on the collective scale is perhaps even more true individually. When a Christian participates regularly in Marxist activities, when he accords "in practice" a certain "justice to anger," even with the militant Catholics who are not aware of it, there occurs a certain pernicious anemia that saps away his supernatural being. This state of being can coexist within him with a faith that seems total; but, little by little, whole dimensions of his life of grace are *debilitated.* This radical debilitation is no doubt the most likely cause of the moral failure and the break with the hierarchy.

It would be particularly dangerous to seek the cause of these tragedies solely in personal circumstances and temperaments.

When the Church becomes a foreign element in so many missionary lives, when the priests are shut out, when the City is preferred to the Kingdom, when salvation is confused with happiness, we should perhaps wonder and ask ourselves above all whether something that is contrary to God because it is contrary to love is not an element common to all of these lives, and whether it is not the common cause of their various failures.

At the same time, we should perhaps also ask ourselves what sort of fruits would grow tomorrow in a climate that would by steps settle over the young missionaries, a climate in which permission is granted to love whole categories of human beings a little less or not at all.

Working Toward Salvation

But there is still the working toward salvation. Is it perhaps because we have not lived it enough in the past that we are incapable of living it in the future?

Over half of the earth, people are not "seated" in the darkness of death, but standing on their feet, so that the apostasy of a class might become the apostasy of a world, and here we go to take our part. . . .

Joining our hearts with those of the apostles of every age, shouldn't we ask that we continue to "be sent"? May those who guide us constantly tell us that we do not love people enough and that we do not hate evil enough.

Seen from God's perspective, Marxists are the most unhappy of human beings, and the sickest. . . . They need medicine. . . . And we have gone to them as if they were healthy, and sometimes as if they themselves were the healers — and that, I think, was our first mistake.

But we know now that their sickness was the proletariat, which was their chosen land, and that by plunging into the proletariat, they were so to speak predisposed to the disease.

We should be aware that this disease is an epidemic, and that it is contagious . . . even before the symptoms show.

The hungry, the oppressed, and the homeless of the working classes so crowded our eyes that we were unable to see, alongside the sins of which they were the symptoms, the other mortal sin that the world was in the process of creating.

Yes, we went there where we needed to go, but, once we got there, we made something other than an apostle out of the missionary.

And yet, vis-à-vis the world, there is nothing else to be. It is not a question of words but a question of a deep reality. We scarcely want to say the word "apostolate" anymore, since of late the word has become oddly denatured.

Nevertheless I believe that by comparing this word with the present sense of the word "missionary," we will rediscover the meaning of working toward salvation.

Love for the Church

It is not something angelic.

It is not drill-sergeant obedience.

It is something "practiced" consciously and deliberately in every moment of life, like the love of God and the love of neighbor that can be lived nowhere else but in "Jesus-now" — in the Church.

That may be why Christians who are officially Catholic are called "practicing."

People look down on this name, and not without some reason. But when a word is worn out and then rejected, more often than not we end up by the same gesture rejecting the original notion expressed by the word.

And just as the "practicing" mentality drained Christian life of its mystical sap and Gospel realism, so too the "anti-practicing" mentality threatens to turn the life of the Church either into a pious dream, a human pastime, or a discipline analogous to that of a political party or an army.

At every turning point in history, it seems clear that the Lord wished to give certain people the vocation of living the Gospel letter for letter, so that their flesh and their blood would become as it were a new edition of the Gospel providentially destined for the men of their age.

But it seems no less clear that their flesh and their blood were of good printing quality only when they were sent through the Church's presses. For those who attempted otherwise, their lives remained like a manuscript that circulates only among small groups of initiates.

We Must Love the Christ-Church
by Practicing His Life

If we are, in fact, participants in the internal life of the Church, the authenticity and intensity of this participation are not only a matter of knowledge.

It is possible to be an excellent theologian and still live God's love very poorly; we can know quite well what the Church is while still being only an anemic cell within her.

By the same token, we can "live the faith" in everything having to do with God-us, and fail to live it while adhering to it merely intellectually in everything having to do with Church-us.

Even when we live a life in close union with Jesus, it is still worth asking ourselves, I think, whether we are not making him or his love into something a little "historical," whether we don't see him above all as he was, and not as *He is,* in the Church.

Have we grasped what Joan of Arc meant in saying "Christ and the Church are one"?

Sometimes we take up the attitude vis-à-vis the Church of someone who is looking for a certificate of good behavior. But the Church doesn't supervise: she exists, and we exist within her. She is the Body of Christ and we are members of this Body. Our dependence on her and our commitment to her, if they entail external acts or signs, are above all an internal and vital dependence and commitment. Our dependence on the body that she is, is considerable.

But our initiative, our responsibility, and our function are also considerable. We are designed as irreplaceable parts of the Church. Both our submissions and our initiatives are matters of obedience, as they would be for a body's cells that want to be at once intelligent and loving. A single cell can infect the whole organism; a single cell can allow the needle that would save it to penetrate.

Our obedience is simultaneously passive and active because it is obedience to a living order, a living rhythm, and a living reproduction.

We don't make good on obedience with a prayer said at mass, with a devotion to a priest or to a movement. We don't even make good on it with a faithful life of the sacraments, or with a fervent life of prayer, but rather by carrying our sacramental life and our prayer life wherever they must go, all the way to the end for which they were made.

Nonbelievers reject the Church either because she is not properly human or because she claims to be divine. If the Church is not what she is meant to be in our life, it is in reality for the same reasons: either we are satisfied to make of her a poor human thing; we lose the Church even while holding onto a mask of her, through a particular liturgical devotion, through engagement in parochial concerns, or through an external discipline. Or else we reject the Church because of lassitude, anticipating that she must be something unknowable and unbearable, like the God of the Jews, to look upon whom is to die.

In fact, the Church is the greatest sign of the mystery of God. For she contains the famous dimensions of love described by St. Paul, dimensions he hopes we can attain with all of the saints. She alone is the sign of the massive breaking open that our entire being has to undergo in order to be capable of God and God's tasks.

We will be incapable of incarnating God's love in the world, we will be incapable of bringing the Gospel, which is but the manifestation of love, to the world, if we do not first accept the incarnation of this love in the Church, in the mystical Body of Jesus Christ.

This body has its own laws, and its inner economy, which is the very economy of salvation. It has its organs — which are not cogs — its blood, its metabolism, its food. I repeat, we are intelligent and loving cells. We need to realize what the love of each cell of our body means for the other cells, for their reciprocal services, for the vital organs. . . . If these cells could only understand and love — at that very instant we would explode with gratitude for every priest who has offered Christ's blood; we would be anxiously praying on our knees for each bishop that had decisions to make; we would have compassion for the Holy Father, and we would thank God that, in the papacy, there exists such a great sign of his own fatherhood.

If the organs of the Mystical Body, which are human beings, are entitled to our faith in their office, they are also entitled to our love for man. And they are also entitled to our charity: though they may be supernaturally weak, their office remains intact: if a heart becomes weak, we do not cut it out. This body has a certain way of eating; it has a certain way of taking care of itself, just as it has its own way of breathing. In all of these things, the Lord did not wait for us to make the decisions. That's how it is, and it can't be otherwise. Everything in the Church shows the movement of Christ's blood, the gestures that offer it, the places where we can place our lips to drink it and to cause it to pour forth.

This is what liturgy is. . . . Are we aware that liturgy is the salvation of the world? If, through the long course of history, it was necessary to adapt the liturgy, to explain it, to translate it, and if it is once again necessary to do so in our time, it never has been and is not today a question of making the liturgy more human. It already is human, and tragically so: it is the Passion of the Son of God made man, made continually present among us.

This is, above all, what a parish is, in the midst of a world that comprehends nothing about such things. What else are bishops with their offices other than the faith preserved and the responsibility for the salvation that is meant to spread to the ends of the earth? Rome, through everything else, is the love of God that has been promised to the Church for eternity. This body wants to propagate itself. The Church will forever aspire to the world. She doesn't need the world in order to accomplish her mission, but without the world, she would have no mission. The world is the stubble and the Church is the flame.

If there is a way of betraying the Church in rebelling against her, which we hear so much about, there is another way of betraying the Church in making her into something she is not, in allowing her to dwindle into something less than herself, into something merely inspired by her: movements, orders, groups, etc.

If there is a betrayal in denying the essential, there is a betrayal in loving and defending as essential what is temporary and relative.

If there is an infidelity in not seeing in each person what he or she is by the order of Christ, there is a lack of truth in making certain people out to be more than they are. Each person must be treated according to the faith, the truth: the baptized, as members of our own body; the priests, as those who dispense sacramental grace; bishops, as guardians of the faith and those responsible for the apostolate; the Pope, as our common father. First let's attend to this . . . and then we'll see what happens.

We'll see that our encounters with Christians will become true bonds; that we will love priests with a grateful heart — without for all that always sharing their particular views on things; that the hierarchy will become our heavy and demanding concern.

At the same time, if a lot of Christians become lifeless in being cut off from the liturgical life, we reduce the liturgy considerably and make it inaccessible to many people by making it merely something formal, if not formalistic. The liturgical life is the continuous actualization within us and beyond us of the mysteries of Christ; it is effective everywhere; it is the hours, the seasons, and the ages of the Church.

We Must Love the Christ-Church
by Practicing His Mission

I believe it was St. Francis of Assisi who said, in tears, "Love is not loved." We cannot always say absolutely the same thing about Christ. Among non-believers, there are many people with a human love for the outward appearance of Christ. But with respect to the Christ who is right now living among us, we can repeat Francis's saying with full justice. We ought to have some compassion for the love of Christ residing in the Church that is despised and hated.

The goodness of Christ, which it is the Church's mission to make manifest — who wants to know this? . . . and, in many cases, who *can* know it?

We must continually strive to make the Church *lovable*. We must continually strive to avoid anything that would needlessly render Christ's love indiscernible in the Church. It is a sin of omission not to give witness to the fact that the joy of being a child of God is something we possess in her, our Mother. There ought to be a certain family resemblance with the Church that shines through our lives. There is a certain witness to eternal life that comes about only in our being a sound in the Church's voice. We must continually strive to make the Church *loving*. Her love is to a great extent in our hands. "It is in her souls that the Church is beautiful," says St. Ambrose. In our lives, the Church ought to be *good;* in our lives, the Christ-Church ought to love as he wishes, according to the movement of his love, according to the rules of his love, according to the demands of his love.

The direction of this love is a movement, an *élan*. From the moment Christ took to the road, he never again left it; at the end, the road was called the way of the Cross.

To St. Peter, to whom he said "You are Peter, and on this rock I will build my Church," the first word he addressed to him was "Follow me," and the last thing he said to him was "Follow me." The final command he gave the Apostles was, "Go . . . ," "I have brought you together in order that you could go out. . . ." This love is like an *élan vital*, surging out toward all the ends of the earth, whether they be geographical or social ends. This love is like an internal *élan* that surges out toward whatever is separated by sin and error. This love is like an *élan* seeking to find once again those whom Christ first set himself to pursue: the little ones, those who suffer, the poor.

The rules of this love are the famous dimensions of charity described by St. Paul, the dimensions he wishes us all to attain, with all the saints, without exceptions, without limits. The name of the game is "loser takes all." But we could not live this love, which takes its measure from the Christ-Church and not from us, except by intensifying our intimate, internal, and living belonging to Christ in the Church. Without this, we would either fall into a ditch, falsify the message, or we would render it sterile.

It is only in and through the Church that the Gospel is Spirit and Life. Outside of the Church, there may be spirit, but no Holy Spirit.

The evangelization of the world and its salvation is the Church's task. She strives constantly towards the world, like flame that seeks stubble. But this striving would be disproportionate in relation to a person who wanted to be merely himself.

The more the world into which we enter is without the Church, the more we have to be the Church precisely there. Mission exists only in her. And she enters the world through us.

The consequences of all of this for us is that our love for the Church ought to bring us to live ever more deeply, with intelligence and with love, with faith and with charity, everything that concerns the inner mystery of the Church. This means moreover that our love for the Church does not necessarily entail that we act according to official ecclesial forms of action or terms, but rather that we have the courage to let the budding of the charity that is our call break through the hard bark, the sap, and the marrow of our lives. We don't paint a budding on a piece of paper, copying from another; a budding pushes out from within. By being strictly faithful to the imperatives of Gospel love, we will be the budding that God wants today, constantly connected from within to the trunk, pushing forth our leaves, one after the other, always prepared to let them fall if they have not emerged in good state, never certain that we will be the ones in the right tomorrow, but certain that there are not two "Spirits," and that if we make a mistake, it is never serious when we know that it is a mistake. On the other hand, we know that a fear of great adventure, a *fear of that Spirit, whom we don't know whence he comes or where he is going,* would constitute on our part, for the Church, our greatest possible lack of love.

The Risk of Submission[11]

The restrictions placed on the Mission, if they entail the danger of insubordination, seem to me to entail another risk that is far less often addressed: the danger of lacking in *realism*.

Many factors present themselves to us with regard to this lack of realism.

If the Mission, for its part, was not entirely free from error, the attacks that were waged against it were not entirely unbiased.

If the Church wants to correct this impulse for the Mission's own safety, there are more than a few people who interpret this correction as a rejection and a self-assured return to the days of yesteryear, the loss of which these people will never get over.

And thus there is a strong temptation to forget that *God is the one leading* and to transform our obedience either into discouragement or a political resignation to the lesser evil.

But if anyone has a sense of History, it's God. If some people think that this present trial will become a thing of the past, are we being realistic if we do not believe that, through this trial, God is pointing out what will

---

11. In this section, we join together two texts, written respectively in January and February of 1954. The title Madeleine gave to the first note applies equally to the second, since everything that is said here about the worker-priests can be extended to every Christian.

be the thing of the future? *Belief* is no doubt our precondition for acquiring the supernatural "genius" we need to take the next step.

The sort of life that the present measures squeeze on all sides is already something that has been *left behind.* People criticize this approach for having gone too far. But are we sure that God does not want this life to go precisely further, and that, in order for it to be able to go further, he is *forcing it to take a different form?*

Perhaps what has prevented it from going further is precisely that upon which the Holy Father has placed the restriction — a priest and a factory worker making their home in the same man.

This restriction surprised a lot of us; we expected the difficulties to come from a different direction.

And yet, when we think about it, perhaps this restriction forewarns us about the potential confusions we were unable to see because of the present moral or political confusions.

Under the protection of this confusion, the term "missionary life" could cease to be synonymous with "apostolic life."

To the same extent that the apostolic life requires the priest to "earn his bread" in certain milieus, in order for it to be genuine, it also requires a constant reordering of every aspect of life, including work, in relation to the goal that is proper to the apostolate. In the apostolic life, whatever does not contribute to "the spreading of the kingdom of God" by the means that are supernaturally accorded it, cannot but take second place.

I think that, precisely here, there are many superstitions lying in wait to ambush our realism.

If one of my coworkers says to me, "it's good to see that there are priests who have hands just like the rest of us," that does not imply that he takes him to be the same as everyone else. And if a lot of workers have their own ideas about "what a priest shouldn't be," their *a priori* notions about what a priest should be are quite far from our own prejudices.

Throughout the modern world, work appears in profoundly different forms. Since society is constantly creating new forms, which give rise to new dangers and new insecurities, what should prevent the priest who, like St. Paul in Corinth, wishes to live by the work of his own hands, from *setting in opposition to common currents* a lifestyle that, though it may be unusual, is true because it results from all of the demands of his priesthood?

In any event, he would be assured of the poverty and the sort of insecurity that is proper to his state of life: the sort of work that would constantly have to be limited, given up, or accepted in conformity to the priest's other demands, could hardly turn out to be "profitable."

I believe that if, in a strictly lay life, work is something that in the first place concerns the "secular" [*temporel*], it can, outside of the priesthood, in the various apostolic missions, ask to be as it were pierced through by the "charity of the Christ who urges us forward."

Just as there are Christians in our age who are called to give witness to Christ by living certain human realities "à la chrétienne" [in a Christian manner], we no doubt need other Christians who have the audacity to allow the various aspects of their lives in society to be completely overturned by a new hierarchy of values.

20 February 1954

For ten years now we have not only with all our heart but also with all our Christian hope watched the young *Missions of France* sprout up like a bud upon the great tree of the Church.

No doubt because it was fragile, this bud has become so bruised that the pain in our heart threatens to overcome our hope. It would be false optimism to deny a mortal danger. But, if we find ourselves in a panic, "God is greater than our heart." If we say "the worker-priests' affair," "the Dominicans' affair," "the affair of the *Mission of France*," we are tempted to set our stakes primarily on human capacity.

If we say, "the Church's affairs," or "God's affairs," we are setting our stakes on God's fidelity; "the shadow that covers us" no longer leads us astray, because it is in this shadow that the promises are fulfilled.

God promised his Church that "the poor would hear the good news," the poor who are "at the ends of the earth" even if today they are right across the street.

God wants us to make him keep his word: but have we put such pressure on God? Have we put enough?

We all know that there are a lot of people right now suffering and praying.

But, because the Mission is able to bring to people the greatest of all goods, we want, in order to save it, to act on people, to inform people, to influence people. Just like for the great human goods — peace, the fight against poverty, life — we want to start a campaign.

But the Mission is also, and especially, a good that belongs to God, a justice rendered to God. We have not started a campaign for God. Publicly, we have not demanded glory for God.

And the ten years that have passed already remind us of this.

Because there are two overlapping maps for a single country — one showing the solid Christian territory, France as a country that sends out missionaries; and one showing the Godless zones, "France as a missionary country" — there has been an evangelization of France carrying all the normal risks but lacking the normal means of support.

When a missionary leaves Brittany or Lorraine to travel to the end of the world, while he is in this new Church, his native Church never leaves his side, constantly nourishing him by the nearness of her prayer, of her suffering, and of her fraternal understanding. The Christians from "back home" celebrate some of their liturgies a little bit in his honor. The people among whom he lives are already familiar to them through large simple images. The errors these people commit are not considered "sins," it is just that they don't know any better. If there are persecutions, people praise the martyrs' fidelity, and it seems as if their persecutors are almost already saved.

The apostle and the infidels are embraced from a distance by a single hope. If the direction of the bud is to grow always further outwards, that of the sap is to follow it.

During these ten years the priests in certain forms of the *Mission of France* have been called and are still called today "unattached priests." This word reveals quite precisely the loneliness of the priests and the laypeople committed to outpost positions. Their only connection to the common life of Christians was through episcopal responsibilities, the affection of a few friends, and the hope of the people whose vocation was related to theirs. They themselves never looked back and hardly ever asked for help.

Can we blame these buds?

And yet information was not wanting: reports, statistics, sociological studies. . . . But, practically speaking, for what audience were such things intended if not for the militants, intellectuals, or already culturally formed milieus? They inspired some to go off and try to penetrate into certain zones of atheism; others were inspired to work for a new awareness or for social reforms.

However, they did not reach the true Christian "masses," to provoke in these people a reaction of faith, and of organic and supernatural solidarity.

For these masses, the atheists have remained less blind than sinful, those who persecute with pen or tongue incapable of salvation and condemned already in advance. And it is even more remarkable that the responsibility every Christian bears in relation to nonbelievers is compounded in Christian countries by an undeniable culpability.

An atheist world does not grow up next to Christian communities without these communities being at fault to some extent, at least guilty of blind selfishness. The secularizing economic causes are themselves the accumulated expression of sinful hearts.

We could no doubt seek the cause of the Mission's present danger in human failings or in excessively strict measures. But why not look first at our own deficiencies? Why should we attribute to their trial today what we did not attribute to their weakness in the past?

Why not — behind all these bruises — awaken the living forces of the faith, and thereby preserve it from being definitively crushed?

God knows better than we do the time and place of new birth; but he saves the life he gives when that person seeks strength in faith.

Not too long ago, we would have been able to find the underground map of this faith in France; back then, each Christian was called upon to make a gift of their faith, to "spread it" to the ends of the earth. Gathered together, one by one, like the threads of a fabric woven in a simple action, thousands upon thousands of people offered up their prayers, sufferings, and the small change that was asked of them for the "foreign missions."

When it is a question of life or death, there is no sense in being creative — in the Church as much as anywhere else, or even more than anywhere else. When there is something threatening the Church's life, she has her eternal remedies; these are what she wants us to use, there is no reason to look for others.

Open minds, creative spirits, and heroic initiatives are and always will be helpful, but what is necessary today are people who believe, who give their prayer and their suffering, as they did for foreign missions; we need people who offer, instead of a little money, the mending of our collective selfishness, our God-murdering selfishness.

Our prayer will be genuine to the extent that it knows what we pray for. It will be genuine, if, when praying for nonbelievers, we put right whatever it is in us that caused their nonbelief.

Wherever we might meet people who truly believe, whether it be at Mass on Sunday, in children's catechism, in prayer groups and in apostolates, we should ask them for this prayer, this suffering, and this conversion of the heart.

We should ask contemplative monasteries and monks, the old Christians in retirement homes, the sick in the hospitals and sanatoriums; we should ask the weak and the lonely, those who have lost loved ones in the war or in the camps.

We should teach them all, in whatever form suits them, through the facts (we don't need to say where they come from), how atheistic our society has become, how much indifference and skepticism there is around us.

We should teach them all, and again through the facts, how it is we got to where we are.

Through the facts, always through the facts, through the infinitely various facts, we should show them all how we can repair this enormous collective sin.

And we should do so in a way that corresponds to the age, capacity, and point of view of each of them — "to say in every case something new to someone new."

And then it will seem impossible that God should not act as God, that Christ should not be proclaimed, and that his Church, even here, should not continue to grow.

PART THREE

A PATH BETWEEN TWO ABYSSES

1955-1960

"This passion for God will reveal to us that our Christian life is a path between two abysses. One is the measurable abyss of the world's rejections of God. The other is the unfathomable abyss of the mysteries of God."

"Light and Darkness," p. 195.

Overwhelmed by the grace that reveals the light and darkness of these two abysses, the Christian "examines" the vital organs of his Christianity: goodness, faith, the Church, obedience. He carries them from the light of Jesus Christ, crucified and risen, to the darkness of a world that rejects them but to which they nevertheless are destined to go.

At the heart of this "Christian dialectic," atheism, far from sapping the life of the believer, becomes a catalyst of love, faith, and hope, to the highest degree: the Christian is "made a covenant."

September 1956. Charles de Provenchères, Archbishop of Aix-en-Provence, approves the foundation of the *Worker Mission of Peter and Paul.*

March 1957. The French Bishops' Conference creates the *National Secretariat for the Worker Mission.*

October 1958. The death of Pope Pius XII, followed by the election of Pope John XXIII.

January 1959. The decision to convoke a council.

June 1959. The first encyclical of Pope John XXIII, *Ad Petri Cathedram.*

July 1959. Cardinal Feltin of Paris receives a letter from Cardinal Pizzardo, forbidding French priests to work in factories, even on a part-time basis.

The reader will notice that none of the texts published here were written between the years 1954-1958. This was a period particularly marked by illness for Madeleine. Nevertheless, she continued to write, and in 1954 began the editing of a series of notes on the religious questions that Marxism poses to the Church; she compiled them and supplemented them in order to make them into a book, *Ville marxiste, terre de mission,* which appeared in 1957. The reader may refer to this book in order to follow the thread of her thinking.

On the other hand, beginning in 1952, Madeleine founded with her Spanish republican friends a Baking Cooperative. Though the difficulties with her health prevented her from taking an active role in the work, she remained no less active in animating it from within, just as she continued to animate the small *équipes* that had received their initial impulse from her and Fr. Lorenzo.

After 1958, Madeleine's health improved and she returned to her normal activities with even greater vigor.

Goodness[1]

Just as love of God is inseparable from love of neighbor, so too is love of neighbor inseparable from goodness.

There is no authentic love of God without love of neighbor, and there is no love of neighbor without goodness.

This keeps us from having a false sense of mystery, from reducing mystery to a place where we hide.

Christian goodness has such a miraculous ambition that, in sensible, tangible, concrete acts, it becomes a visible sign of the Mystery. Vis-à-vis human wisdom, it is as extravagant as the Cross.

The First Thing Is to Be Good

Without wandering into areas in which I have no competence, I would like to explain what sort of life a Christian, whether priest or lay, ought to embody and maintain if it is to be a genuine apostolic life in the world of the working class, which I do know.

To ask for and receive faith as on the day of baptism, the faith such as the Christian asked for and received, such as he continues to receive if he asks for it, the faith that he received from God through God's Church.

To possess eternal life, from day to day, by living the two commandments.

Being rooted deeply in the Church, having become Christ, being the

1. Personal notes, 1959.

son of a God who is father, a brother to all people, streaming forth for them the goodness by which God loves us — this is what faith must constantly mean for us; all of this is what we must obey without respite in the faith, what ought to be as it were within our very eyes no matter what we are looking at, within our very mind prior to every reflection, within our very will before we make any decision.

We should be obsessed and possessed by this, simultaneously fascinated and captivated.

Every flicker of reason, every particular attachment ought to be able to be assimilated to the ordering of our spirit in faith, to our being taken over by charity in faith. Whatever is incompatible with them, or even whatever stands in competition with them, should be placed outside of ourselves.

Such a life founded on faith, on the heart of faith, presupposes that we have the means capable of maintaining, developing, and spreading the faith: the light of the Gospel, the nourishment of the sacraments, a deliberate and living adherence to the Church, to her movement, to her fruitfulness.

We thus acquire an ever more realistic awareness, an ever more concrete awareness that is ever more willing to believe in that which constitutes our essential functions in the Church, and our relations to the other functions entrusted to other members of the same Church. We should learn ever better to make use of whatever the Church has made out of us, of whatever the others in the Church are, the same way we make use of our arms and legs: as the hand makes use of its fingers without ceasing to obey the head; as the hand can touch but cannot see except for the head. This supernatural reality needs to become a practical and active realism in us; it is crucial that no particular social aspect of our life, whatever it might be, become more habitual to us than our inner life in the Church.

If Jesus today were to walk through our streets, there would be many among the "simple people" who would no doubt say about him: "He is so human!" In all of the social classes I have come to know, I have often encountered threats to humanity in various forms coming from one side or the other.

Indeed, it is not unlikely that the attention, sympathy, dedication, or affection that we give to the people of one social class, by bringing to light the particular sufferings and joys shared by this class, might blind us to that which causes suffering or joy for all people, from every age and every part of the world. At this moment, then, it might be the case that our love of neighbor, that the goodness that springs from this love, grows in "depth" and even in "height," but at the same time loses precisely that universal "breadth" that makes it what it is.

"I Will Teach You a More Perfect Way . . ."

Love is the one means that we cannot do without. Love can bring everything in the world into her service. It is love that hurries us, because there is nothing in the world that can keep her waiting. Love does not wait around for a means that might seem better suited; instead, she uses something else. But everything she thus makes use of — every circumstance, event, reconciliation, or distancing — is already in advance placed at her service: when love takes hold of something, it will have to suffer violence in order to be made useful by love for the Kingdom of heaven. All circumstances, events, situations, and relationships will burst open under her pressure, like the bark that is forced open by the sap so that the buds may sprout forth, like the seed that breaks open so that the germination may be accomplished, like all things living in their rendering service to life.

The words used in a given social milieu, the meaning these words acquire, reveal the sorts of realities or substitutes for reality that this milieu lives.

Knowing a language is thus not something abstract. It is not possible unless our life in the milieu has genuinely brought its influence to bear on our sensibility and our way of thinking, making them capable of perceiving and appreciating the share of real goods that each of our neighbors desires, the share of actual evil against which he defends himself, or which he rejects, or which leads him to despair. This is what it costs us to keep us from underestimating anything about the things that make up the lives of others; this is what it costs us to be able to speak a language that they know, that shows them we share a true familiarity of heart and spirit with them.

But at the same time we have to realize that sharing the way of thinking and the sensibilities of the working class, sharing their loves and their hatreds, even if we correct and purify them, if it is our sole witness, constitutes a counter-witness to our actual mission. We must never allow there to be any ambiguity about the fact that God is for us the only absolute good, and that he thus relativizes all other goods because they are so only insofar as they come from him.

But this God of ours, this good that we call absolute, would strike people as a reasonable possibility only if we took seriously, as things that come from God, all the real goods that man desires, and the real evil that the lack of these goods represents for people.

If we do not refer to God, our witness is a counter-witness; if we do not exhibit a realistic goodness as extravagant as charity itself, it would be as if we were bearing no witness at all, because it would be beyond the range of human eyes, ears, hands, and hearts.

In both cases, and in an equal but opposite manner, it would represent a betrayal of the whole of gospel witness.

It has many times been said that the word "charity" lost its meaning the moment it began to be uttered and heard by those who did not live their faith.

But it is less often said how often we hide behind this word only to betray it, even if we do try to live according to the faith. Because it is of God, because it comes from God, charity is a mystery. It is just as hard to bear its mystery as it is to keep from hiding behind it in order to escape what represents at least part of what charity would mean when translated into our human life among men: namely, goodness, such as Jesus Christ showed and taught us in his human life.

Goodness is beyond mystery. There is no escaping it. The Gospel defines it, specifies its nature, and unambiguously demands it. But if Christ expanded goodness to the utmost, since before him it had only ever been something simply human, human beings have all the same shrunk it, deflected it, and lessened even its properly human significance. Nowadays it has become almost something pejorative. No one wants to be a good girl anymore, or a good egg. . . . Who would want to devote his ambitions to a good work? Who recognizes the word "good" in "a good mess"? Is there anyone willing to bet that "good Christian" means the same thing as "saint"? Haven't we all heard the expression "goody-two-shoes"?

And this deterioration of a word is almost always a sign that the reality it signifies has disappeared. Indeed, there is nothing rarer in our world than a good human being. In this same world, everything that has replaced goodness — solidarity, generosity, dedication — is accompanied in the various realms by a blind indifference to whole hosts of other human beings: in the economic realm, by an implacable cynicism; in the political realm, by cruelty; in the international realm, an enormous disregard for the hunger of others, for the dying of others, for the physical or moral oppression of others.

The hearts of those living in the modern world are slowly and imperceptibly suffocating from the universal absence of goodness.

Thus, coming into contact with a genuinely good man or a genuinely good woman causes in other people something that transcends the realm of thought, a veritable instance of the heart getting back its oxygen. These men and these women realize that they are getting back something that is essential to their human life.

Goodness is truly the translation of the mystery of charity. That is why it is authentic, full, robust, not puffed up or full of holes, only when it flows from the charity within us, only when it comes from God, when it is a reflection of God.

On the other hand, a single act of true goodness that is fundamentally connected to God can lead to God in a manner that far surpasses our comprehension. "Whoever does the good comes to the light" here takes on such a real and tangible meaning that if there is anything surprising it is that we do not see that this goodness, which is the sensible body of charity, is perhaps the greatest sanctifying force of the "saints," of the "conversion" of us poor sinners, of mission to the lukewarm, the nonbelievers, and those who are completely cut off from the faith.

I am convinced that this is the case wherever you go. . . . That is why, in making this judgment, I hesitate to accord the working class a privileged place. But I will mention certain observations on this subject because at the moment we are more directly concerned with the people in the working class than with people in general.

The goodness that I am talking about here is not having a good heart, being by nature someone with a good heart. But this goodness can turn a bad heart into a good heart. It would not be the goodness of Jesus Christ if it could not manage this. Nevertheless, the Christian cannot count on his newly renovated heart as he would on a definitive gift. What is definitively given to him is the heart of Jesus Christ, the permanent capacity to be able in every moment to make his own heart new.

But, if I do not mean to say that having a "good heart" is the same as having Christian goodness, I do mean to say that the working class is made up of many people who often show a good heart. Many, though, is not the same as all; often is not the same as always. But to have such a good heart that you do exactly what that good heart commands at the drop of a hat is a normal, common, and automatic reaction in the working class — so automatic, however, that the actions thus engaged can come to a sudden stop or quickly run out of steam. So automatic, that is, that they can sometimes lead to little apartment-floor or neighborhood wars, with their summary judgments and their condemnations that brook no appeal . . . although these, too, tend to be short-lived.

Through all of this, one thing remains the case: the proletariat will always show sympathy for anything that recalls goodness, genuine goodness, however much or little it may be. Yes, a genuine sympathy: they have a feel for it, they know what it means. In earlier aberrations, goodness — or at least a certain form of goodness — had little concern for justice. But now we have come to realize what dry bread justice is when it is not preceded by or completed with goodness. When public funds are distributed on the occasion of an accident, when they come to provide assistance with the burdens of having children, when they accompany old age, these subsidies, pensions, grants, and benefits correspond to a sort of justice — and moreover increase the already great differences between the rich and the massive poor countries — but they do not in any way substitute for goodness. In such cases, it is not James or John himself who, in his misfortune or well being, finds help; instead, it is a condition or situation that is helped. General measures regulate collective categories. I resist criticizing the justice that society is able to achieve; criticism serves better to provoke progress in what remains to be achieved. What I am trying to say is that goodness is something else; it achieves something else.

For a person to encounter the goodness of Christ in another person is in particular to encounter himself for what he really is. The world forces us to be ourselves plus something else: family, profession, nationality, race, class. . . . It necessarily groups us in series. It judges us according to what counts for the world as qualities and deficiencies, but does not touch who we really are. Each person in society feels himself branded by the original sins that vary according to the milieu and that are treated as incurable. But in relation to the goodness of Jesus Christ, it is the individual person who exists, and everything else is relativized in one fell swoop.

If the catalogue of what is good and what is evil does not correspond with what is actually good and evil, each person nevertheless — and this time it does touch who he is — feels burdened with his deficiencies and limitations. No society is kind toward what it considers vices or a disgrace.

But in the encounter with the goodness of Jesus Christ we do not automatically become innocent; we may learn that we no longer have to feel guilty about certain weaknesses, but we learn quickly which weaknesses really affect us. Nevertheless, the goodness of Christ considers them all curable. It teaches us that this "who we are," which has been so manhandled by the world, possesses a value that is absolutely independent of wealth, power, smarts, influence, strength, and success. The goodness of Christ works with us; even more, it hopes for something from us, from each one of us. The goodness of Christ is above all something else: an encounter that affirms for us that we exist, that makes us present to ourselves, that walks alongside us in a common life.

We sometimes start to think that goodness has left the world because the world chased it away. Among us Christians, I wouldn't say that it is absent, I would just say that it has become the poor relative. I am not saying that there are no Christians left who are good. I am saying that they are good in spite of the unfavorable environment in which we have engulfed goodness.

I say "we" not out of politeness or in deference to our Communist neighbors, but because in all of these things I must in the first place think "me."

This brings us to an example. I will permit myself to cite only one.

Since I do not keep track of my life in a journal and have not yet started my memoirs, the fact that I can remember this event that was recorded in me so many years ago proves its peculiarity and its vivid truth. For, before I speak of goodness I want to give a snapshot of it that was taken right where I saw it, in one instant among others. I am leaving out more than other snapshots: I'm leaving out the portraits of all the people who have given me an unforgettable contact with goodness. Because of the sort of people they are, acknowledging their goodness would not be rendering them any service.

I will most likely never know whether the woman about whom I'm going to speak was Christian or not.

I was in a big foreign city many years ago, coming to the last few hours of the several days I had spent there. I was almost entirely out of money, completely exhausted, and was suffering the pain that shakes the animal in the rational animal that we are: the pain of loss brought by death, by the several deaths of those who were of the same flesh as mine. I do not believe that I represented any social category. The clothes I was wearing had nothing particular about them.

I had been walking through the streets for several hours while I waited for my train. And why not say it? I was crying. But I didn't care anymore, and I waited for it to pass. A foreigner. A stranger. A sorrow that all people know, one that brings tears just as certain forms of work bring sweat.

It started to rain; I was hungry. The few coins remaining to me determined what I was permitted to eat. I went into a tiny café that also served food, and ordered what I could afford: some raw vegetables. I ate them slowly so that they would be more nourishing and also to give the rain a chance to stop. Every once in a while my eyes filled up with tears. Then, all of a sudden, a warm and comforting arm took me by the shoulders. A voice said to me: "You, coffee. Me, give." It was absolutely clear. I don't remember exactly what happened afterward, which is lucky for me because I don't much care for melodramatic scenes.

I have often spoken about this woman, thought about her, and prayed for her with an inexhaustible gratitude. When I look today for an example of goodness in flesh and bones, she is the one who comes to mind.

What makes this woman a Christian sign, a distant but faithful image of the goodness of God, is that she was good because goodness dwelled within her, and not because I was "one of her own," familially, socially, politically, nationally, or religiously. I was a "stranger" without any identifying marks. I was in need of goodness, and even that goodness that goes by the name of mercy. It was given me by that woman. Today she represents an absolute example of goodness because I was just "anybody," it didn't matter what or who I was, and because what she did for me she did simply because there was goodness in her. In her simple gesture, I discovered everything that goodness has to be in order to be goodness.

Some Confusions about Obedience and Love of Neighbor[2]

Obedience to the Church

Disobedience to the Church is one thing . . . — everyone knows what that is. But what about false obedience . . . ?

If children were to obey their mother like a drill sergeant, like a party leader, like a foreman, or like a boss, it would not hurt her in the same way it would if they simply revolted, but it would nevertheless wound her heart — differently. And it's not clear that it wouldn't cause her even more suffering. For there are children who disobey their mother as if they were disobeying someone who is in fact their mother, and there are children who obey their mother but in a way that amounts to treating her like a stranger.

When a mother asks for something and you give it to her — as if she were the Revenue Service, to avoid paying a fine; as if she were a cop writing out a ticket, so you don't have to go to the station; as if she were someone getting on your nerves, to make her go away; as if she were from Social Security, to make sure you have a retirement plan; as if she were an investment company, to have an even better one. . . . When a mother recommends or forbids something and you comply just to avoid a scene; or to keep your stake in the family business; or because you'd prefer to do what she says and then get on with things rather than have to discuss it; or because you're worried about your inheritance — for your mother, it's as if she were childless.

2. Notes from a conference given to a group of Action Catholique Ouvrière from the Paris region, January 1959.

With the Church, it takes us a long time to come to understand what her maternal bonds with us mean. For, what happens with her is precisely the opposite of what happens with our mother: with our mother, birth was the initial separation. Our life as a whole was made possible thanks to the life she gave us, but it finds nourishment, develops, and reproduces outside of her.

When the Church gives birth to our Christian life, by contrast, it is like a seed, a beginning. All of the grace that we receive throughout our human life is given to us constantly by the Church; it is she who constantly nourishes it, develops it, and reproduces it. Our Christian life, that which was transformed in us at our baptism, that which is Christian at the heart of everything we do, comes from the Church, and remains a part of the Church.

Moreover, the obedience we owe her ought to be a free submission to the laws of her organic life, just as the cells of our body — although these are not free — are subject to the laws of our life. It should be a free, but organic, obedience.

Moreover, when the Church addresses us in order to advise us, or warn us away from something, or forbid us certain acts, the words we hear or read ought to be listened to or read the way the intelligent human being that we are (in principle) listens or reads. But not only thus. They should be read and listened to by a human being who has received his Christian life in the Church, by a Christian human being who lives at once in the world and at the heart of the Church.

A *human being* — not a little kid — a human being who not only has the right but has the duty to understand what is requested of him and why it is requested of him; who has the right to find himself not in complete agreement, but who has the duty, even if he disagrees, to accept in faith and to do so with that piece of humanity called a heart — that is, heartily; a human being who has the right and often the duty to say why he disagrees; but a human being who has enough good sense to know that, speaking simply humanly, it is possible that he is wrong and that being wrong is surely something that happens to him from time to time; who has the duty to say (but like someone who even on the human level might be wrong) what seems to him not quite right with the people among whom he lives, in the piece of the world in which he lives, in the world where the Church is present through him.

A *Christian human being,* a child of God, an adult, a confirmed soldier, a member of the Church militant, knows that Jesus Christ is not always recognizable in him, a member of the Church; he knows that he can distort the Gospel in his attempts to live it, that he sins, that he is weak, but that all of that does not keep him from being a member of the Church, or from being able to work toward the Redemption brought by Christ.

He knows that the same thing goes for the other members, and that their office remains in spite of their weakness. He knows that we all live with a sick heart, sick stomach, and sick liver, but that we would die if we eliminated our sick heart, stomach, or liver. The body cannot be anything else but a body: if it is healthy, so much the better; if it is sick once in a while, so be it! . . . To dismember the body means death.

This is how we have to understand the things that are sometimes hard to understand. When a member is weak, the others come to its aid, even if they are "less essential and less noble." The whole body works together to make a leg walk that has grown stiff from coxalgia; it does not leave the sick member all by itself.

When we have reasons for not understanding, we have to pray twice, to reflect twice, to forgive twice what we do not understand. Whenever our charity is put to the test, we have to ask twice for charity. . . .

And if this Christian person does not spontaneously come to agreement, he has to have not only the good sense but the humility to realize that, from where he stands, he cannot see the whole world; where he stands there is not the grace to judge the whole earth. He has the duty to speak about his brothers if his brothers are misunderstood, but to speak about them to the Church as one would speak to a mother, in the name of those things that she herself has the task of *guarding, giving, saving,* and that *she alone* can guard, give, and save.

When My Neighbors Are Communists

The highest authorities in the Church and the highest authorities of Communism are in complete agreement, and for the same reasons, concerning the radical incompatibility of Communism and religious faith; they are likewise in agreement about what happens when certain contacts are established and the ways they are established between Communists and Catholics: religious faith is lost.

And if, at root, militant Christians and Communists come to agreement on the only questions they address in consort, it is only to the extent that both sides pay no attention to the Church's fundamental views on

146

Communism and the Communists' fundamental views on the Church as well as on itself.

Nevertheless, the Church does not cease being the Church regardless of whom it is that stands before her: she would no longer be the Church if she did not make Christians live the Lord's Commandments: "You will love the Lord your God . . . *and* you will love your neighbor as yourself." She would no longer be the Church if she gave up a single human being for lost; but she would also no longer be the Church if she conceded the loss of some of her children in order to give birth to certain others.

Here, in these three sentences, we have to find the answer to the question: "To what extent can we work together with the Communists?"

There are two things that we cannot allow to mesmerize and thus paralyze us: what the Church asks us not to do; and what the Communists ask us to do. Holding only these two aspects in view would be exactly like wearing blinders that transform our horizon into a metro tunnel: two rails, each bearing the sign, "Warning: Do not touch! Possibly fatal!"

Now, what lies before us is not a metro tunnel, but *life*. And life overflows, infinitely surpasses the rails of these tracks, which would threaten to make us their prisoners if we saw only them.

The Church makes contact with the world through us, in a manner that ought to take the form that our lives already have: directly — indirectly. Whether the Church helps us to carry out our human task, or whether it is a task that she herself entrusts us with, we have to approach everything our lives contain with a Christian responsibility. It is from this perspective that we have to consider whether we come into contact with Communists in our life *as a matter of course.*

This seems to me crucial. To try to make our way toward Communists who do not live, or sleep, or work near us, would raise certain questions. To content ourselves with getting to know only those Communists who want to get to know us, would raise other questions. . . .

What is extremely important is that we *first* focus on those who are our actual neighbors, or members of our family, or coworkers, or people we exercise, or camp, or vacation with — in a word, those people we did not decide to get to know, but whom God willed or allowed to be *in our lives.*

For at that very moment they are no longer merely our neighbor like all the other people on earth, whom we owe a love that they will most likely never recognize, but they are our actual neighbor; they are the "man" —

regardless who it is — that the Good Samaritan encountered on the road to Jericho. All of the duties laid out in the Gospel fall to us in our relations with this man, as with every other human being. The fact that he happens to be a Communist makes no difference regarding our obligations. We have to live the Sermon on the Mount with him just as with anyone else; if we do not, it is no more or less deplorable than it would be for anyone else.

If we don't have Communists around us, there's no reason to waste time trying to figure out what we would do. . . . Let us do for all those in the world what the Church asks us to do for each member of the whole human race when we do not know them.

One of the reasons that seems needlessly to increase the difficulties in our encounters with Communists is the following: before we take up the normal Christian attitude, which is always apostolic, with those with whom we come into contact — I mean with those who happen to be near us — we allow the initiative to be taken by those among them who have received the mandate from their Party (which would be the Communist equivalent of an apostolate) either to exercise this mandate on us, or to involve us in roles that serve this propaganda.

When we remain in this passive acceptance of an encounter with those Communists who have been "instructed" to encounter us, not only does this meeting necessarily become more political than human, but it is likewise deprived of a Christian attitude — open-heartedness — that is the first step toward those who avoid us: "If you welcome those who welcome you. . . ."

For, the Communists do not hide the fact that each renewal of the "outstretched hand" offered to us is not equally and spontaneously welcomed by all the members of the Party. Indeed, if not all the Communists understand all of the reasons for the anti-religious foundations of the Party, many of the Communists nevertheless hold personal grudges against religion, the Church, or Catholics. These grudges might correspond to the Party's own grudges, but they could also be different. They often go back longer in a person's history than his adherence to the Party.

Moreover, when the directors ask that contacts be made, renewed, or intensified with us, they often run up against what certain Communists call the "prejudice" of their comrades. Some of them grumble about it. Others bow to the external act, but it is not rare to feel among them a world of contempt and hostility.

If we do not let ourselves be mesmerized by what the Church forbids us to do and what the Communists ask us to do, not only will we find among all the people we have in our life some who happen to be at the same time our neighbors and Communists; but, even while never losing sight of what it is the Church forbids us, we will no less lose sight of what the Church asks of us and what she asks of us because Jesus asks it of us.

The Lord and the Church never cease to ask of us, before all else and continually, before all the other commandments, before all those things these commandments advise and suggest: *the two commandments of charity, of Gospel love, the second of which is similar to the first,* and which will always be the first two commandments: "You shall love. . . ."

We remain free to accept or reject the Lord's will. But there will always be something in the Lord's will that we indisputably *know*: we *must* love the Lord. We cannot love him *without* loving each human being as much as ourselves (that's the minimum); it is *not possible* that our love for human beings would get in the way of our love for the Lord.

And this is so huge, so absolute, so indisputable, so much the fundamental law of our whole existence, that everything else is nothing but a secondary issue, everything else poses questions that are necessarily marginal.

And then there is *the* commandment of Jesus Christ that, as it were, is pasted onto the two commandments of love, the commandment that represents for us the supreme law governing all those who believe in him, the commandment that specifies everything we must be along with everyone who believes in him and every member of the Church: "Love one another as *I* have loved you."

Regarding all of the Communists we know, this translates to: Jean, Jacques, and Pierre are Communists, but they are also human beings, and therefore our neighbors.

There are perhaps certain things you can and certain things you cannot do with him, but what remains certain is that you must love him at least as much as you love yourself, you must be and do for him what the Sermon on the Mount and the Parable tell you: "I was naked. . . ."

Nevertheless, this love can never lead you to perform any acts that would prevent you or others from loving God; that would prevent you or others from loving all human beings.

Nevertheless, this love should never prevent us from loving each and every Christian, whether known or unknown, as Christ loved us.

AND THAT MUCH IS CLEAR — INDISPUTABLY SO.

In the Wake of a Decision from Rome[3]

The following reflections have absolutely nothing to do with the obedience we owe to the decision from the Holy Office — which is an actual obedience for the worker-priests, and an obedience in spirit for all of us.

Since the letter from Rome has been put into print, we can no longer pretend we don't know anything about it.

We should not reflect on the obligations that are recalled to us and underscored in the second part of the letter without first trying to understand the warnings that are suggested in the first part.

Understanding this letter is not an easy task, and it will no doubt be interpreted differently by each person.

The following reflections represent my personal point of view.

Should certain symptoms lead us to suspect that the missionary apostolate is suffering from a disease?

It is doubly helpful for us to pose this question: first, because the decision affecting the worker-priests is accompanied by encouragements to continue and to promote other forms of apostolate to the working class. This prompts each of us to figure out where we stand.

---

3. On September 15, 1959, the newspaper *Le Monde* published a confidential letter that the Vatican Congregation of the Holy Office had sent in July to Cardinal Feltin of Paris. This letter explained that the worker-priests, who had been initially given permission to work part-time or in small factories, now had to stop this work altogether.

Second, because it forces us to consider whether the missionary apostolate to the working classes has a sufficiently resilient foundation to keep its present forms or its new initiatives from becoming, in their turn, the object of concern tomorrow.

Finally, it is useful because certain other people are raising the same question, either in order to categorize it without trying to understand it; or to answer the question with the diagnosis that what we have here is one or more heresies waiting to be born; or else, finally, to conclude that we are dealing with episodic occurrences of a chronic and fatal disease.

For my part, I am convinced that both facile and condemnatory judgments are equally harmful to the missionary apostolate.

As for treating the mission as though it were sick, that would certainly do some good to the extent that it is in fact sick, but it is possible to believe that it is not.

The following reflections seek to lift out the common symptomatic features, whose presence is indisputable. But they intend above all to propose that we consider these features not as so many symptoms of a disease, but rather the result of a lack of awareness.

To the extent that this gap exists, I would not trust the solidity of any missionary initiative that rested on a fundamental weakness. Nor do I trust the effectiveness of emergency measures taken here or there, and which are felt by everyone to be a discipline or reprimand. Whether they are good or bad in themselves, they are not what we need in the present situation; addressing merely the effects, they do nothing to prevent the cause from producing further effects.

Finally, to the extent that such a fundamental weakness remains, there will always be the danger of assuming the influence of the working classes as the principal factor in the breakdown of missionary life. On the contrary, it is our own weakness that makes this factor decisive.

The Christian Missionary in Good Health
(An Amateur's Sketch)

The Christian missionary is at the same time and to the same extent a human being, a Christian, and an apostle. The invariable and necessary condition of becoming a missionary, becoming more and more a missionary, is not only not to become less and less a human being, a Christian, and an apostle, but remaining and even becoming more and more all of these.

The Christian missionary lives many realities that he was not consulted about beforehand and concerning which he is *incapable* of changing anything: namely, human life, Christian faith, and the Church's apostolate. For the Christian missionary, there is only one death that is absolute: losing the faith. If the missionary life were to become impossible for him, he would nevertheless remain fully an apostle in mission; if the apostolic life were to become impossible for him, he would nevertheless remain fully a Christian in the apostolic Church.

On the other hand, the Christian missionary is one who has decided in advance:

- to change, the moment the apostolate demands it, whatever can be changed in his human life that is not necessary to his life or to his Christian vitality; to change, the moment the missionary life demands it, whatever he is free to change that is not necessary to his apostolic life;
- to allow himself to be changed by the milieu that is the place of his mission, if changing allows him to live there in the same condition as the others; if changing permits stripping ourselves, not of those things in the Christian life that are "alien" to people, but those things in us that make it alien, and sometimes even hostile, to certain people; to change our mentality and sensibility, if changing allows us better to be heard and understood, if it helps us not to be a mute among the deaf.

The Christian missionary is thus one who has to tread simultaneously over the ground of the permanent and unchangeable as well as over the unpredictable tracks laid by particular circumstances, immediate events, chance encounters, and influences. Insofar as the realities that constitute this life are for the most part invisible, and those that affect it are extrinsic and for the most part unknown in other Christian or still Christianized milieus, the missionary life is necessarily something atypical. It is therefore easy to mistake the expression of its apostolic life for a symptom of a falling away from the Christian life.

Since it concerns milieus that are new, sterilized, destroyed, or ravaged by skepticism, unbelief, or a new atheism, the form that the missionary life has to take in this context has not yet been assimilated by the missionary apostolate, and it will necessarily appear strange. It is therefore easy to mistake it for the symptom of a falling away from the apostolic life.

The Christian Missionary Who Seems Sick
(A Sketch from Memory)

If, in regard to the "worker missions," some people cry heresy, and others by contrast utter nothing but justifications, it is because the facts in question could at the same time be the manifestation of a way of living that is odd because it is missionary, or else the symptoms of disorder. In comparison to the general structure of good health, these symptoms would consist in the protuberance of an element that is peculiar to the missionary life. This area starts to become feverish, extremely sensitive, and congested; it throbs in echo of the heartbeat; and by drawing all attention to itself, it gets special treatment to the detriment of the rest.

Now, all of these things occur when the Christian missionary undergoes the normal changes from living in the new milieu. It is impossible to touch life without a reaction from life, and without these reactions provoking disorder more often than order. But such reactions do not normally become permanently established.

When, however, they do settle in, or if they are eliminated only to reappear time after time in more extreme forms in relation to a particular point, they start to take the shape, not so much of chaos, but rather of an inverse order. We are thus all the further away from the disorder of normal reactions when another series of symptoms arise as it were to complicate the first. In conjunction with each protuberance, there occurs a correlative deterioration, as it were, of an element that is necessary either to the Christian life or the apostolic life.

I would be surprised if many Christian missionaries did not at some time or another show these twofold symptoms. The recurrences of these symptoms over the years in particular missionaries might help us to reconstruct the problem that lies at their source. It may also be the case that the problem as a whole develops in a single life.

It can settle onto the missionary life itself, and transform its growth into a cancer, diverting the forces of development in order to distort and force things out of proportion. It affects all organization and warps every dependence. We might have the normal Christian life topple under the hypertrophy of the apostolic sense, the apostolic life wither from an exclusive focus on one particular mission, the missionary life become emptied out by an obsession with being present to the world, or being present to the world become eclipsed by the worldly vocation.

It may be the case that these symptoms reveal a lack of health; but it is clearly the case that they reveal a lack of knowledge.

If the Church did not teach us "the truths that God made known to us," we could neither believe them, nor live them out, for the excellent reason that we didn't know them. Whatever is based on the truths of faith in the Christian life can be lived by us only if these same truths are not merely taught, but also only if we have learned them, if we know them, if our *belief in them is solid.*

Our missionary life is the actualization of the truths of faith. It is necessary for us to believe them, to know what they are and how they fit together.

Since these truths were made to be lived, it is necessary that we understand what sort of education and formation they entail in the lives in which they are lived. For the Church never teaches us the truths of faith without educating us in them and without forming us in them.

Now, keeping with the facts that are familiar to me, it would be impossible for me not to see in them a lesson about the things that illuminate and outline precisely what lack of knowledge we are suffering from, in the very realm of our own vocation and even in those areas in which we are best taught, educated, and formed by the influence of our milieu.

On this point in particular, the practical ignorance of our faith does harm to our entire life. Our ignorance is made up of *forgotten truths:* I will try to show how we forgot them; it is also made up of *truths we have never learned:* I will try to show how they can be discovered.

Our Lack of Knowledge: What We Have Forgotten

The Way We Came to Forget

We got involved in our apostolic life by "believing firmly all of the truths that God revealed to us" and that "he taught to us through the Church."

And no doubt all of us would have been able to repeat faithfully the same words every day. However, they would no longer refer in our memory to the same things. As amazing as it may seem, we came to lose, along the way, a few of the "truths that God revealed to us" and that "he taught us through the Church" . . . simply by forgetting them.

The only thing we do not risk forgetting is what we live in faith, because it is then no longer simply a good left in our memory. But the moment we begin to live it a little less, or a lot less, we are once again at risk of forgetting.

Before We Forgot: An Ordinary Christian Life

As people who have been Christian from time immemorial or as converts, we generally lived an ordinary Christian life — which does not mean mediocre, but rather in order, according to the order that belongs to it. If this stage is lacking in some people — the newly converted who become militants overnight, the indifferent who have been stirred to life precisely by the apostolate — the other stages have been, in general, the same for everyone.

What were the essential traits of this ordinary life? It was marked out by our "obligations" toward God: Mass, liturgical prayer, personal prayer, meditation for some, adoration for others, spiritualities for many, visits to the Holy Sacrament, rosaries . . . , all of this betraying a hint of rote rule-following in some, smelling strongly of mysticism in others, but considered by all of them as things owed to God, as representing the most important relationship in our life: our relationship with God.

This ordinary life recognized its primary citizen's duty in becoming conformed to God's will — not always for the purest of motives, admittedly, but nevertheless in such a way that it did not keep God's work in us from retaining its priority.

If we frequent the sacraments more or less regularly, with varying doses of faith and feeling, we would not end up looking elsewhere for that which the sacraments were meant to give us; though we might not always know how to make the best use of them, still we don't try to replace them with an ersatz.

This ordinary life was thus a normal Christian life: of course, we did not live out "all of the varieties" of faith in this life. But nevertheless the basic aspects I have just enumerated enable us to live what was most essential to them. Even if faith was not the only thing we lived, all the dimensions of our lives were nevertheless enlivened by faith.

How a Person Comes to Forget

The indispensable prerequisite for the apostolate, that which it is our first concern to fulfill, is that there be a real and concrete intimacy between those to whom we go and ourselves. But this cannot take place for anyone unless there be some transformation, whether small or large, in our way of living. We have to be cognizant of the fact that we are treated as a "foreign body" in our milieu — even more than we already feel so ourselves.

That our faith be something foreign is already written into the logic of things: and we have no idea how far this logic may unfold. But we make a promise to Christ that we will not allow our body to be a foreign body, our heart a foreign heart, in the place where we are. We are even prepared to keep our head from becoming a foreign head.

And this is how we learn how good a teacher the influence of a shared daily life can be. . . . Thus, the old foreign body feels itself slowly melting away, bit by bit, in this corner of the world where sympathies and revulsions stand out as clear as day, where everything is learned in the doing, where the tasks at hand are so urgent that everything must be simplified.

Another change takes place, more unconsciously. Our judgment may perhaps have remained the same, but we begin to use it a little less often. What has become different with respect to most things is our point of view. We grow accustomed to looking at the world from the vantage of the milieu in which we live, in perspective, in light of our pressing immediate plans. Equally automatically, we find a new hierarchy of values and priorities settling in. This new "way of seeing things" seems to justify itself by virtue of all sorts of things that have been brought close or kept distant. Our choices begin to seem surprisingly simple to make. The repeated decisions they entail give us a real ease in responding. We are no longer paralyzed by moments of hesitation.

After the overtaxing work at the beginning, our attention shifts to focus on trying to observe and understand. But once these exhausting stages have passed, our attention finds itself effortlessly and constantly occupied by what goes on immediately before us.

These immediate events gradually become the basis of reflection at the community meetings, in which we share with each other what we have learned to live or to do, what we have come to see more every day, and what we have to learn and receive from our neighbors.

And it is especially through this information that we discover how much and in what ways the Church is foreign to the world, and foreign to our milieu.

What Comes of Forgetting

When we have come to this point, the time has already long passed since we knew with certainty that the Church can only be to some extent or even completely a foreign element in her encounter with people in mission, just as she must remain to some extent or even completely foreign in us. The time has passed since we knew with certainty that if the dynamism of the faith presses for all time toward every human being in every corner of the world, that faith is also for all time a gift from God and so for all time remains something foreign.

Over the course of this long time, we genuinely loved our lives' companions. This love sought out and found what was common between them and us. It came to see what was more human in them than in us. It joyfully recognized those aspects of the Gospel that they were living more and better than we were. On the other hand, we have become more than ever desirous of sharing with them the Good News that we have received. Just as we have let our hearts be molded so that they may appear more fraternal to our neighbors, just as our language and thinking have gladly spent time in their school in order the better to be at God's service in them, we start to think that the faith ought to accommodate itself to them just like everything else so that it might be more familiar to them. They will later come to see that the faith can be at once a sister and a stranger.

But the abrupt aspect of the faith, which we do our best to attenuate, will necessarily show itself one day or another: the Church makes it manifest.

On the occasion of some minor incident, of a position we take, of bitter memories carried over from some corner of Europe, our friends rise up against the Church with bitterness, rancor, and rebelliousness. What we once thought was evidence in them of a far-off movement toward God seems to be obliterated in one fell swoop. We painfully begin to take stock of the "scandal of the Church" that stands between us. That which would allow us to understand the difference and yet the relation between this incident and the necessary scandal of the Church — necessary like the scandal of the faith, like the scandal of the Cross — lies beyond our field of vision.

It is almost always by virtue of some such incident, in which the conflict with our milieu is brought out into the open, that the *violent dimension* of our missionary life is also brought out. This incident likewise becomes the test of our endurance. It produces victims or survivors: in such incidents, there are no victors. Without outside help, we emerge from these situations spent and broken.

Our endurance proves inadequate — why? Is it the intolerance of the normal Christian life to the influence of a particular milieu? Can such intolerance be overcome only through an extraordinary Christian life, provided with supplementary structures and gifted with special means?

We were convinced at the outset that the more missionary we wanted to be, the more genuinely Christian we had to become. Convinced, too, that the apostolate forms part of the Church's role and mission, that the Church's means are the only ones open to the apostolate, and that the good of the Church is the sole good that the apostolate could propose.

We knew that, if the scandal caused by the Church because she comes from God was not the same as the scandal that we, the members of the Church, present to others, these two scandals are nonetheless both part of the mystery of the Church. The way we participate in this mystery is to remain within it.

But when we were put to the test, we partially forgot some of these certitudes. Partially blinded, we have grown weak. For us, everything in the Church that was not apostolate became obscure; and so did everything in apostolate that was not the missionary apostolate; and sometimes everything in the missionary apostolate that was not mission.

For us, the Church's treasure becomes the treasure of a Church that has been "reduced" in this way, i.e., becomes the treasure of mission.

The sacramental priesthood, bishops as well as priests, the Eucharist, and the Gospel, are no longer visible in relation to the Church as such, but only in relation to the Church as we see her, in relation to mission. That is why we so often give the impression of being outside the Church, of seeing her from outside, of discussing her as outsiders.

But there is something else. In practice, the Church is turned into mission and nothing more; we end up being in the Church only where she is visible. We no longer live out of the Church where we no longer see her, but rather where we see a mere social structure or a historical facade. When we criticize or discuss the Church, it is no longer the Church we are talking about, but merely an appearance.

Our Lack of Knowledge: What We Never Learned

The Fundamental Reality of a Missionary Situation

Our forgetfulness alone does not account for why our journey thus far has been so arduous and exhausting. The forgetfulness was compounded — and perhaps caused — by our initial ignorance.

We were instructed about the missionary apostolate in the Church and for the faith, we were instructed about what the mission ought to be and *to become* in a particular milieu; we received enough information to know, in general, why and how the goal, the activities, and the means of our life are related to our faith. We were also instructed about the forms and approaches that it would be our responsibility to figure out and that would *situate* us in a milieu.

But we did not learn what supernatural reality was underlying the visible situation.

We were blind to the *supernatural state of affairs* that is constitutive of all missionary situations. Let me explain. The circumstances that arise in the missionary situation are perhaps more *immediate* than they are anywhere else, in the sense that we do not have the time or space to stand back and get perspective. All of the realities surrounding us force themselves onto the already cramped surface.

By contrast, the realities of the faith are not represented here; we do not know where or how to get a hold on them. The instruction we were given took too long to think through, was too far away to be at hand. If it is not immediate itself, if it is not present where we are, if we do not have it before our minds, we are condemned to live the faith only by miracle.

The Violent Character of the Missionary Situation

The previous observations are based exclusively on the facts. They seem to me sufficient to suggest how I learned from them an "objective lesson."

In the working world, the Christian life of the missionary only rarely avoids taking on a violent character. We are not expecting to have to undergo such a thing, and so we are rendered helpless for being taken by surprise. It is easy to hold the living conditions of the working classes responsible for such a situation. A couple of questions might be helpful in this context.

Should we blame the living conditions of the working classes just because they are working classes?

Should we blame them because they are the new conditions of a milieu that has been more or less broadly and deeply secularized and because they themselves are more or less the cause and the effect of this secularization?

How do we explain the fact that Christians (workers or not) in fact encounter this crisis only when they become the advocates of an apostolic movement or when they become involved in a mission?

In order for Christian life to be confronted with this trial with more regularity, two conditions have to come together in one: the living conditions of missionary apostolate and the living conditions of certain working milieus. This convergence constitutes a missionary situation.

Now, if this situation *appears today* necessary to the apostolate of certain working milieus, it is precisely in these milieus that the Christian faith runs into dangers. But this poses an absurd dilemma. All throughout these notes I have pointed out what the symptoms, ignorances, and weaknesses have revealed about the contradiction between their disorder and the order of the missionary apostolate. I have also pointed out everything the life of the Christian missionary contributed, in contrast, to missionary possibilities, or to Christian impossibilities. This all-too-ordered disorder suggests an encoded message, for which we must find the key.

A Normal State of Violence

Doesn't proposing the faith mean proclaiming the Father's love in the world? Doesn't the Gospel require, from one end to another, that it be proclaimed in the world and against the "world"? Doesn't the Gospel present the faith as a choice to be made in the world, between the "world" and the Kingdom of heaven, a choice bought for us by Christ, and for which he gives us the strength? . . . And, lastly, in order for the faith truly to become this choice, doesn't it need to be connected with the "Be converted!"? Isn't faith for us a "turning back" and a "reversal"?

Can the apostolate be anything other than a living contradiction between that in us which God has made his own and the things before our eyes that remain foreign to us? Is the Kingdom of heaven not suffering violence everywhere we look? Doesn't this violence pervade and penetrate the world from one end to the other, through all its parts, wherever God's Dominion runs up against the Prince of this "world"? Wherever Redemption runs up against sin? Wherever the Church runs up against the world?

Is there any way for apostolate to skirt around this accidental but constant, unequal but fundamental antagonism? And if it does have to face up to this antagonism, how would it be possible for this confrontation to keep from taking indefinitely new forms in the changing places that it occurs?

To the extent that the faith does not speak out loud and clear in this confrontation, the world can maintain a surface ambiguity. But the moment the faith shows itself to the world, the world can no longer remain ambiguous; the "world" that tries to hide within it is forced to come out and present itself as being *at odds* with the faith.

But we know that this antagonism is not traced out like an abstract idea hovering over the world. Every Christian knows that this antagonism cuts through him to the core, and that he is always free in this battle to choose God, often in the choices he encounters in day-to-day living.

We are well aware that neither the Church herself nor her various offices are affected. But we, the little ones of the Church, just as much as all the others and the greater ones, we too are penetrated to our very core.

Do we have any reason to think that an apostolic situation would not involve some violence? On the contrary, isn't it obvious that a certain violence would be inherent in it? Perhaps violence is easier to "tolerate" when one becomes accustomed to its manifestations and when faith encounters familiar forms of unbelief in equally familiar contexts.

But isn't it also to be expected that a situation that is not merely apostolic but also missionary must necessarily be subjected to a sort of normal violence that is nonetheless not yet familiar either to Christians or to the Church?

To respond affirmatively to these questions would raise even more. Is not the Church, simply by virtue of her situation, the "violent" who bear away the "Kingdom of heaven," knowing and teaching that it "suffers violence"? Does she not carry out her mission by transforming this violence into a correlate of Redemption? Would she be able to do so if Christ did not provide her with the means?

But, if an apostolic life entails participation in the Church's apostolate, if it served the Church for her own mission, how could it ever deplete its resources if they are the very resources of the Church herself?

Finally, doesn't the "absurd dilemma" we denounced a moment ago seem to arise again with the same absurdity when events of some significance in the apostolic and missionary history of the Church create the need for new apostolic forms?

Let me offer a striking example. The externals will seem a complete contrast with the externals of a missionary apostolate to the working classes. Nevertheless, even in completely different forms, there is a clear state of violence here, and the risks are just as clear. What we see in this example, ultimately, are the permanent and inexorable foundations of an apostolic situation.

I am talking about the Carmel, at the moment of its reform, and of the Reform, at the moment in which the contemplative life of the Carmelites, which was becoming fragile and lifeless, was about to turn into the contemplative apostolic life it would one day be for the Patroness of Missions. If the Carmel had not accepted to live the Church's violence as an essential feature of its vocation, it would not carry as its slogan the flamboyant word "zeal." And yet, if St. John of the Cross had not found this Christian life in such a bad state in its contemplative lives, he no doubt would not have published his "clinical notes." These notes bear witness to a fairly widespread and serious illness. Now, he had so little doubt about being able to overcome this sickness that he simultaneously worked at a renewal of the life at Mount Carmel and at the flourishing of its apostolic dimensions.

The approach followed was not a discipline but a *reform*. We are perhaps familiar with the sketches in which St. John of the Cross outlined several times the same spiritual journey. The basic direction of an entire life, as well as the step-by-step development of each moment, are embraced in a single vision.

It is a journey proposed to all Christians who would love God as quickly as possible and as best they can. Perfect love is represented as the peak of a mountain (for the Carmelites, this is Mount Carmel). A pathway follows a steep slope, and separates from all the "stray" paths winding back and forth along the way. A lot of people must have gotten lost and a lot must have gotten held up for there to be so many false paths blocked off, so many ill-advised roads. Without a map it would be hard to do otherwise, because the through-way, the "short cut," is a single path among a multiplicity of possibilities.

It is not a question of finding new means of transportation. It is a question of climbing higher as we walk, without getting lost as we climb. The step of our climb becomes the step of the mountain, but it always remains a step-by-step process, touching ground, detaching from the ground, and then beginning again, etc. No one offers advice in flat terrain or on the streets, except to young children: "watch your step." But in the mountains, it's different. In one of his sketches, St. John of the Cross tells us where to put our feet. He *shows*, in a particular apostolic situation, how to keep sight of the goal without breaking our necks.

If we had to picture the profile of our *missionary situation*, we would have to imagine a high mountain ridge traced out at every moment within us and in front of us. It is the sharp convergence of two slopes. At odds with each other, they come together in us. The one has its roots in God's promise; the other descends all the way to the rejection of God. But our line of vision does not reach to the end on either side. Between the point where our vision trails off and this high mountain ridge emerges, everything comes into view from a dizzying perspective. If we have come to know through experience the existence and presence of an abyss and a mystery, we will be able to reconstruct the actual incline of the slopes, to interpret their perspectives, and to understand that in terrain such as this, a false step means a long fall.

We will understand that if these two slopes seem to mount an attack upon each other, they nevertheless come together in us, and so will ultimately bear the emblem that stands over our missionary situation as a whole: it will say either "I will not serve," or "God alone saves."

Characteristics of a Missionary Parish[4]

These parishes encounter a new form of unbelief: the progressive atheism of "our world," the atheism that is overtaking most of the countries in Europe that were once Christian.

This growing atheism, whether it be aggressive, indifferent, or "tolerant" of God, possesses everywhere a common characteristic: the rejection of a creator God who would place the world in the position of being a creature. It gives rise to very diverse forms of secularization.

This growing atheism does not leave Christians unharmed: they are unconsciously forced to allow the aspect of faith that binds them to God in the depths to deteriorate; for that very reason, they risk having their entire Christian life become dried up and "humanized."

A world that once was Christian seems to be in the process of being emptied out from within. It first loses God, then the Son of God, and then everything divine that the Son would communicate to his Church. It is often the surface that is the last to collapse.

And yet, if this world no longer bears even a single reference to Christ on the surface, it is nevertheless a world that was long nourished on Christianity, which digested it; and it is still pervaded by Christian "by-products" that linger confusedly and archaically in its institutions, its mores, its ideologies, and its politics.

If very few milieus in France are genuinely Christian, it would never-

---

4. M.D. was invited to Toulouse for a conference during Lent and participated in a series of discussions about parish life and evangelization (1960).

theless be no doubt impossible to find a single one that is *totally dechristianized.*

> *These parishes, which have the place the Church has willed for them, must become missionary wherever they happen to be, or they will no longer be apostolic.*

Their missionary situation is almost the exact opposite of other missionary situations. They have no need to go anywhere: the missionary "countries," "lands," and "regions" are themselves coming to meet them; they are becoming thicker, more vast, and are penetrating into the parishes.

The world to which "foreign missions" were sent lacks the social traces of christianization; it was not — in general — molded by Christian influences; however, this world remains — also in general — pervaded by religious faith, or belief in God, or reference to the gods; it remains strongly or obscurely religious; it has certain cults that can on occasion become monstrous: the sacrifice of children or criminals leave few countries without some acknowledgment of dependence on something divine.

In "foreign missions," priests or lay missionaries enter a world in which the Church has not yet been implanted, of which they represent the first seeds. God willing, this seed will sprout, will grow into a "tree" under the guidance of a bishop who himself is called missionary because the whole Church under his charge follows the same law of germination and implantation.

The missionary parish, for its part, is often an old Christian community that is unable to destroy the tree that it is, or reduce it to a few seeds; even if the parish is new, it is made up of people, a certain proportion of whom have been Christian from their birth but who are rarely missionary by conscious vocation. The priests of these parishes are not necessarily especially "missionary." The bishop of their diocese is the bishop of a long-standing Christian diocese.

> *From another perspective, however, the "foreign missions" and missionary parishes face, at bottom, the same questions.*

In foreign missions, the Church remains an outsider to the country, the race, and the regions whose peoples remain outside of her.

The missionary parish is in a city, a sector, or a neighborhood made up of people, mentalities, and destinies that likewise remain outside of the Church; it is in milieus in which it is not part of the family, in which it is poorly tolerated, as if it were an alien body, without a soul, and without kin.

For both forms of mission — though of course for the missionary parish the frontiers are far more difficult to make out, far more roughly drawn, far more uncertain — it is a matter of knowing and being known, of understanding and being understood, of speaking and being heard, of being received as people who are entitled to be there.

Missionary parishes are able to draw analogies between their situation and the situations brought about by the various heresies or schisms. These analogies break down once we begin to compare the forms of unbelief in question.

Apart from a fractured unity, the Christian faith in God was never compromised. By the same token, if missionary parishes have to become aware of the traces of Christianity that characterize their world, they know that beyond these there exists an absence of God that is more absolute than anywhere else in the world; this absence is evident in all of the new sectors of human activity, in particular those that have to do with technology.

They know, moreover, that these vestiges of Christianity are ambiguous and that they can sometimes fool us: we might easily mistake them, in certain individuals or in certain ideologies, for points of openness to the Gospel, while they are much more often partial aspects of the faith that have become irrational or merely reasonable.

The missionary parish, as a cell of the Church, must live the two-fold vocation of being at once ever more deeply "rooted" and ever more radically "sent."

Rooted

The people of God the parish assembles must vigorously cultivate and develop the Christian life in tandem with the human life of its children who are becoming children of God.

The life that is specifically theirs is *supernatural;* its authority, its teaching, its mission, and its means possess a divine dimension — they come from God and exist for God. It is a life because God is alive.

It is a religious life that can endure neither the absence of men nor the absence of God. Its form of worship is the form that God willed for his glory. Its law is the law in which God tells us how he wishes us to live. Its sacraments are the means of living, of becoming strong, of growing, that God chose for us. Its word is the self-revelation that God has made to us.

It is a life that is inseparably both filial and fraternal, because the living God is our Father, because being his children makes us all brothers and sisters in relation to each other.

The ultimate goal of this life is something that is "impossible for man."

Sent

What the missionary parish has to propose to those who are indifferent or who don't believe is precisely what makes it most alien to the world formed by them: it proposes *its faith*.

But in order for the faith to be heard, for its message to be understood, those that proclaim it must be willing to be separated from the world by their faith; they must desire to be united to the people of this world as brothers and sisters of the same blood and the same destiny; they must be aliens because of their faith but not because of anything that they themselves add to it.

Faith in itself is essentially foreign; the hostility we undergo because of faith causes us to distort it, to present something other than our faith. The clarity of the missionary parishes has been and should be sufficiently strong to keep us from making it, not a foreigner, but rather the partisan of a social clique; not the mistress of eternity, but a specialist of the past; not the purveyor of eternal life, but of a temporal lifestyle; not the translator of the mystery that belongs to all people, but a scholar who cannot speak the common language.

At the same time, even if the world rejects God, the heart of every human being was "made for God." But if people must come to recognize God, they will never do so in the form of the "miniature God" we have reduced to our size. If the God "whom no eye has seen" can be known only through Christ and through his Gospel, he cannot be known through a Gospel that we have accommodated to our own understanding or our own strengths.

If God has given his law to men, it is only a sign of God if we observe it with a solemn fidelity and not haphazardly. At the same time, if we show ingratitude in the way we live, if grace is something we take to be our due, it will be impossible for us to understand what it means to be without faith, without reference to God in a world that finds it has thereby become formless, random, and blind. We will speak "naturally" about the single reality that can genuinely transform life, and when one makes faith into something natural, it becomes for the nonbeliever something absurd.

Finally, if we resign ourselves to living on the margins of human life, to being amateurs in life's affairs, if we find it the normal course of things to remain mute among the deaf because we do not share "the same world," "the same ideas," "the same political party," "the same education," "what will we have done for our brother" when we have to leave the same street to appear before the Lord?

What the parish must live in order to be ever more deeply rooted, in order to be ever more deeply itself, is precisely the same thing it needs to be ever more radically sent. It is exactly what the parish needs to bring to the world, so that it can proclaim it.

The missionary parish is a militant cell of the Church militant.

It is a cell that participates in the life of the whole body. It is one; it has the unity of a living tissue; it is not a collection of "practicing Catholics," of militants. It is made holy by God. It is catholic, a cell that lives a universal life. It is apostolic because the Church's mission is to preserve in order to transmit and propagate.

The apostolate is essentially a battle; it is the battle fought by the Church militant; a battle between "the world" and the Kingdom of God; a personal battle, fought out in the heart of each one of us; raging in each member of the Church; fought one on one, body to body, between the mystical Body of Jesus Christ and the social or political bodies of nations, states, races, and civilizations.

The missionary parish cannot rest content with having a few "militants" who are involved; it is a parish at war, and so the whole parish is militant. When a nation is at war, what it is fighting for is not suicide. Rather, in principle, it fights for something alive; it is for the sake of life that it risks death.

In a much more absolute manner, the Church fights in order to give life; this is why the Church is missionary and why a parish becomes missionary. This battle is going to require the mission to sacrifice certain ways of living; to take up other living conditions: but the battle will never require the sacrifice of any living reality that is supernatural. If it were to do so, it would by that very gesture reveal its absurdity.

Mission ought not weaken but rather should require and encourage the strengthening of everything essential to a living parish.

Trying to make "mission" into a new kind of expertise rather than a renewal of vital forces threatens to weaken the parish. (For example: creating a missionary liturgy in order to make it accessible to nonbelievers; a missionary spirituality by giving a central place to certain aspects of life that are useful for a militant Christian; missionary preaching, not only by accommodating a certain mentality, but by shifting around the contents of the faith in order to emphasize what is most accommodating; missionary evaluations of things connected to the Church from a perspective linked to the reactions of a particular "sector," etc.)

It makes a lot more sense to worry about these specializations *after* having worked at building up what is *constant, permanent, obligatory, and indisputable* — in other words, by building up what all Christians have in common.

Public Worship

That the liturgy be accessible to nonbelievers is helpful. But it is not what is most needed. What we need most is to make the liturgy more accessible to believers; to make it more effective in strengthening *the apostolic vocation* in the lives of the members of a missionary parish; in strengthening the role of their prayer, which is to link together their nonbelieving brothers and God; the word they must speak on behalf of their brothers to glorify God in their brothers' place; the living bond they must be between God and those to whom God is unknown.

We need a *spirituality*, rigorously true and rigorously simple, where the Christian accepts precisely the place allotted to him between the Omnipotence of his Father and each person of the whole human race who is known and loved by God. The Christian keeps to this place because it was given to him, but he knows that it doesn't take up the whole stage, that it is far too narrow for all of his dramas to be played out, be they personal or missionary. It is simply the place to ask and to receive, and in this way, to give glory to God.

Resisting Evil

One and the same apostolic trial falls to the lot of every apostolate. In the missionary apostolate, this trial becomes more brutal; in particular, it takes on an unfamiliar form. Mission is the intersection of God's love and the world's rejection. The Christian is penetrated to the core by the one just as by the other, and the two converge in him. Because it is a trial that belongs to life, there is no way he can avoid suffering from it. But this trial is a participation in the apostolic trial of the Church; the Church is armed to overcome it; the Church is equipped with the strength to resist it and triumph over it.

The Good News[5]

Can the Gospel, the Good News, Still Be News?

Can it still be "news," that is, the announcement of a "current event"? Something we didn't already know about? For whom can it be something current or new? For whom is it not something either already known or poorly known?

We would have no problem finding a relatively large number of people who do not know anything about the Gospel, but even for them, the contents of the Gospel cannot be something wholly new. The lingering existence of ideas and values that were one-time effects of Christianity, and are now defaced and deformed traces of it, fundamentally silence and falsify even the very words of the Gospel message.

But there are even more people who know the Gospel as a report of what Christ did and taught. Some of them have formed a particular idea of the message based on the behavior of Christians and the way they have used it; others were baptized in the faith and practiced their faith when they were young.

In either case, they have a generally uncertain, fragmented, and disfigured knowledge of both the Church and the Gospel. For those who were never baptized: what they have heard or observed might have awakened their curiosity in the way a quaint social custom would. For those who were baptized: some have forgotten their Christian education all the more

5. Cf. the note on p. 164.

171

easily for never having "learned" it; others have flushed it from their memories like so many boring facts.

Finally, alongside the Christian influences that have been assimilated or digested are the Christian truths that have sometimes become irrational, but more often rationalized or naturalized, and then assimilated and proclaimed by various ideologies and movements. Sometimes nonbelievers have been taken in by these secularized truths; sometimes believers have been won over to them, some as if they are discovering the adult form of their childhood faith, others in order to make real what Christianity teaches but does not put into practice.

The majority of these people — the atheists, nonbelievers, and agnostics — seem to be immune to the Gospel in the same way a person can be immunized against a disease. Faced with such an immunity, which reason can ascertain and prove, every missionary effort is tempted to become discouraged.

Not only does the Gospel seem no longer to be news, but it seems as if it cannot even be *good* news anymore. Everywhere mission tries to make a start, the same echo is heard: "Faith? That's not what they need. . . ." In our world, needs are rekindled and multiplied, but the riches of the Gospel are not quoted at the marketplace; they are out of circulation because they are not in demand. Such as they are known, nobody wants them, even for free. They have become somewhat like the outdated leftovers of an inheritance, which are useless and a burden, and so are passed off to a pawnbroker so he can get rid of them.

What the Gospel riches are in truth is not missed by anyone; but what they are, people are not even aware that such things exist; and what is unknown or ignored is necessarily not wanted. The world presents itself to us as self-sufficient. It suffices for whatever can mold it. No room for whatever does not.

And, in this case, the problem is not a Gospel that is either too distant, or proclaimed in a language no one understands, or betrayed by poor witnesses. The problem is rather an intellectual deafness to what it is we want to say: not only to the supernatural but to everything in the human being that is not satisfied by the world alone.

The Good News about God

To the extent that our world tries to break itself away from God, that people believe they can get by without God, that they can organize things apart from God, God becomes for the world something new, and the living God of the Gospel once again becomes news.

In the face of secularization, the Christian often fights against the new facts and events so that the faith may live on where he is; he seems to everyone like someone stuck in the past. On the other hand, in the face of atheism, the believing Christian, because he believes, posits through his life a living hypothesis of God precisely where God is no longer presupposed. His faith in God is for this brave new world an even newer phenomenon.

For his brothers and sisters around him, the Christian is a man who loves the things of this world as they really are, according to their true value, but he is also a person who prefers the God in whom he believes to all other things. This preference leads him to make certain choices. People see him choosing the invisible God. These choices pose a new question to the world, a question about whether there may not be something greater than the world.

When people forget the fact that God is their good, we do not have to collude with their lack of awareness, their poverty. We should not only believe, but also understand that the living God of the Gospel can be for them not only news, but *good* news. For this, however, we have to understand what it means to be an atheist. Do we in fact understand?

The person who lives as if God were absent, whether consciously or not, is often poorly understood by us. We know what he does not believe, but we fail to grasp what difference this lack of belief entails between his way of seeing things and ours. That is why we sometimes remain barred, as it were, from entering into his mentality, which we cannot get a hold of.

The convert, on the other hand, has a grasp of these differences. His conversion divides his life into a "before" and an "after" because he has passed from death to life, because all of those things that once made up his life have been as it were snatched away from death.

It does not occur to the convert to explain to us how all things were made new, to tell us the nature of the happiness that was his. It does not occur to him that his is an experience that we have not had, and that we are the less for it. Let us take two particular examples that are very much in season at present.

The Christian who has always been Christian because he possesses faith, even if he lives his faith only weakly, automatically establishes a connection between everything that goes on in the universe and God's providence. This sometimes imperceptible connection forges a chasm that divides the believer's mentality from the nonbeliever's.

The believer has no means of comprehending — and it does not occur to him to try to comprehend — what sort of fears assail modern men, at an insane pace, when they do not relativize them in the context of an almighty wisdom. The anxiety of such a person rarely comes to expression. And yet if we only knew how such fears account for so many disorders, even among believers, a little reflection and a lot of love would allow us to perceive what is softly spoken in the silences the nonbeliever keeps, what he perhaps even keeps from himself.

Collectivisms create islands of *loneliness*. Modern conglomerations pile solitudes on each other and intensify them. There are more and more categories that are better and better known, and all the while individuals are more and more overlooked. These social forms of loneliness aggravate the loneliness that is inherent to man, the loneliness we have all suffered from and will continue to suffer from, even those with faith.

The believer, even if his faith is weak, is never completely alone, never completely without help. The nonbeliever is one who knows loneliness in its absolute form, an inhuman loneliness. He is deprived of the relationship that most fundamentally belongs to him.

Let us take another example, the example of death: indeed, the believer has passed from death to life. But in general he considers this transformation only in relation to the great moments of this "passage," the death of a family member or loved one. He doesn't realize that, for the nonbeliever, it is life itself that is afflicted by death. Everything he deems valuable in the present is condemned to death in the future. Everything snatched away from God is destined to death. The inner support that holds all things in being crumbles from within. No matter what we love, what we love must die. Life becomes life in death, and all things are swallowed up in nothingness and meaninglessness.[6]

Once we realize this profound misfortune that besets the nonbeliever, will we ever more dare to infer from what he says, from what he does, from what he seeks, that the Good News of the Gospel would be use-

---

6. This favorite theme of the author's is repeated almost word for word in the section called "Light and darkness," p. 194.

less to him? Can we continue to disbelieve in his disbelief? Or wouldn't the living God of the Gospel rather burn in us with an unbearable intensity to the extent that we did not cry his name out loud to those living in quiet desperation? If, in hearing us call upon God, they were to turn themselves around, it would be for them the beginning of the one and only *good* News.

An Examination of Faith[7]

Faith is the engagement of eternal life in time: are we temporal enough?

Faith is asked for, received, and lived in free acts: are we free enough?

Vis-à-vis the world that is created to serve him, and vis-à-vis God who created him, man is free. He is free to accept or reject his vocation to live as a human being and his vocation to live as a child of God, but whether he accepts or rejects them depends on his choice.

On the other hand, man does not have the capacity to create. He cannot recreate man: he cannot invent some other child of God. He nevertheless retains the capacity in freedom to live what he was given in a way that degrades, destroys, or falsifies it.

The only thing that counts between us and God is what is free. God judges us according to our choices. Faith is given to that in man that has remained free. It is the science of eternal realities, of all that God has told us about himself and all that he has told us about ourselves.

It is the art of knowing how to do God's will, the science of charity. It governs our choices.

It was given to us so that we might attain eternal life, but that we

7. Cf. the note on p. 164.

176

might do so in time; it was given to us so that we might live God's life, but that we might do so in our human life; so that we might bring about the salvation brought by Christ, but to bring it about in the world and in history.

It is given to us so that we would choose God with human acts; so that we would *do* God's will in human history, in the human world, with human acts. It is as temporal as we are; it will pass away when we die.

Faith is given to the human being we are on behalf of all the human beings that we are not.

Moreover, faith teaches us that the Christian life should be structured like a living tissue, according to eternal laws, but that it must be lived in the immediate, in the moment, in the particular. We are destined for the eternal love of God. But we can only come to this love in our human life, in the time that belongs to us and others, in the world here and now.

All other dialectics seem relative compared to the dialectic of faith: all existentialisms seem repressive compared to the existentialism of faith. The "loser takes all" of faith is new in every moment; it destroys memory in order to be constantly reborn. It engages us in time for eternal goals.

It strips from us every past honor and every future ambition that does not serve the glory of God.

We know for the most part what our faults are and what imperfections drag us down. But we know less well that certain things, which we forget in practice, end up trapping us in false slaveries or leading us to confuse the love of God with fatalism.

If, in certain, particularly weighty circumstances, we make such poor choices, the practical cause is that we choose so little and we choose timidly. God does not give us pre-cooked and ready-made circumstances. The circumstances he gives us are "do it yourself"; he gives us these circumstances so that we can do his will in time.

Faith is our guide. Without it, we would either work rarely or poorly, and in any event, we would only be doing the work of an artisan. Faith allows us to be an artist. But the artist at work will always make work for the artisan.

Choosing to do God's will in every situation as it presents itself means choosing how to do it with all the human work we can furnish, and bringing our heart, our mind, and our will into harmony with our faith, in order to love God as he wills to be loved, so that "his will be done" on earth, in all the days of the earth, with the humanity of the earth, as it is in heaven.

We are entangled in a false obedience that can transform us as much into false rebels as those who falsely obey.

Moral obligations, the obligations of the Church, perhaps also the obligations of social or professional customs, constitute the regulation of what we call our religious duties. This smells of discipline or the fear of punishment. It smells above all of Christians who have not had their dose of truth, or who perhaps received it under conditions that made it indigestible.

Some of these people risk sliding into a slavish form of Christianity; the others risk sliding into anarchy. But both would be saved from these opposing risks by doing an examination of their faith.

The certainties of faith are absolute certainties. It is only by faith that we are able to discern God's will and live it freely. The obligations established and regulated by the Church are the application the Church makes of these basic certainties to her common life. They are for us a reminder of eternal life, what it is and what it requires.

We do freely that which for us corresponds to a necessity. Obligations render us free when we see what we need to do in the light of faith, and when we make these obligations our way to attain it.

A Christian Manifesto
to the Atheist World[8]

The conversations between you and us easily turn into dialogues of the deaf. And that is often because neither of us has correct information about the other. We know people who are Christians or Communists; we observe or read what certain Christians or Communists do or say. And we supplement this with commentaries that Christians have written on the Communists, or Communists on the Christians.

We need to understand why you are Communists and why we are Christians, the purpose of the Party and the purpose of the Church — in a word, your program and our program. So I propose an exchange: let us tell you ourselves what our program is, the only one that is truly and historically ours. Then it will be easy for you to argue whether or not our actions are in agreement, not only with you, but with our program itself. The polemics between us often become an idealism sung in two voices, because each of us often possesses spurious information about the other.

The history of our cowardice as well as the history of our fidelity to Jesus Christ has been going on for two thousand years. A hundred years were no doubt enough to teach you that if a person learns how to give up his life, he has also been known once in a while to take it back. But you also know — a hundred years again sufficed in this case — that if it is just you who are accused of something true or something false, there's no harm done. But if an ideal is accused, an ideal that is not merely an idea but

8. A personal note. M.D. is here trying to formulate a presentation of her faith that might be accessible to an atheistic world. She addresses herself to this world, which extends beyond her Communist friends and neighbors.

something for which a man and in fact hundreds of thousands of people have died — that cannot be tolerated. Please be sure, when you accuse us, that you know what the facts are. The choice is yours.

If you criticize the mediocre Christians that we are, you can do so. However, we will not accept disputes over definitions that have never been applicable to Christians, over figments of the imagination or caricatures. The Christian seeks to resemble Christ. Discuss Christ, and then we'll talk.

Christian as Technicians of Mystery: The Christian and the Unknown

The only unknown that the Christian accepts for his reason is the same unknown that scientists accept for their reason. The Christian strives as much as anyone else to participate in everything that science discovers, explains, or applies. But the Christian will not accept without examination that the limits of scientific knowledge are the final borders of all human knowledge.

He realizes that as the circle of scientific knowledge gradually expands, the circle of what science does not know expands right along with it. We know more and more how reality — and this includes humanity — exists; but the question of the wherefore and why of all reality — and this includes humanity — becomes greater.

For the Christian, this increasingly vast question remains open. Accepting without further ado to remain in ignorance before this question constitutes for the Christian a veritable alienation of the wonder and the vital instinct that belongs to all human beings by nature. Faith, for the Christian, is the science of mystery, of the true mystery, not of the mysteries concerning the origin of life, its laws, its evolution, and its development, which gradually receive elucidation.

The true mystery: how is it that the world is so intelligible? What makes us able to understand it, to be as it were students in the world's school? Why are people not able to make something new except by receiving what already exists and learning its lessons? Why have human beings interpreted the enigma of the world as a work produced by a great artisan?

The Christian's Good Luck

Good luck! We all agree what luck is, even if each of us expects different and incomparable things from it. Luck is receiving from life or finding in life what we desire.

I don't know if anyone has written a history of luck in the lives of geniuses. Of course, they all worked hard, struggled, kept their eyes open. . . . But without even speaking of the great luck of having particularly well-equipped brains, we could take all the instances of luck they had in coming across certain aspects of reality, coming across the precise fact that set their research going: for example, Denis Papin's chance meeting with the cooking pot. And that's all luck.

Christians are human beings with good luck. They have learned that among the circumstances that make up the events of history, events that bear scientific examination, God wanted certain people to learn where the world came from and where it is going, to learn for the sake of all people the very law of their ultimate destiny.

Christians are those to whom the good luck has fallen to learn what God has said to a certain group of human beings for the sake of us all, which was transcribed and repeated down through the centuries. Christians are given the responsibility of repeating to all human beings what God wants from them; they are given the responsibility of living in accord with what they have learned.

Being Christian is not a matter of cogitation, invention, and imagination; it is a matter of speaking and acting: to speak in order to say what God has said to say; to act in order to do what God has said to do. Being Christian is not being an idealist. If Christians have ideas or an idea, it is because they are human beings with ideas, and not because they are Christians. It is not the Christian's responsibility to have ideas. Christians have the responsibility of acting: God is the one who invents; it is God who creates.

God Is "a Somebody"

When someone says, "he's a somebody," everyone knows what he means. For me, to say "God is 'A Somebody,'" is one of the best ways to translate "I believe in God." Why? Because it really says something, while all the other words one uses to try "to give an idea of what God is" speak only about an abstract idea of God and not a living, not an active God, not a God who has an effect on reality — in a word, not a somebody.

For a lot of people who are not Christian, God is "a Somebody." They did not invent this idea, but arrived at it by contemplating God's handiwork, life itself. The more these people love life, the more they sense God. It doesn't matter what they love among life's gifts: the love of their mother or their wife; the man who is growing up in the child; the laws of life teased out of the earth or chased down on the moon; the forces of life running free in nature, or the same forces captured and put to use in the laboratory; the swirl of life's movement, leading to who knows what over the course of time, or this same movement harnessed by men in the course of time to multiply their working power, their possibilities for exploration, or their making use of the world.

Through all these things, people sense somebody, they sense God. But none of these things can teach God. God cannot be learned. A somebody cannot be learned. You can learn the scientific laws that Marie Curie discovered. But you could not have learned Marie Curie when she was alive. And you cannot learn her now. People knew her and they will always know her; when she was alive, she was known in varying degrees by people who had never even seen her. And she is still known today. Those who have never seen her, those who will never have the opportunity to see her, know her because of what she said and which has been repeated, because of what she did and which was written down. Because Marie Curie is a "somebody," she is not a thing that you can learn, but a woman you can know. However, if she had never spoken, and if her family, her friends, and her students had never spoken about her, no one would ever have been able to know Marie Curie.

The people who sense God in and behind life are like me standing before my radio set. I don't know who invented the radio, but I can guess that "someone" or "some people" invented it. People are free to say to me: "What I'm interested in is my radio, and it won't work any better if I knew who invented it." Christians, for their part, are like scientific researchers: scientists, students, inventors, or technicians, who, each in his own way, know Marie Curie well enough to continue her work, to make use of it, and to apply it.

There are plenty of things we do not know about God. He wanted us to know that He is Somebody, that He lives, that He acts, that He loves; and he wanted us to know this more than everything we are able to know about life, action, or love. But what we know is that God is with us, we know what

God is for us and what God makes and will make of us — that is his work. We know how God loves us and we know how we must and can love.

If we do not yet know all of the secrets contained in life, in our own lives or all those things that human beings have yet to discover, we do know that, having their origin in God, and as they evolve and develop through history, the world and all the people in it are progressing step by step toward God.

But the Christian also knows the law of the eternal history of humankind, of the eternal destiny of each human being. His purpose in being Christian is to take responsibility for all of this.

Our Dialectic: Life and Death

Let me first make a comment. There is already such a serious opposition between Christian faith and Marxism that we have no need to add other differences that are not true. False differences arise when we have false ideas about each other.

Not infrequently, a Christian will attribute to the Communists goals they do not pursue, or doctrines that are not theirs. But the same can be said for certain Communists who propagate notions about Christian faith that are not true.

Thus, certain Christians confuse the Marxist dialectic with some of its particular applications, ignoring — like Monsieur Jourdain with his prose[9] — the rigorous dialectic that Christian life itself involves. And thus Marxists reveal to Christians the basic dialectic that they fail to see, though it is open to simple common sense in its engagement with day-to-day life.

The Christian believes, on God's word, that man is immortal, that all of humanity has an eternal destiny. The Christian believes in the resurrection of all the dead of the human race, of every body. He believes in the immortality of humanity. But he believes on God's word and not in some sort of magic trick, which would be grotesque. He believes in the continuation of life's mysteries beyond death, that through death life is brought to fulfillment; he believes that even death has a purpose; he believes that death remains a horror, indeed, but that it is not a senseless horror.

---

9. In Molière's *Bourgeois Gentilhomme*, Monsieur Jourdain is astonished to learn from his language teacher that he has spoken "prose" for forty years without even knowing it.

Like any reasonable human being, the Christian sees his life, from his birth to his death, as a continual coming to be, accompanied by a continual passing away. But the Christian believes that in this coming to be and through it, the immortal person he is is being born and growing, the human being he is is being fashioned day by day and he will remain what he has become in and for eternity.

We fashion the immortal being we are through our choices. Through our choices we bring the man in us to the fullness of life or to the worst of human suffering. At the hour of his death, each human being has become either a person who will live with God forever, or who will be without God forever.

God's Law: Good and Evil

The divine law for which the Christian is responsible, the law of immortal man, is the law of freedom. It is a law that speaks to what is free in each person. In fact, it speaks only to what is free in each person.

It says to man: "You will love the Lord with all your heart, with all your strength, with all your mind and above all things, and your neighbor as yourself for the love of God."

Translated: "You will love God more than anything else, and to love him, you will love others as yourself."

For the Christian, it is impossible to love God without loving humanity; it is impossible to love humanity without loving all people; and it is impossible to love all people, without loving the people he knows, with a concrete and active love.

This law by itself is the law of good and evil. This is the law that separates humanity out into the good and the bad. This is the living law of immortal humanity. To know this law is to possess the basic science of our coming to be.

Each person is an active cell in the body of humankind. Each free act of each person works for the body as a whole. It either follows the dynamism of life, or it yields to the drying up or deterioration of death; it is either a seed of growth and development or a catalyst of decomposition.

The ultimate usefulness of the world lies in the use man chooses to make of it, because the world itself is not free. The world is at man's disposal. Man's actions are what make use of the world. But the fundamental rule of this use follows from the fundamental law of humanity: the world must be used by each one for the benefit of all.

The choices that determine a person's action are the most powerful capacity a person has of having an effect on the world. When a person sets to work on the world, on its treasures or on its natural secrets, on its laws or on the course of its history, he works for the good of all people and for his own good, simply because he is a human being; he works to kill death. He battles against it; he becomes its master. That is why the action of human beings is related to the purpose of man's mastery of the world: his imaging God.

So, to love all the people making up humankind is to image God, because God loves them.

We Believe in What We Do Not See
Because of What We Have Seen: Jesus Christ

Let me repeat: faith was not made to teach us what reason can know. Faith was not made to teach us the mysteries of nature and the mysteries of human life in nature. Faith is made to teach us the mystery of our very existence: that we exist because God exists; that we are alive because we are loved by God; that human beings are immortal because they are eternally loved by God; that love for all people makes each one of us the living creature we will be for all eternity. The believer is able to say of God alone: "I believe God." The unbeliever, by contrast, says "I don't believe in God."

On the other hand, the unbeliever will say about Jesus Christ: "I do not believe Jesus Christ." For all of us, Jesus Christ is a man. We know what he did, what he said, the country he came from, his profession, and his age.

But for Christians, Jesus Christ is not only a man, he is God.

What I am trying to get at is that, if all of this has been merely made up, we have to say that it was made up by Jesus Christ himself, his own insane idea. We cannot say that it was made up by Christians. It is not, for example, a sort of legend that gradually over time grafted itself onto a real person like some of the legends of Antiquity or the Middle Ages. It was Jesus Christ himself who said, who repeated, who affirmed, and who proclaimed that he was God.

If today there are a lot of people who claim he was insane, the people of his own time made a much more serious claim: namely, that he was guilty of blasphemy. There is no group of people who have insisted more

185

than the Jews that anything that makes God "something" human or limited is a sacrilege. God was for them the immense, almighty, and incomparable "Somebody." God, for them, was truly God and not a great man or superman.

So what is at issue is not a legend that we have stuck onto Christ, so that we now have to decide whether or not to relieve him of it. No, what is at issue is believing or not believing Jesus Christ, believing or not believing what he said about himself; refusing to believe him just as those who lived around him constantly refused to believe him. The Christian believes Jesus Christ when he affirms that he is God.

But if the Christian believes by faith in Jesus Christ, true God and true man, the basis of his faith is not only the words Jesus Christ spoke about himself — words that are facts — but the deeds of Jesus Christ, which are also facts. These facts, even if they lie within the realm of reason, cannot be accepted unless faith as it were perfects our reason. For reason, these are real but inexplicable facts. For reason perfected by faith, they are real facts whose causes are evident to us.

Among all of these facts, the one that is the most crucial because it is the most disconcerting, is that Jesus Christ, who was sent to death because he claimed to be God, was raised up again, and became again a living man. Indeed, his friends doubted . . . and doubted again, and continued to deny it until they saw it for themselves, and even touched, felt, and proved it to be so.

These people did not want to believe Jesus Christ when he claimed to be God, did not want to believe in the life of this body that they had themselves felt with their hands when it was dead, unless they could feel for themselves that it was alive again; they set out throughout the world of their time, not to proclaim in the first place and loudest the universal love that Jesus taught them, the justice for the little ones, for the weak and the oppressed, the goodness for each living person on behalf of each living person — but to proclaim first and loudest that Jesus Christ, the man who was our friend, Jesus Christ, the friend of the poor and of sinners and of the downtrodden, Jesus Christ who threatened the selfish and the proud with an eternity of suffering, Jesus Christ who was spat upon, mocked, struck, and scourged, who was tortured amidst laughter, Jesus Christ who was hung upon a cross, who was bled dry, who let out his last breath with a moan, Jesus Christ who froze upon the cross, who no one doubted was dead, Jesus Christ with whom we lived, who died before us, who was buried in a grave not far from us, with a great stone rolled over where his body lay, and where soldiers stood to keep us from opening the tomb and stealing his body, this Jesus Christ is risen because he was, because he remains today, tomorrow, and forever, truly man and truly God.

Christians believe what these people went to proclaim to everyone who would listen and even more so to everyone who did not want to listen. They did not present themselves as the witnesses of the doctrine of Jesus Christ, as its most perfect observers. It did not even occur to them to do so.

They presented themselves as witnesses of Jesus Christ, of his life, his death, and his resurrection, as witnesses of the Law that he taught, of the examples he gave and the promises he made. They presented themselves as the personal witnesses of the very person of Jesus Christ.

Twelve out of twelve of them suffered martyrdom one after the other because they refused to keep quiet. What they said and what they wrote we continue to read even today; we continue to repeat even today.

It is because of these facts that we believe Jesus Christ, that we believe what he told us about God, about what interests man in God. We believe Jesus Christ who taught us and who showed us how a person ought to live in order to be God's image, how a person ought to live the law of the immortal human being, the human being that God wills, the human being that God loves.

The Church: A Single Life in a Single Body[10]

Perhaps it is the "definition" of the Church that each of us has stamped in our memory that leads us to live the Church like individuals who happen to be grouped together in a society rather than as a single life in a single body.

Of course, to be baptized means to be a citizen of the People of God, and this entails for Catholics certain obligations that will always possess a certain social dimension. For example, a person lives in a particular Christian community in a particular country, and not simply according to one's own taste. A fault that might remain personal in one setting would reach scandalous proportions in another. Likewise, a simple life of selfless love in a Christian country might become in another, without changing anything about it, a proclamation of the Gospel.

But plunging into the inner mystery of the Church, into the Mystical Body to which Pius XII devoted an encyclical a few years back, makes us aware of our place and the place of our brothers not only within a larger society, but within Jesus Christ. It is altogether something different to be a person in a society and to be a cell in a body. It is altogether something different to participate in the Church's external activity in the world and to bring salvation to people as a hidden part of a saving organism, in a way that requires us to be both living and life-giving.

Unless we make a gift of ourselves to the invisible power of the Church, our commitment to her visible power will build only what is hollow and fragile.

10. A personal note.

The Church must be visible in the world, the Church needs each of her members to make an effort so that her outer clothing reveals who she is. But, if it is the case that she must be visible, it is first necessary that she *be,* and it is through each one of us that she *is.*

What St. Paul wrote long ago to our fathers in the faith still applies: his explanation of how we were supposed to be members of a single body, having different roles that complement each other insofar as they have the same goal is something that we can read over and over again, and then learn from it how we are to apply it.

We could even say that all the things science has taught us are particularly illuminating for the Christian who seeks to live the Church deeply enough to be able to live an authentic and courageous Gospel in the world.

I have neither the qualification nor the competence, and even if I did, what an immense book would be necessary to say all there is to say about what the Church means for the Christian and what the Christian means for the Church.

Thus, I will stay within my own limits and will just give you certain examples, which I hope will serve you as well as they have served me.

The Church, like any other society or any other body, is made up of relations. It is not our responsibility to invent these relations, but rather to come to know them and submit to them. We have to submit ourselves to them unconditionally, just as we are subject to social rules that no revolution will ever destroy, to the laws of life that we can become aware of but that make us what we are through our free or instinctual submission to what they are.

What we Christians come to know first are the social rules that govern our relations to those who are citizens with us in eternity, our relations to the clergy, to the hierarchy, and to the supreme pontiff. And yet, even in this realm, we tend to fall into concepts drawn from human societies. We try to "join forces" among ourselves; the clergy receives our respect, the hierarchy, our obedience, and the Holy Father, more still. But this union of forces often turns into a defensive and offensive fortress, this obedience often turns into external discipline, and this respect into "leaving each his own."

Even when we think of the Church as a society, it is not about being citizens: the most unknown baptized person *is* our brother in a mysterious life. The most hidden priest has received the power to carry out certain functions belonging to Christ himself; he is a miracle of fruitfulness. The bishops and the Holy Father bear for us the crushing burden of preserving and transmitting the faith of Jesus Christ, and it is only because of them that we can participate in the most invigorating of tasks: the revelation of God, the communication of the Gospel.

It is very important for us, I believe, religiously to "conform" our religious acts to the profound realities they concern. These acts, which are borrowed from normal life in society, tend to "naturalize" the face of the Church, as it were, vis-à-vis nonbelievers: the priests of Christ become for them party leaders, directors, or full-time members, etc., a political enterprise for some people, an ideological one for others. And we do not merely "naturalize," but even "denature" the Church when we transform the human gathering of people into a mere army, when we transform knowing one's proper place into acting like a child, and discipline into petty officiousness.

In all of the external obligations that the Church asks of us, we have to remain human beings, true in who we are, and true in what we do. We may end up being humiliated, mocked, and scorned, but even if we are, we must remain fully living creatures, living the same life as other people. We must remain people who have freely chosen to submit themselves to their Church, even if it means, in the end, being thereby crushed.

But it is even more essential that we *believe* — in the fullest sense possible of the word — that we are living and extraordinarily active cells of the Mystical Body of Christ. And insofar as we believe this, we must *be* these cells.

If our belonging to this people of God which is the Church requires from us or forbids us certain activities or acts, our incorporation into the same Church must transform us in the deepest aspects of our being and grant us obligations and abilities that nonbelievers cannot even begin to suspect.

These *obligations* are our submission to the living exchanges of grace just as they are a doing justice to the constitutive relationships of the Mystical Body.

Exchanges and relationships always have an aspect of mystery, even when they occur between saints. But we should be well aware that this mystery is doubled by the reality of what a human being is. An important function of grace might be clothed in a mediocre or problematic personality. A particular bishop, apart from his being bishop, might be someone gifted with remarkable human abilities. Another may seem to have received relatively few. Here or there the face of the Church may be a little worse for the wear, but on the other hand the life of grace of each person, if his faith remains realistic (if he understands the bishop as a pillar who pre-serves and communicates the Lord's Gospel), may become all the richer and stronger for it.

I believe it was St. Ambrose who said, "Become who you are." "En-counter in them the person they really are" — this ought to be burned into our hearts with a red iron. Those who make up the "hierarchy" weigh not according to their human weight but according to the weight of God's Omnipotence. We cannot pass judgment over the office of priesthood, but we can give it our faith if we meet it in the place where it acts.

And our "brothers." . . . Do we even dare to call them "brothers" when human beings have become for us mere catalogued and labeled val-ues, sitting on a shelf, waiting to be sold? And I am not talking only about money, but also about the various talents that some people have and oth-ers do not; I am talking about anything that divides people. ("What a poor fellow he is. . . .")

And this Church, which is made up of human beings, which is made up of us, has the responsibility of continuing Christ's relationship with those who turn away from him. A life that does not pass itself on is not a life. Every authentic Christian works to contribute to this passing on, ei-ther directly or by giving life to those who bear this task under its various names: evangelization, mission, apostolate. . . .

Light and Darkness[11]

At the present hour, in the place we live, the words "light" and "darkness" seem to me to be taking on a more pronounced meaning. What the biblical word "darkness" means is illustrated by the people around us — a darkness that is more impenetrable than in any other time or place.

It is not only the living God, who has definitively revealed himself in the Gospel, who has been rejected. Along with God, every reflection, every trace of him has also been rejected. Man desires no other light than his own.

Objectively, the Christian has the capacity to see a trace of God in every person insofar as he can see in that person the work of God. Subjectively, these traces can be hard to see for many people.

Moreover, when the Christian manages to penetrate the mentality of his brothers and sisters, he comes into contact with a darkness of an extraordinary density. This density is increased, for the Christian, by the contrast with the light that he himself bears. The density is increased still more by the contrast with the light that has been chased out of whole sectors of humanity. And the more the Christian is illuminated by God's light, the more tragic this contrast becomes.

It seems to me that precisely this contrast ought to be the point of departure for mission in our age. This in particular is where missionary love has its roots.

Missionary love discovers the intensity that belongs to it in the contrast between the light that formerly Christian milieus once possessed and

11. A note written at the request of a group of students from Lyons (1960).

the darkness in which they now wallow. What we have are no longer countries that are unconsciously waiting for the Lord. Instead they are countries that once possessed the light of the Lord and subsequently rejected it.

However, the encounters with contemporary atheism or nonbelief or indifference should not be only catalysts of missionary love; they should also serve to generate and quicken faith, which then expands so as to be able to take in more light.

Indeed, such encounters lead us no longer to take for granted the gift of faith we have received and the capacity it gives us to contemplate God, but rather to see it as an extraordinary treasure that has been given with extraordinary gratuity.

These encounters teach us to be dumbstruck by grace. They then lead us to live the state of soul of a neophyte, which we too rarely realize we are. They reveal to us a depth of thanksgiving that we would never have known without them. As a rule, if they lead us into the inside of a certain anxiety or a certain missionary sorrow, they illuminate the true foundations of Christian joy.

For the faith that we have received from Jesus Christ enables us to love God because it enables us to know him. But because we often tend to live our Christianity like a habit, we do not make use of this ability, or at least we do not make sufficient use of it. We love God only with a mediocre love because our knowledge of him is mediocre. Now, it would therefore follow that the first of our tasks in time is to know God as much as possible, in order to glorify him as much as possible and to compensate as much as possible for our neighbor's lack of knowledge of him.

If we are fully convinced of this first temporal duty, I think we will be able to confront all the rest of our temporal duties without unbalancing our supernatural life: for these duties carry us implacably deeper into the first and second commandments that the Lord gave us.

Does Our Faith Seek the Light of God in a World That Has "Lost God's Light from View"?

Our missionary immersion into the depths of our age reveals to us the world such as nonbelievers see it. We do not always take into consideration how different their view of the world is from ours.

In contrast to the field of vision possessed by people who have remained pagan, this is a field of vision that was once illuminated by the light of God. Those who possess it have become blind to every supernatural or religious reality.

If, to a vast extent, the world has remained closed to Christianity, the world has nevertheless remained to a large extent open to the divine sense, in varying degrees of purity.

On the other hand, in the dechristianized milieus in which we live, the divine sense is what people tend to lose first, and they lose their "Christianity" only later.

What characterizes the field of vision of the neighbor with whom we interact on a day-to-day basis?

In comparison to our own way of seeing the world, its first characteristic in our day is that it is illuminated by the light of the human spirit alone. The next is that it is not illuminated by anything that transcends man.

A whole new scale of values follows from these two characteristics, concerning the reality of things and concerning their necessity.

Within this field of vision, each particular thing acquires a certain utility or reality. This reality or this utility is *true;* but what is irreparably false is how it is integrated into the scale of values, because all the lines of vision have been blocked.

We could say that everything that has thus become blind to God is in a certain sense conquered by death, swallowed up in the "shadows of death." Each thing thus finds itself raised up in the present and struck down by death in the future. This gives rise to despair. Everything that is snatched away from God is condemned to death.

Everything that is alive, everything that is loved, loses its foundation in being and thus crumbles from within. Everything is swallowed up in nothingness and meaninglessness.

But when the life of faith comes into contact with this disaster, it reacts. The Christian examines his Christian life. He asks himself about God, about God's importance, about God's place, about how he seeks God's protection.

He then begins to realize how easy it is to lose God in Christian life or to lose him in Christ; and then how easy it is to lose Christ in Christianity; how easy it is for Christianity to continue on at first without God and then without Christ. Finally, he has the vertiginous realization how easily such breakdowns can occur.

Two Abysses

If our greatest strength is our passion for God, we will turn off of dangerous missionary trails without our even noticing it. The path left open to us
will scale dizzying heights, but it will not be dangerous. Or more precisely,
its danger will be no match for our strength.

This passion for God will reveal to us that our Christian life is a pathway between two abysses. One is the measurable abyss of the world's rejections of God. The other is the unfathomable abyss of the mysteries of God.

We will come to see that we are walking along the adjoining line
where these two abysses intersect. And we will thus understand how we are
mediators and why we are mediators.

We will understand what sort of "covenant" we have been made
guardians of, a covenant of which we are both the beneficiaries and the
stewards. We will cease being perpetually distracted: distracted from the
world by God, and distracted from God by the world.

We will be faithful to God personally, with the name by which he has
called each one of us, and we will be freely subjected to his glory.

But it is on behalf of the world, it is on behalf of each person, of every human being that we will be personally faithful to God, that we will
personally place ourselves in the service of his glory — and we will do so,
not because of the world, not because of people, but because of the God
who loved the world and who loved all people with a first and gratuitous
love.

Salvation and Happiness

In the age in which we live, we must listen to the word of God with all of
the resonances it acquires here. For example, the passage from Isaiah: "I,
the Lord, called to you in justice and I will hold you by the hand, and I will
make you strong: I will make of you a covenant for the people, a light for
the nations, to open the eyes of the blind, to release prisoners from captivity, and from the dungeon those who are seated in darkness" (Isa. 42:6-7).

Listen to this passage within our age, at our historical moment,
within our day-to-day life, within the here and now of our existence, our
permanent relation to God, our changing relations with people. God has
made us a covenant. We are a fact of the divine covenant. Each Mass reminds us of the universal breadth of this covenant.

But in order for this fact to be true, in order for us to live this covenant, universally in spirit and in grace, it has to be lived out concretely right where we are, in our day-to-day lives, among the people that we know.

We have been "made" a covenant for these people, for their families, for their nations, their blind, their prisoners, as if it were a duty of personal honor.

In order for this fact to be true, it is necessary that the people, the nations, the blind, and the prisoners, be real for us, be present in us, just as we are real for ourselves and present to ourselves.

They must be flesh of our flesh, the very fibers of our heart; they must be constantly recollected in our thoughts. They and we must be inseparable, a single organism. We must make their destiny one with ours, the destiny that is for us the fulfillment of salvation.

It is our duty to know the concrete and particular conditions in which their salvation is being played out. It is our mission to make them feel the presence of God through us. This is the temporal service we are required to perform and for which there is no one else to take our place.

Our time within time, our place in the world, these human beings among all people are for us the concrete face of the people with whom God wanted to make a covenant. The Christian who is animated by a passion for God will feel rise within him a passion to imitate God's paternal goodness by means of a fraternal love that is always more demanding and always more authentic.

But this same Christian, who is more and more captivated by the meaning of the divine covenant, will more and more want to bring people closer to salvation, which is the crowning work of God's goodness towards them.

The Christian will feel compelled simultaneously to be more and more at the service of each of his brothers, and more and more at the service of their salvation.

The happiness and the salvation of human beings will confront each other in the very depths of his being.

But this confrontation will not create confusion or sterile tensions. The service of human happiness, which he pursues in the likeness of the heavenly Father, is ordered, hierarchized, and brought to completion within the vast horizon of salvation.

PART FOUR

THE BATTLES OF FAITH

1961-1964

The Christian has to realize that, by virtue of office, he has
*   the means to see things clearly and the means to fight.*
To fight, he must be in good health, and not weighed down
*   by useless habits.*
The "nothing more and nothing less than the Gospel" is what
*   helps us discern in each situation that presents itself:*
*   what is certain, what is necessary, and what comes from faith;*
You shall love God more than all things.
You will make those around you your neighbor.
Go, proclaim the Gospel,
Pray.

What is neither important nor permanent
are our mentalities (either old or new) that must be revised
in accord with charity and proclaiming the Gospel.

> *Two golden rules:*
> "Be prepared to change everything we are free to change."
> "It would serve no purpose to be close enough to be heard, to
> speak the language of our peers, to be present and there for
> them, if, having fulfilled all these requirements, we ourselves
> had not discovered the total message that we have *received* and
> that we have to *pass on*."
>
> (Atheism and evangelization, 235)

December 1961. John XXIII's Christmas message: *Peace and Goodness*
October 1962. The opening of Vatican Council II.
April 1963. The encyclical *Pacem in Terris*.
June 1963. The death of John XXIII and the election of Paul VI.

As of 1959, Madeleine Delbrêl was once again able to stabilize her health and thus found it easier to respond to her frequent invitations to conferences.

She found many opportunities in various encounters to let her life and thought radiate outward: at an ecumenical session in Bossey in 1959, in various sessions and meetings, at the *Pax Christi* meeting in Geneva, the Action Catholique Ouvrière meeting in Marseille, the A.C.G.F. in Paris, etc., not to mention the less formal discussions with various groups.

At each encounter, she adapted her thinking and its developments to the public she addressed. There are countless notes from these last years that could not find a place in this volume. In addition, she composed travel memoirs: there is one of a trip she took to Poland at the bidding of several close friends, and another of a trip to Abidjan [Ivory Coast] where one of her *équipes* had been founded in 1961. Her thinking broadened to embrace the problems of the third world, and at the same time her missionary reflection extended beyond her dialogue with Marxism and became more and more occupied with contemporary atheism and the problem of technology in our age.

Now Is the Time for Our Faith[1]

To start things off, I ought to warn you about my vocabulary. Now,
you are all specializing in various areas in order to get "qualified" in
something. I myself am not a specialist in anything, and the lan-
guage I use is not specialized either. The most everyday sorts of
words can sometimes contain a scientific, philosophical, or techni-
cal meaning that is hidden from the uninitiated. I ask that you take
the words I use in their most ordinary, everyday sense.

What I would like to speak to you about the faith can be
summed up in the title, Now Is the Time for Our Faith.

Time — you can already see what a verbal adventure we could have if we
wanted — time in the common meaning it has today as it had yesterday is
a "film" that records the history of things and the history of people, or to
put it simply, History in general, *our* history.

But it seems that never before has this film recorded such a mass of
unrelated footage as it has in our age. It also seems that never before has
the film had to run at such a quick speed.

Today, in this one day alone, we have accumulated as many facts as
would have sufficed to record the whole history of certain peoples, at least
as far as we know. Now, although there are some exceptions, faith seems to
make a rare appearance in this film. It seems that the action of faith has left

---

1. A conference given to a student chapter of UNESCO, at the Centre Richelieu
in Paris, in preparation for the annual student pilgrimage to Chartres (March 1961).

little or no trace, and that even where faith is persecuted, where people are suffering and dying because of it, it is persecuted because of yesterday, because of the past. It seems that the persecutions unleashed against it, as well as some of the campaigns that seem on the other hand to be led on its behalf, are merely aftereffects of what faith long ago inspired and that has continued on in the world.

The topicality of the press, the radio, and television does not provide us with the voice or the image of faith that would be a faith of our age. Faith seems to get into the media only by accident, not on account of itself but on account of the things it has produced, and even when these things are masterpieces, we have the constant impression that they are ancient masterpieces.

Nevertheless, we call this time, this film we are watching, "our age." We have the right to call it our age, because it is always something that concerns us, and we are often actors in it. These events are not simply things brought to our attention, but they are brought right into the heart of our lives, and they have sometimes even disrupted or changed our lives. Even the things in this film that do not touch us directly still constitute as it were the very air we breathe, the air that surrounds and pervades us. It establishes relations with us, natural and living bonds. By virtue of the "today" that we are all informed about together, that we live together, we are made contemporaries in a way that would have been totally foreign to the people of past ages.

To be contemporaries in our age is somewhat like being compatriots. We are thus, and sometimes even without our knowing it, formed into a people with a shared mentality, identical sensibilities, and common desires and fears. We tend to become contemporary citizens of a country that no longer has its roots in any particular land.

Now, we notice a certain absence of faith in this film of time, of our age. The storyline does not in the least seem to be determined by faith; faith is as it were crowded out by everything that is going on, by goals and desires for which faith does not seem to be needed. It seems to be too much in the way to take part in the action, it is tempted to slink off into the margins, to take leave of our age, to withdraw.

But it gets worse: some of the most modern milieus have the reputation of being harmful to the faith, of being intolerable to it. This reputation did not come about for nothing; it has some foundation in the facts: within such milieus, many Christian lives grow thin, get warped, or crumble altogether.

However, whether we are talking about wavering attitudes, or actual deteriorations and breakdowns, it is worth pointing out that this is not the fault of faith but the fault of what Christians sometimes call the faith; it is in fact a mere representation of the faith that becomes abridged, deformed, and deprived of certain essential elements; or else a representation of the faith that is weighed down, encumbered, and adulterated with elements that do not belong to it — with mentalities, principles, and goals that are more or less foreign to it. In most cases, what is at fault is a faith that strives primarily to maintain and preserve itself and in the process forgets its own effective presence and fecundity.

Genuine faith holds firm.

It would be absurd to think that faith could not survive precisely in those milieus for which it was made.

It would be absurd to think that the Christian is inescapably doomed to lose his faith in milieus in which faith has not been proclaimed.

If we are so often partial and practical apostates, it is because we tend to be people who forget. Whenever we discover or rediscover one aspect of the faith and allow ourselves to become fascinated by it, we are constantly tempted at the same time to lose interest in another truth, which we very quickly end up forgetting altogether.

All of a sudden we remember that faith exists in an age and for an age. And at that very moment, we are tempted to temporalize or naturalize it. All of a sudden, we are awestruck by the glimpse of eternity faith affords us, and we begin to think that we can best be faithful by being immobile. But, if God is immutable, standing still is not the way to image him.

Genuine faith is wholly made to guide us in time toward eternal life, to make us live eternal life already in time.

But we cannot attain to eternal life through faith except in time and through time, because faith itself is temporal. Faith must pass away, as St. Paul says: "It will pass away"; faith is temporary; there is no age that is impervious to it, and it is not impervious to any age; it is made for time; it is destined to every age; and when an age seems to be impervious to it, it is no doubt impervious to us because we carry around with us the residue of a past age that sets itself in opposition to the age in which we must live.

Nevertheless, genuine, naked faith never finds a comfortable welcome in time. Faith is beset with the questions of an age, it is sometimes questioned by the age, and it is often called into question by the age. And the rule of the game is the law of Redemption.

But if we take our faith as sufficient for us, if we do not add anything to it, or take away anything from it, we will be able to be questioned and called into question along with it: but faith will give us life, will tell us how to act and what to say, no matter what sort of age we live in, even if the age is our present age.

Moreover, I have no other aim in speaking to you here than to present you with the facts, with the steps that brought me to this conviction. It grew within me over the course of many long years spent in a single non-Christian, I would even say atheistic, milieu.

If this milieu is generally a Communist city, that does not mean that my conviction is valid only for Communist cities. But this milieu casts the sharpest light on what is at stake in the Christian resistance, and the trials and temptations it is undergoing.

On the other hand, it doesn't bother me that it is a Communist city because Communist cities are taken to be the most dangerous and destructive for Christian life.

Even if I do not leave you with a certainty, I would nevertheless like to leave you at least with the hypothesis of an uncertainty. I would like to tell you that, though I am a convert, I found in this non-Christian milieu the conditions favorable for a new conversion, a conversion to a more genuine, truer, and healthier faith.

And I would like to tell you, with the same firmness and the same conviction, that I found in this same milieu conditions that were just as favorable for the evangelization of this milieu.

I will go even further. I would say that in a Marxist milieu, that living near Communists, you can find conditions that are particularly favorable for evangelizing, because Communists are people who ask questions, questions that we can silence only by refusing them the Gospel.

I would say that the Communists themselves can evangelize with their own "good news" and that if we do not evangelize them, then we are accepting to be open fields for their propaganda. Thus, they unmask our silence, which might remain masked in other milieus. They teach us that the silence of Christians is often either ignorance or cowardice.

If you will permit me, then, I will take two slogans to guide our line of reflection:

- To believe is to know (and to know how).
- To believe is to speak.

In an atheist or modern milieu, we are constantly compelled to take up one of these two Christian attitudes.

To Believe Is to Know (and to Know How)

To Know

Contemporary society, in general, is dominated by the notion of reality. Those whom society takes for its heroes — and they often are heroes — are those who have a passion for knowing life or a passion for living it.

Those who are not heroes are most often the ones who have a passion for things, for things that distract from daily living, or make it easier or more comfortable. Whoever is not a realist is not a contemporary.

What we believe is generally not what interests the people living around us. The people we run into in contemporary milieus usually do not start out asking us about what we believe. What their questions — even the ones that remain unspoken — boil down to is this: "For you, what does it mean to believe?"

And sometimes it takes us too long to realize that even we cannot say for sure. We end up asking ourselves the same question that others ask us: What's the use of faith?

Now, if we don't try to dodge the question, if we face up to it, we come to see that faith had unconsciously become for us merely a way of thinking, a way of looking at things, a way of visualizing our interior life, but that we rarely use faith much for acting, for doing. Faith, in us, was not being put to its full use, because, far more similarly to the modern milieu than we ever realized, we haven't felt the need for faith. It wasn't very clear to us how faith could help us to do what we needed to do.

And the first step in our reconversion to the faith is to discover that faith is, itself, a realism.

If we wanted to find an analogy that could help us understand what faith is, we would not be able to find such an analogy in the systems of philosophy, in the rules of morality, or in the dreams of artists. We would find it in science, in one of the life sciences — for example, biology. A life science teaches the laws of life; it teaches a reality upon which we can act according to the laws we have therein discovered.

From the very first conversations you may have with your Communist comrades, you quickly discover that, for them, you are "an idealist." And to get to the heart of the issue, you realize that you have to understand the word "idealist" in its philosophical sense.

To believe, for a Communist, is to adhere to an idealist philosophical system. And, receiving unexpected help from Communists, we are forced to take stock of the extent to which our Christian lives have remained idealistic. We are shown a true disorder within our life of faith. What the faith teaches us, we understand poorly and inadequately, and what we do understand, we apply it only partially, or we apply it to things that in fact do not concern faith.

After much seeking and much trial and error, certain very simple practical truths begin to emerge for us. We begin to take faith seriously as *the science of a reality that concerns us and yet transcends us.* A reality about which God himself has taught us. This reality is called eternal life.

The laws that God has pronounced for us are thus the laws of a life. We have nothing to do with changing the reality of this life and the laws that govern it. We are not asked to imagine what they would be like if they were different. We are simply asked to take them for what they are, to live them as they are.

No one asks for our initiative or creativity to change them; on the other hand, everything that has to do with our natural human life requires all of our initiative and our curiosity and our imagination and our involvement.

Now, in those matters in which we are asked simply to conform to the reality that we know and to obey its laws of life, we tend to be particularly active. On the other hand, in matters that have different laws of life, which require us to be active and creative in order to obey them, we tend to be particularly restrained.

What's the use of faith, and what does it help us do?

We are harassed in ways that make a deep impression on us with questions about our effectiveness; but there is a misunderstanding about what effectiveness might mean in this context, and I am ashamed at how often we become paralyzed with inferiority complexes, for reasons that are groundless.

With respect to these questions about effectiveness, we have better things to do than to get complexes. These questions themselves should prompt us to enquire what sort of effectiveness is proper to faith; for faith is not only a science, it is also a practical science, it is an applied science. Faith gives us knowledge, but it also gives us know-how.

Know-How

We might be able to get an idea about this know-how by taking a step back. But these practical activities happen nowhere else than in what we ourselves do, in what we are called to do with others and for others. Whenever we forget the temporality of the faith, we forget a whole aspect of the true work of the faith, and thus of its effectiveness: faith is to live as Jesus Christ told us to live and to do what Jesus Christ said to do; and to live it and to do it in *our* age. It is a life that cannot be translated into any clichés. It is a work that has no blueprint.

The will of the Father is always the same, but it is carried out always anew. His work is always the same, but we must always work anew at the part of it we are asked to complete.

The task of faith is to bring about the eternal in time. Its task is to bring about our history within the universal history, to form an eternal event out of each of our history's passing episodes — an event that is eternal not only for us but for all of humanity.

Faith is the temporal engagement of God's love; it is the engagement of eternal life in time. It is a lack of faith not to allow faith to teach us the meaning of temporal events, just as it is a lack of faith not to allow it to teach us the meaning of the eternal.

When we learn through faith what eternal life is, how to live it, and what to do through it, it is then that we are God's students. There is no greater joy for human intelligence. We have so little idea of this joy, and we have so little grasp of the responsibilities that follow from it.

To believe is to know God from the inside, by participating in his Spirit, by participating in his work; it is to enter into the inner life of God in order to receive a science that we would never have been able to achieve on our own: the science of eternal life.

People talk a lot about the honesty and the humility of science; before the reality of God, we ought to have an infinitely greater humility and an infinitely greater honesty:

- To hold as certain that which is certain; and faith does not provide us with that many certitudes.
- To hold as necessary that which is necessary; and faith does not show us very many necessities.
- But not to overburden this web of necessities and certainties with "maybes" and with "obligations."

That which is necessary binds us to obligations. But an obligation is merely something that follows from a necessity. Obligations do not exist in themselves. They are completely relative, which does not mean that they are something optional for us.

Now, one of the necessities revealed to us by faith is that those who have received the faith proclaim the faith to those who have not yet received the faith. In other words, a necessity that they say what they believe to those who do not know it. And because the contemporary milieus around us are always made up of nonbelievers, we who live in these same milieus are required by supernatural necessity to evangelize.

Today, we will always find around us people who would say with Prévert, "And we do not know what life is and we do not know what day is and we do not know what love is."

Faith is the science of our fundamental ignorance.

I do not need to tell you that in order to know, you have to work, and in order to work, you sometimes have to suffer. The know-how of faith cannot be won without suffering; and the sorts of practical work one has to undergo contain a sort of quasi-permanent common element: being put to the test. Now, it surprises us to be tested, because we complain about being tested. And because we are tested, we excuse ourselves when we do things our own way.

But being put to the test is in fact a great fortune: it means having the chance to know. A single example will suffice: We believe that fraternal charity is easy enough to understand and that we all know what it is. I can say, however, that I do not know what it is, or at least that I have a poor understanding of it, in light of a few experiences I had with the Communists.

The Communists that live next door to each one of us are our neighbor, and the first thing that faith asks of each of us in relation to them is that when you are a disciple of Jesus Christ you must treat these people as your neighbor: all of the instructions for this have been given in the Gospel, particularly in the Sermon on the Mount. The Communists have a right to the whole Sermon on the Mount, and we can make no objections.

However, in trying to treat them truly as our brothers and sisters, we begin to realize that these people are as it were indwelt by a doctrine that is not at all brotherly to us, that is even our adversary and our enemy. And so we are tempted to treat the Communists as we believe the doctrine that inspires them deserves to be treated. Thus, certain Christians take up an attitude we could call warlike towards the Communists, even though it cannot be here a question of doing spiritual battle.

But, if we manage to escape this temptation, that doesn't mean we are safe: another one is lying in wait for us: sympathy. The love that we bear towards the Communists affords us a sympathetic knowledge of their doctrine, their system, and their goal; we see it as though it were an essential property of those we love. At this point, we begin to judge them according to their intentions, and by the same token, we begin to judge their doctrine by the same intentions. We may even end up seeing in them perfectly innocent human beings, and even being seduced by their doctrine because they themselves have won our hearts.

But if the first temptation reminded us that the Sermon on the Mount could never be denied its rights, the second temptation reminds us that the Lord's second commandment, "You shall love your neighbor as yourself," can never cancel out the first: "You shall love the Lord your God."

But there is still more. In the light of our relationships with the Communists, we discover a truth that may strike us as peculiar. We are required to love the sinners that these people are, who are conscious of their sinfulness to varying degrees, but sinners who at the very least participate in a public, collective sin, not counting the fact that some of the ways they behave or see things might seem to us to be very actively sinful with respect to truth or in terms of violence. We might thus start to think we can take certain liberties with fraternal charity, with love of neighbor.

But if we stick to the absolute aspect of fraternal charity, its boundless and exceptionless character, we will come to understand that *what seems a surprise to us is in fact the very basis of the normal condition of a love of neighbor.*

As long as we are on this earth, when we love our neighbor we will be loving people who are sinners. As long as a Christian is on this earth, he will be a sinner loving another sinner, because there is no such thing as a person who is not a sinner. And as long as a Christian is on this earth, he will not be able to love his brother with anything other than a redemptive love.

And I could give you thousands of examples of various adventures, short ones, long ones, dramatic ones, or funny ones, in which we come to discover, through temptations, the real nature of God's will for us.

To Believe Is to Speak

In the most modern of milieus, to believe is not only to know but also to speak.

I don't know how the idea became so common today that speaking is something optional for a Christian.

I mentioned a moment ago that it is a Christian necessity to proclaim the Gospel in a nonbelieving milieu. Let me add something: if it is true that you have no choice whether or not to proclaim the Gospel, whether to speak or to be silent, you also do not even have the choice *what* you have to speak *about*.

One example among a thousand: One night there was a meeting of about fifteen people, mostly men, all of whom I know quite well. One of them said to me: "Listen, you're not going to try to make me believe that you yourself believe that Jesus Christ came back to life after his death. Do you really believe that?"

Let me tell you, if there is no difference in content between saying in the Credo "on the third day he rose from the dead" and responding to such a question, "yes I do," there is certainly an amusing difference in the impression it makes.

If it were up to us, the resurrection of Christ would no doubt not be the first topic we would choose to embark on in our proclaiming the Gospel. But when you are in the midst of a milieu that has no faith, especially a Communist one, you have to answer the questions that are put to you, and you do not always get the chance to decide yourself what they are.

It is also essential that we keep in mind that to evangelize is not necessarily to convert. That to proclaim the faith is not to give faith. It is our responsibility to speak or to keep silent, but we are not responsible for the effectiveness of our words.

God is the one who gives faith. And there are a number of things to get straight on that score. It often happens that we "lose the forest for the trees." The nonbelief or the religious unrest of some people that we might be close to can threaten to enslave us to them. Nevertheless, even if we have a certain responsibility toward them, it should not prevent us from seeing a bit further; it should not restrict the scope of our vision.

To evangelize is to speak; it is to speak in order to proclaim the "Good News." It is to speak to someone in order to bring the good news to *him*.

To do so, the first thing we need to do is to be what people would call nowadays a "reporter." For the people who are our neighbor, for whom we are neighbors, we must be the "reporters" of a particular message.

To report means to use practical means to proclaim to these people news that they do not yet know. But if you proclaim it to them, it is because it concerns them and, in order for them to hear it, they must feel that they themselves are the subject of this news, it must arise from within the field of things in which they are interested. They have to know you as a reporter who can be trusted.

The person who "reports" the Gospel must be someone who, in areas other than the Gospel, is respected for his integrity, for his precision, for someone who is not easily taken in by "fantastical notions."

It is all about a current event, something that is just now happening, an event that is underway. It is not a lesson of ancient history; it is information about our age; it is a fresh piece of news.

As for making contact with the working class, or more precisely with the working classes, people often talk about the importance of vocabulary. No matter what milieu we are speaking of, I believe, vocabulary is equally important. The vocabulary that is most familiar to one milieu is generally the same vocabulary that estranges another. You have to acquire the habit of spontaneous translation.

People talk less often about the danger presented by a dead language used to communicate everything that has to do with religion. And they talk the least about the muffled mumbling of words that are understood everywhere in themselves, but which, because of the muffling and mumbling, cannot help but conjure images of death and boredom. A vocabulary that is outside of life cannot communicate anything to people but things that lie outside of life. And a bored manner of speaking cannot communicate anything either other than bored realities.

If you want a lesson in good pronunciation, I advise you to listen, for example, to Edith Piaf singing *l'Hymne à l'amour*. Words like "eternity," "immensity," "God," and "heaven" take on a very clear and tangible meaning.

And don't think that the question of vocabulary only concerns helping others. It is helpful also for us, because we are incapable of talking of life with dead words. Either these dead words are a sign that we are not treating these supernatural truths as things alive, or else just by speaking of eternal life with dead words, we begin to think of it as something dead.

But now I have to conclude, because, like all the things of this world, even this long-winded speech must come to an end.

So what should we finish with, among all the reflections that I have left in the lurch? Well, I suppose I shall add a brief remark about *the language of the Gospel.*

To proclaim the Gospel in the language of the people with whom we are speaking is not enough. We have to proclaim the Gospel in the language of the Gospel, in the language of Jesus Christ.

The language of the Gospel is accompanied everywhere by words related to goodness, to the goodness of Jesus Christ. There is quite a lot to say about this goodness, quite a lot for us to learn.

Its name has been cheapened and blackened — you hear about a "good" mess, or a "good" girl, and you begin to lose respect for the thing itself. Now, the goodness that Jesus lived, and which we try to live in all of its breadth and depth, without limit and without exception, for each human being, is a miracle all by itself because it is the visible sign of God's love.

We should not forget that even if the news that we proclaim strikes our brothers' ears as something genuinely new and relevant, that is not what makes it *good* news. This news will manifest its goodness if it is proclaimed by someone who gesticulates with the goodness of Jesus Christ, with both visible and invisible gestures.

This news will manifest its goodness if we fulfill the second characteristic of the language of Jesus Christ, if we, like Jesus, speak as one human being to another, as one free person speaks to another, as one free heart calls out to another free heart. The whole Gospel is full of such personal calls to a freedom, which is free to say yes or no.

For, in liberating humanity from what we call its alienations, it sometimes happens that we alienate freedom itself such as it exists, such as it lives, such as it is concrete, in the heart of each person making up humanity.

The battle for freedoms is not a modern battle, though some of its episodes are taking place in our time. The way things stand for freedom today is that it is freedom that is putting the questions, freedom that is questioned, freedom that is put in question. This age assigns to the freedom of each one of us the same destiny that the age assigns to God.

I could start a whole new lecture on this point . . . but have no fear. I will only mention to you what in this context concerns you in particular.

In the past, youth enjoyed two different conventions with respect to time: a person had the likelihood of being able to enjoy the strength of being young and the probability of living into old age.

Today, these conventions have been broken: youth is shut out from

211

its freedoms from the beginning. The future no longer possesses its usual coefficient of possibilities.

Today, in the time that is ours and that could come to end tonight, faith is, as it has always been, a sign of contradiction, but its contradiction is timely, as it has always been. It erupts into the most immediate of our present-day events, because it bears witness both to God and to us by designating as God's sole dialogue partner, both in ourselves and in the world: our free heart.

Communist Hope and Christian Hope[2]

My sisters,

You have assigned me such a beautiful topic. It may even be too beautiful. If I weren't from the south, I would probably have stage fright. So, just in case, and without asking your permission, I brought along a nun to participate in our work this evening and to give us her help along the way.

This nun died a few years ago. I have good reasons for wanting to call on her help. As a matter of fact, even though I have never seen her, I feel as though I know her well, through her brother who is a strict Communist and holds important responsibilities in the Communist Party. He was never Christian, and he is to this day an atheist. He has spoken to me often and at length about his sister, and he loves her as such, but he also loves her as a friend whose faith, vocation, and even religious community he holds in respect.

He also told me, with deep emotion, that no one has ever understood him better than his sister. And so I too have turned to her during these last weeks as I sought, researched, and noted down things that we could speak about together today. And that is also why I turn to her at this very moment to ask her for clarity and sincerity of heart, which is what we need in order that this conversation unfold in truth and in love.

2. A talk given in Marseille at a regional meeting of the Union of sisters of hospital and social service, 1961. [In the title, and throughout the text, Madeleine distinguishes Communist *"espoir"* from Christian *"espérance,"* espoir being a human aspiration and espérance the theological virtue of Hope proper. The distinction can be rendered only periphrastically in English. — Tr.]

Under the banner of two different hopes, the Communist Party and the Church exist in the world, act in the world, and work towards a future for the world. For the sake of this future, they both strive to extend themselves universally through the world, to continue through time, to gather together people whom they teach, educate, and organize.

But their two hopes are essentially opposed, because they hope for mutually exclusive futures. Moreover, these two living organisms, these two universal, permanent, and combative bodies that constitute the Communist Party and the Church are intolerant of one another. They cannot coexist without opposing each other, and they cannot encounter one another without conflicts. Nevertheless they are by vocation condemned to encounter one another, because each of their members is required to go everywhere and to prepare wherever they go for the whole future.

If the Communist Party and the Church seem to be pulling the world in two different directions, it is because their partial or widespread coexistence will never raise merely practical or merely theoretical questions. Every question they raise always becomes both theoretical and practical because if, for them, hoping means waiting, it never means only waiting, as we say in the south. Even as we speak, both are working toward the future: they are preparing for it, accomplishing it, hurrying its arrival. For both of them, to hope means to be certain and to act with confidence.

The hope of one is inseparable from strategic action because its doctrine is a system of action. The hope of the other is an active love because its faith is nothing but the knowledge and know-how of love.

Moreover, I cannot speak to you about Communist hope and our own without speaking of it as a hope lived by people who are our neighbor. Now, when Communists are our neighbor, their hope can become for us either a temptation to despair or an occasion to hope more and better. It is a difficult subject, but it becomes simple the moment we highlight the words: *When Communists are our neighbor.*

Indeed, in 1961, the Communists are necessarily our neighbor; we need only look at a map of the world to be convinced. Whether we know Communists or we do not know them, no matter what sort of encounter we have with them, the true encounter between them and us takes place in the core of our being. This encounter is an inevitable consequence of our living of faith, of our living in the Church in this age. If this profound encounter with the reality of Communism did not take place in our being, all of our external encounters would remain superficial; they would be without Christian value. Indeed, our vocation to Hope is one with the Church's vocation and it is to be expected that countless Communist people should weigh upon us because they weigh upon the responsibility, upon the mission, upon the love of the Church.

We love Péguy's verses about the little girl Hope. They speak of very true things, but, let us make no mistake, the hope that we need to live in the presence of Communism cannot be a little girl. The little girl has to grow up. What we need in order to face up to the Communists is a hope grown into womanhood, the hope of a woman who loves, the hope of a woman who, driven mad with anxiety, leaves the city and asks the soldiers and the guards, "Have you seen the One my heart loves? Do you know where he is?"[3]

This hope must be strong, and it must also be true. What we owe to the Communists — and we owe it to them because they are our neighbor — is supernatural hope, the hope that God gives us, the hope that we must constantly beg from God. It is desire for God, passion for God, compassion for the world. It is made to take flesh in our heart. And there it gives birth to Jesus' own hopes, the hopes of God's passion and his compassion for all people and for each person.

You doubtless know better than I that faith in God rarely comes without a test of hope. It seems that, for the Lord, genuine faith cannot exist when certain things get confused; when we mix up what the Lord gives us as things that remain his and what he gives us as ours to keep; what will always be gratuitous and above us in his gifts and what we can make use of somewhat as if they were our property; what comes from him and what comes from man. He does not like it when we mix up faith and reason; he does not like for us to mix up God's hope and human hope.

Now, the great advantage of the encounter with the Communists is that sorting these things out becomes easy with them because they constantly force us to go back to what is basic in Christian life, insofar as they contradict it or threaten it. They don't worry so much about the details. Moreover, with regard to hope, they attack what is essential in it; but precisely for that reason, we are prompted to examine our hope and to live its reality to the full.

3. Song of Songs 3:3.

Communist Hope

The word "hope" [*l'espoir*] is too modest to express what the Communists wish for the future. It is also too weak. The French word "hope" [*l'espérance*] works better, but we cannot lose from sight even for a moment that Communist hope and Christian hope are two fundamentally different and opposed things.

The word "hope" applied to the Communists designates a human hope, a hope that concerns human objects. The word "hope" applied to the hope of the Christian is a reality that comes wholly from God, to which we do not as human beings have a right. It concerns a supernatural hope, a divine hope, a hope that is bathed in the very mystery of God's inner life.

We will not try in this context to understand the Communists' hope as you would a theory. We will not try to raise our awareness of it as you would for a political or economic program. I would rather we try to understand it in a brotherly fashion; to understand it as being the hope of our present neighbor, of people who are brothers with us in the present age. I would like us to understand it as the nun I just told you about understood it.

So what does the Communist, the brother that we often hardly know, hope for?

A Response to the Hope of the Poor

In practical terms, hope is a sort of hunger and thirst in man's heart. Afflicted by certain sufferings, certain lacks, certain privations, man's heart aspires to what would still this lack, this privation, and this suffering. Hope is like an answer or a promise that lies beyond his wildest dreams: the promise of satisfaction.

In the Communist Party, countless hearts harbor, call out to, and give voice to the hope of the poor. The very doctrine of Communism is an answer to this hope that many people live. It describes a future in which all the things the poor wish for will come about: a future that represents a certain happiness, because it represents the disappearance of that which causes the suffering of the poor.

Suffering, for the Communists, results entirely from economic sins, the commission of which is called inequality, injustice, and oppression. The Communist future is a future liberated from this economic sin. If, even without God, the world to come is supposed to be a paradise, it is because the world to come will be a world without poverty.

Hope for the People of the Future

The hope of the Communist Party is truly hope in the deep sense, because its members do not merely hope for themselves individually. Each person works towards its realization, dedicates himself to it, but does not expect to reap its benefits. Communists hope for others; they hope for a future for the people of the future. For those who would dispute this disinterestedness, allow me to cite a passage from Gorki: "He who works for the future must abstain from all things in the present."

Nevertheless, if Communism thus satisfies one of the aspirations of the human heart, we must not overlook the fact that it takes no care for the heart's other aspirations; that it goes so far as to suffocate them if these aspirations distract man from the only future for which he is supposed to hope.

Hope for a Love

In the Communist Party, I am convinced that love is often, if not always, the most powerful force motivating any particular Communist. Communist hope is hope for a love, a love that hopes for something.

I am too much aware how strange this affirmation sounds — not to take refuge behind the nun, the Communist's sister, whom I have been referring to over and over again. Indeed, it is only looking at things with a brotherly eye that we are able to understand the role of love that remains predominant in the actions, not of the Communist Party, but of the people who make up the Communist Party.

Even if, like everywhere else, there are among the Communists false brothers, people who in their membership seek their own interests, or else those who as they got older lost the primary objective they entered with, I maintain that most Communists became Communists only because they love human beings, only because they did not want to participate in that which causes needless suffering in the world. Because they did not want to participate in injustices that seemed to them remediable.

What their love hopes for is a world to come in which, because money no longer exists, we will never see children thirsting after a chance to go to school, a chance that never materializes. We will never see people working to produce goods that they themselves will never have a right to use. We will no longer see machines produce luxuries for some while they threaten the lives of others. In such a world, you could be a manual worker without being a slave, standing next to skilled workers who seem to receive the privilege of freedom as a matter of course. In such a world, you would no longer have to cry over needless suffering and you could take joy in pleasures that in our world are made for everyone but that, sporting price tags, have become the pleasures of a few.

It is with all of the joined strength of their collective hearts that the Communists hope for happiness. And if this happiness is of the economic order, founded on a better distribution of wealth, it is not for all of that a happiness comprised of material things. The absence of money, in fact, entails the loss of goods that are not merely economic, such as culture, a certain freedom, and a certain form of human flourishing. When we speak of such happiness, it is crucial that what we say be precise and properly nuanced.

The Communist hope, throughout the world, pulls countless personal hopes along with it: the hope that the day will come when what we suffer from will disappear; the hope that wears a different name, bears a particular desire, in each person's heart; the hope of the woman who says, "One day, there will no longer be any men whom work forces to drink"; the hope of the woman who says, "One day, there will no longer be wars that murder twenty-year-old kids"; the hope of the old man who obsessively scrounges and saves in order to survive: "One day, when you're old, you won't have to live under such tight reins." Each Communist hears in these various hopes an echo of his own suffering. Each sees his own misfortune identified and wiped away, identified as the true evil from which man must be liberated.

It is because so many personal hopes enliven and inspire the Communist Party's hope that it is a great hope. You don't have to look anywhere else for the cause of the spread of Communism, the cause without which all of the means set in motion by the Communists would be incomplete and ineffective — for this hope constitutes their proper impetus. This hope is what explains the unanimous fervor of the most insignificant militant, the one who hangs the posters, or the one who hands out flyers in every corner of the world. And this hope explains immediately some of the day-to-day experiences we might have: I ran into a Communist friend of mine on one of the last days of the year and said to her: "Now it is time to wish each other a happy new year. . . . Let's hope that it will be." She immediately answered: "It will most certainly be happy, because it will bring both you and me closer to the goal."

A Solid Hope

Human hopes, as a rule, are not impervious to doubt.

Christian hope is certain because faith is "the substance of things hoped for," and faith is certain.

Communist hope, too, banishes all skepticism. The Communist doctrine makes precious little use of the word "hope"; it affirms for its truth what it takes to be solid realities. But because this truth represents for them the response of hope to hope, we can speak of Communist hope.

If human hopes are satisfied by Christian hope, Christian hope is not in turn founded on them. By contrast, if Communist hope satisfies a certain longing of the human heart, it is because it is an extension of this longing, it flows from it.

Nevertheless, neither Christian nor Communist hope can be separated from human hopes: Communist hope because it stems from them, and Christian hope because it justifies, renews, and fulfills them.

What Do Communists Hope For?

Christians hope in God. Communists, for their part, do not hope in something small: they place their hope in the world that God created, though they themselves would deny it.

They place their hopes in the world of which humanity is a part, of which humanity is a product, with which humanity is in solidarity, outside of which nothing exists; in a world that has existed without God, a world that exists alone. World, nature, universe — any of these words would serve to translate what the word "matter" means to the Communists.

Indeed, I have met Christians who do not have as vast and deep an awareness of God and faith as the Communists do of matter.

We often find in the Communists a fraternal love for nature. For them, nature is good; she is the one who knows; she harbors within herself the secrets that science seeks to disclose. She is the one whose laws tend toward the fulfillment of life, whose laws tend irrevocably toward happiness. That is why, even when they are not themselves scientists, Communists bear a tender love toward scientists, since they are able to penetrate nature's secrets. The discovery and bringing about of the secrets of nature, ideologically speaking, interest them as much as the fulfillment of their own lives. Nature is a mother, and it is not she who causes human evil.

Moreover, to know the laws of nature is to know the laws of happiness; to apply them is to hasten the arrival of happiness.

Communists do not hope blindly, but according to laws, by applying laws, by means of which one can be sure to possess a certain effectiveness with respect to the future.

Moreover, if we wonder how the Communists hope and how they practice their hope, we will find that their lesson of hope is a lesson about the inner laws of nature.

For Communism, life, the whole of life, is an evolution, a continuous transformation. The engine of this transformation of all things, and of the entire world, is an internal battle raging deep within everything that exists; a battle that rages between that which is already living and that which must come to life; between that which was living yesterday and that which lives today; a battle between the forces of death and the forces of life; between generation and decay; between degeneration and growth.

Evolution and transformation thus follow along a broken line, through downward swings and upward surges, the line of a constant progress with respect to the fulfillment of each thing that is to come, a progress that each thing must serve. This is what is called the dialectic, and if this word seems a little out of the ordinary, it is common coin in the Communist milieu.

The history of each individual person within the history of all people, the history of man in conjunction with the history of all existing things, is governed by the dialectic. When applied to human realities, it takes on the name "historical dialectic"; it is the meaning of history, the scientific march of history; it explains history and can be applied to history. Whoever knows this law and subjects his activities to it can hasten the arrival of the future.

This historical force guiding humanity nevertheless has a dimension of choice: this is the peak toward which progress aims, the evolution of human labor; it has its own law, its own dialectic: this dimension is called the class struggle.

For Communism, the battle going on within all the things in the world becomes in human history the battle of labor. According to Communism, it is labor that has divided and continues to divide all people into oppressors and the oppressed, the exploiters and the exploited, the rich and the poor, the powerful and the vulnerable. It is the history of labor that endlessly splits humanity and every aspect of humanity in two: those among men who cause suffering and those who suffer. However — and here we touch on the culminating point of Communist hope — this suffering turns into the condition of possibility of progress itself, the distant but necessary condition for happiness.

Because this suffering always ends up becoming intolerable, those undergoing it refuse to tolerate it and they revolt, destroying the social order that crushes them; they initiate a revolution. For the Communists, history is thus a chain of countless cycles of oppression and revolt giving rise to one another. And this will go on until a state of total Communism comes to pass.

To the extent that we neglect the fundamental role suffering plays in the Communist worldview, and the profound significance of the class struggle, we will fail to understand the positions the Communists adopt in the face of various events. Nor will we understand the initiatives they take, which we often find outrageous. This concern to apply the dialectic to history, and to redirect circumstances into the current of history in order to provide them maximum effectiveness explains the various turnabouts of the Communist Party that can leave us bewildered and scandalized.

It is the Communist Party that safeguards and spreads the Communist hope. When we have not sufficiently grasped the nature of the Party, it is hard for us to avoid becoming either too timid or too bold with the Communists themselves.

The Communist Party is not a collection of people who adhere to the same program with the same enthusiasm. It is a veritable political body, a living organism, animated by a common spirit, set in motion by the same impulse; fitted out with the same reflexes, strictly organized and strictly hierarchized. This body requires the same characteristics of all its members. It wants them all to be bound back to the body and all open toward the outside, even to the point of self-sacrifice.

Its place of work is the entire world; it aspires to the whole earth and all of time. Its tools are human beings, and its goal is man. To make the future it remakes each person, by means of its education, its instruction, and its discipline. It considers itself the leader of the human race, and the proletariat represent a sort of chosen people. In effect, it is at once the leader and servant of the proletariat. Insofar as it draws into its activity the men it has attracted by its word, the Communist Party attaches new members to itself who, in turn, preserve and proclaim the Communist hope.

This political body, which so uncannily mimics certain aspects of the Church, represents for the Church precisely a counter-hope. That is because the Communist Party as a whole hopes in some*thing* while the Church as a whole hopes in Some*one*.

The Communist world hopes in itself. It breathes its own air. Even when it includes people who hope, it remains a finite and self-enclosed world.

If, for the Christian, the future is in the making, as it is for the Communist, the world represents for this future and this development something relative that God alone can sow with his eternity. The Church herself is altogether something relative; she continuously receives from God that which brings her continuously to be what she herself is.

Communism does not wage war against God, because you do not wage war against what doesn't exist; instead, it does battle with the faith in God that exists in each living person. It battles in particular against the aspect of faith that hopes, because the believer's hope distracts him from the only future for which Communism fights and works.

Body to Body

Before taking a look together at what represents the true test of our own hope among the Communists, I would like to turn again to our contemplative nun.

Certain of her flesh and blood union connecting her indissolubly to her brother, as we said earlier, she was also certain of a tragic contradiction standing between them: because he was a cell in a universal organism, in a universal political body; and because she herself was a cell in the universal body of the Church of Jesus Christ; and because these two bodies, having different natures, were irreducibly opposed to one another, contradictory and incapable of coexistence.

She, better than anyone in the world, was able to measure the breadth, depth, and drama of this contradiction. She knew that belonging to God, being *disponible* to God, for his service and his work, is what constitutes the unity of the Body of Jesus Christ. She knew that the unity of the political body of Communism was brought about by a spirit that was hostile, not to the God that it does not know and that it denies, but hostile to all faith in God that subsists within the human heart.

She knew that the scope of the Church's aspirations, the aspirations assigned to the Church by Jesus Christ himself, was the ends of the earth and the end of all history; but she knew as well that the Communist Party also aspired to working on the whole earth, and transforming every inch of it and all of humanity until the end of time.

She knew that the vocation of the Church of Jesus Christ was connected with the mission of evangelization and proclaiming the faith and spreading the faith and the Kingdom of God. She knew that the Church cannot live without speaking, but she knew just as well that the political body of Communism was diffusive by nature, diffusive and contagious, and that its contagion spread through words; and thus that it had to speak if it wanted to live.

She knew by heart and flesh that the Church requires those who give themselves to God through the Church to become authentic sacrifices, to be no longer anything but people offered up, expropriated of themselves. But she knew too that the body of the Communist Party requires of its members a self-denial that is extreme, that might often entail self-sacrifice, but might also entail the sacrifice of people who are unknown, indifferent, or sometimes even friends.

And above all, she knew that there is an implacable hatred separating God and evil, a hatred that the Christian necessarily shares. But she also knew that, for Communism, evil is whatever hinders the future, and that hatred is not only extended to evil but also to anyone who slows the future's coming or impedes work toward it. The Communist is obliged to hate people today for love of humanity tomorrow.

The Lord's two commandments: "You shall love the Lord your God; you shall love your neighbor as yourself," these two commandments formed so to speak a living contradiction, a dual contradiction between this nun and her brother.

The nun speaks of this contradiction with a loving truth, because though her life was publicly and solemnly given to God while her brother's was opposed to God, these two contradictory lives remained nevertheless radically fraternal through what they had in common in the blood of their veins, the tissues of their heart, in their form of character and in their memories.

You can't stop being brother and sister; of course, you may become divided in what you do, but you cannot divide what constitutively unites two people.

By the same token, when we as Christians deny by our actions the reality of our brotherhood with others, the brotherhood that each person joins simply by being born, then we are liars, as St. John says. We deny what God has created, and we deny what we ourselves are.

Conversion to Hope

In a sense, the Communists are a reminder to us that Christian life is a battle, because they call us to a battle that is essentially their own, and in which their hope condemns the very purpose of our conversion, our combat, and our work, to absurdity.

Their hope in a practical sense tests the certitude of our hope; it tests us to see if our hope is real. If our hope were merely a peacetime hope, a fragile and forgetful hope, we would go from retreat to retreat, from failure to failure, indeed, from ruin to ruin.

If we do not take care to examine our hope, we will become obsessed by the contradictions that disorient us and by the temptations that are unconscious because they are unforeseen. And the day will come when we finally succumb to them and take the proposed good as the real one, a good that outshines the treasure our hope had been set on, because we have to some extent forgotten what exactly it was.

It may happen that our ultimate temptation, whether it be ours or another's, will be to recognize in Communism a force that is stronger than faith. We would in this case give up for lost the people who live by this force out of fear of becoming lost ourselves. We would judge the Communists as being unworthy of receiving Christ's salvation, and would separate ourselves from them. And in this way we would claim to remain true to a faith whose hope we betray.

And too many recent events would seem to justify our conclusions.

But if, by contrast, we discern in each contradiction, opposition, and temptation a provocation to expand our hope, to hope more and better, our Christian life will recover, through the battle it was made for, its normal condition of vitality and growth.

Please note what I am saying: it is not a matter of seeing in Communist hope a sort of help for Christian hope. And even more so, it is not a matter of seeing in it a sort of complement or even less a corrective of Christian hope. I would rather say that it is by a sort of backlash that Communist hope leads us to reexamine our hope and to reexamine the realism of our hope.

This backlash compels us to reexamine what we had managed to forget as well as the measure of living credence we give to what we haven't forgotten. It allows us to become more faithful to a genuine hope and to become more realistic with respect to it.

Insofar as we have not in one way or another encountered people for whom faith has no plausibility whatsoever, or even more, people who have not heard about what faith has taught us, it is impossible for us to realize the aspect of faith that is essentially "unheard of," unheard of in the strict sense because it lies beyond the scope of human hearing.

Precisely to the same extent we thus lose sight of the fact that faith is a gift from God and that every life that stems from faith continues to be a gift from God; that faith has nothing to do with human aptitudes or with being well-meaning people. Faith is a divine reality that God reserves for himself.

The Realism of Hope and the Interior Life

The fact that faith and what comes from it are unheard of explains why, most often, the activity of eternal life in us offers so little foothold to our impatience or curiosity. The bottom of our soul does not have tangible images to hook into. What stands most sharply to view of God's work in us are the obstacles that we ourselves place before it. I have no experience of the religious life, but if women who are not nuns often have a taste for introspection and are not quite as good at simplifying what is complicated as they are at complicating what is simple, it is perhaps because, unless they did so, they would have the impression that the interior life did not exist.

Now, Christian hope creates within us a capacity to desire and to receive what by ourselves we would be unable to desire, receive, or even to recognize. Before we recognized the unheard of gratuity of faith, the interior life of grace was often for us simply the most precious part of our own life, a part "set apart," privileged, and in a certain sense autonomous.

The contact with Communists, and with atheists in general, shows us that the place of God's gift is the whole of what we are and nowhere else, that our whole being must become the living soil for his mysterious seed. We begin to discover that the interior life is internal to a life and, to the same extent, it is internal to all of the activities of that life. Hope is like the constant breathing of this life. We breathe in order to live. There is no particular age or hour for breathing. We don't quit breathing so that we can work.

225

The contact with the Communists and their materialism places life and all it means to them before our eyes and in our ears. Nothing escapes the unity of life, and this unity is always made concrete for them in action. We have to ask ourselves whether we have not taken the word "life" out of the Gospel, which can be found everywhere in it, without translating it into our Church.

Our Lord talked about a life; he did not speak of a program of studies you would have to take in order to pass an exam. He did not speak of a political system for organizing life in society; he did not speak of a philosophical doctrine contrived to give an objective view of the world. He did not even speak of a treatise on God devised to delight our minds.

He spoke to us of a life that, if we accepted it, would allow us to live by it. He spoke to us of a life in which knowing that God loved us and being able to love him in turn was one and the same; of a life lived by each person with all people, and with all people for God and by God. Could such a life possibly be less alive, less real, or less dynamic than the life on this earth, the life of the world, or the life of creation? And yet don't we often turn it into a routine program, a system of thought, or a philosophical doctrine? Or an inert contemplation of God? Let us take the fundamental realities of this life, its vital laws, and its organic functions, just as they are, for what they are, as unshakable realities that we cannot in any way change.

Do we have in relation to this life the same simple, practical, and direct certainties as when we don't think of walking any other way than with our legs, of picking up objects in any other way than with our hands? Do we have the same realistic reflexes that fill our daily lives whenever it is a matter of using the technology that science provides? When, for example, though we have never taken a course on electronics, we rely on an electric switch? Are we sure of the certitudes of faith, are we sure that faith is the applied science of a life and that it is the know-how of that life?

Now, to apply the laws of faith, to conform ourselves to the rules of its know-how, is necessarily to become converted. For these rules and this know-how run counter to our inherited inclinations, and they surprise — as they surpass — our natural habits and abilities.

Moreover, wherever there is conversion, suffering can be found. It would be worthwhile in this context to gather together all of the lines in the Gospel where the Lord sets the price of a person's returning to him. It is a "fixed price," never to be paid off; faith cannot be anything but a violent state for us. But if suffering clings to us, hope clings to this suffering;

whether this suffering be temptation, failure, rejection, or lassitude, hope gives it its true name and transforms it before our very eyes. Hope calls it conversion, that is, turning back to God, return to God, access to God.

For if hope plays a role that concerns eternal life, it does so already from time and within time. Its role is not to make us have patience, to live on earth while waiting for an eternity that's held in reserve beyond death. Even if hope aims at eternity, it hopes for the present, because that which it eternally hopes for already exists in its fullness. Christian hope hopes for Jesus Christ, hopes for God. What God was yesterday he still is today and will be tomorrow. And Jesus Christ has been raised from the dead forever. Hope, in our interior life, possesses an extraordinary activity and effectiveness. It allows us, by the dust of lowly battles, efforts, and labors, to transform the circumstances or events of our life into eternal events. We insert into salvation history the events that we were destined to accomplish.

The Realism of Hope and the Life of the Church

What we are trying to do is realize that, while we are on earth, faith places us in the heat of battle, a permanent struggle, a constant choice between Jesus Christ and that which in the world remains hostile to God; to do so is to accomplish within ourselves the Church's own vocation.

On the earth, the Church is made for fighting; by vocation, she wages war against evil; by mission, she stands on the front lines of evil; by office, she delivers from evil.

The Church's combat will never cease to be bloody: the frontiers she defends will never cease being attacked and the liberation she fights for is always violent. A realistic love for the Church necessarily entails taking your blows and living with bruises. Now, what gives the Church's combat meaning, what outlines the meaning of her history, is hope.

To march ahead, to multiply, to liberate, the Church must fight, with her eyes and her heart set on God's promises. Locally — or we could say physically — the frontier of the Church passes directly through each one of us. This is the line that divides good and evil; it is the line that separates the "with God" from the "without God," the "for God" from the "against God."

The place that Christian hope assigns to us is that narrow ridge, that borderline, at which our vocation requires that we choose, every day and every hour, to be faithful to God's faithfulness to us. While we are on earth, this choice cannot help but tear us in two. But hope never allows us therefore to fall to self-pitying. It is the suffering of the woman who is bringing a child into the world. Each time we are thus torn apart, we become as it were breaches in the world's resistance. We open up space for God's life to pass through. Nothing can carry us more deeply into the inner reality of the Church.

Christian Hope and Fidelity to Human Hope

If a heart is poor in human hope, it will have very little divine hope, even if it is a Christian heart.

The hope by which we hope for fidelity to Jesus Christ gives us — as a compulsory and constant citizen's duty — the goodness of Jesus Christ, which is the human translation of divine love.

No matter who the neighbor is next to whom we must live, no matter what activities we are involved in, or works or duties we have, they do not allow us to shirk the absolute obligations of goodness. We cannot hope for love without hoping for goodness.

Moreover, and no matter what variety of encounters with the Communists we may have, or what sort of complications they may entail, one thing remains certain and simple: we must do all we can so that, whenever they encounter us, they encounter Christ's goodness.

Often, when we speak about Jesus' heart, we use a vocabulary that we hardly ever use to talk about love, friendship, or affection. Perhaps it is safer to revise our convictions by rereading the words of the Gospel, in order to see and to hear the beating of Our Lord's heart. This heart, which is the *raison d'être* of our hope, is a heart overflowing with human hope.

We do not always notice that the Good News of the Gospel constantly crosses the Lord's lips in words addressed to the human hopes of the human heart. The Lord proclaims the eternal Beatitudes by appealing to those who weep and hope to stop weeping, who hope for peace, who hope for justice, who hope to escape from the extremes of poverty. These are the people he calls to Christian hope.

When we address ourselves to others, the Lord does not ask us to be any less human than he is, to betray human hope any more than he did. He is a God who is faithful to the hearts he created, and their vocation to divine hope is not a betrayal of their human hope. In his school, we learn to place our hearts in listening attention to the hearts of others, in order to hear their whispered hopes. We learn to recognize in these hearts the prefiguration of Christian hope.

We saw at length earlier what it is the Communists hope for: their hope, which is a magnification of certain great human hopes and a multitude of personal hopes, born in love, work, or suffering. If the Lord had come into contact with these Communists, he would at once have called them by name and appealed to their hopes. So too must we call the Communist that we know by his name and not by the name of his ideology or his Party, and we must appeal to the hope of the poor that dwells inside his own hopes; we cannot allow his heart to be foreign to us, and we cannot allow ourselves to become numbed to the evil of the world.

Is it possible to hope genuinely and decisively for the Redemption of the world without possessing a heart passionately determined to see an end to the injustices of the world and their effects, even if these are not all of the evil or even the cause of all evil? Is it possible to hope sincerely for the Redemption, with genuine, divine hope, and not at the same time hope for the cessation of all the consequences of the sins we call selfishness, injustice, and repression? Does the fact that the Communists aspire to revolution in the name of everything we have mentioned mean that we, for our part, have to participate in the suffering and sin of others?

When we learn to weep with those who are weeping over the death of a child who died for no reason; over a man who was crippled for no reason; over a man who has spent twenty years in prison for no reason — then we will have learned to hope, with a heart that resembles in hope the very heart of Jesus Christ.

Atheism and Evangelization[4]

I. The Distortion and Debilitation of Faith

In an atheistic environment, we ourselves undergo a distortion and debilitation of faith.

4. This text, which was composed in 1962 with the aim of providing information for Vatican II, was originally preceded by a study on *Contemporary forms of atheism,* which could not be included in this volume. Nevertheless, we present here that study's conclusion:

"*A silent atheism.* Next to the old French atheism, which was doctrinaire and professorial, and its raucous political, philanthropic, and even satirical variations, Communism has stolen the role of tenor, and forced all else to become background music. Its propaganda, which inspires some, has sown seeds of panic in others.

"But the atheism we encounter today is altogether different. For we have to realize that, in spite of what it says to the contrary, Communism is already becoming 'dated.' Of course, it still carries off victories, and no doubt will continue to do so. But its seed, its doctrine, and its initial inspiration are over. The various scientific discoveries that Communism shoves into the spotlight as representing its most up-to-date façade do not in fact belong to Communism proper. No matter how advanced or behind a particular nation may be, its scientific communities, which arise out of the research itself, are in their fundamental essence all strictly related.

"If the problems of class relations have had and maintained their importance amidst the problems of secularization and evangelization, in the new milieus it is the man-matter relation that ought most to occupy Christian attention. This relation has been forged in complete silence about God. By a strange act of substitution, creation has taken the place of the creator. And

230

The seeming abruptness of the secularization of certain milieus, the seeming collapse of the faith precisely where it needs to be proclaimed (in the Communist milieu, for example), and our seeming incapacity to evangelize atheistic, Marxist, and modern milieus, are three disturbing facts that tragically question Christian consciousness.

1. A Single Cause Stands Behind Each of These Three Facts and at Least in Part Explains Them: Namely, "Our" Faith Has Become Naturalized

In the milieus that Christians have occupied for generations, people have begun to confuse faith with a Christian mentality. In this mentality, the gratuitous gift God gives us — the gift of knowing who he is, the gift of acting according to his will, the gift of created life and eternal life, the gift of creation, and the gift of the saving Incarnation — have become a sort of innate property of the Christian stock, a sort of inherited good passed down through Christian families.

Slowly but surely, faith in God, a living faith in the living God, began to be mistaken for simple good sense, the good sense of believing in God. Slowly but surely, the Gospel virtues became and then were confused with the virtues of the well-meaning individual.

Hence the partial debilitation of a life of faith partially practiced but not exercised — in short, existent but not altogether living: the interior life became equated with the cultivation of personal gifts, no longer a vital and urgent striving after what God offers and *gives;* prayer is deprived of its

---

since it has happened in silence, we haven't been alerted to it. A fundamental danger has been noiselessly overtaking the Church: it is the danger of an age and a world in which God will no longer be denied or forced away, but simply excluded. He will be merely unthinkable. It is the danger of a world in which we will want to go and cry out his Name, but we will be unable to, because there will be no place for us to get a foothold.

"In discovering the laws that God has woven into creation, we learn how to 'create' as he does. Things pass at an extraordinary speed; each year seems to bear the weight of centuries of history. The eternal life that we have received in order that it may inhabit the world will be betrayed by us if we attempt to moor ourselves to that which stays behind rather than let ourselves be carried along by eternal life into the age that is ours."

foundation in adoration; Christ and his Gospel become less a source of life and more a savings account for life.

Hence, this Christian life, which has grown weak in some of its most fundamental characteristics, acquires a surfeit and overburdening of convictions and obligations that do not belong to it: attachment to certain forms of moralism, a commitment to certain political alternatives, an adoption of certain lifestyles and customs, which are all indifferent in themselves, but start to be taken for Christian duties and mistakenly equated with the life of faith.

2. The Debilitation of "Our" Faith and Dechristianization

Because we have confused faith with a Christian mentality, faith in particular has gotten formed in areas that have nothing to do with common sense and simple kindness. Education in the faith has become primarily a training in certain forms of worship, rites, and a practical "discipline" in the Church. And these areas themselves have been only insufficiently infused with the first sap of faith in God. Everything begins to take on human dimensions and value (obedience to the Church, for example, is reduced to a simple external discipline).

We slip from a realism about vital supernatural necessities, to the obligations that translate them according to place and time. Once the vital connection that binds these obligations to the necessities of faith has been severed, the obligations of "religious practice" fall prey to the whims of the prevailing mentality.

If the Christian modifies the convictions that he is in fact free to modify, but that he mistakenly took for faith, the obligations that were not based on faith will fall apart. The external expression of faith, even if it is perfect, becomes fragile in the extreme if the faith that it expresses is dead. Three years ago, a beautifully constructed dam in France was washed away like a piece of straw; no one knew why, until they discovered that the stone it was anchored to was completely decayed.

3. When Faith Is Faith, It Holds Firm

Faith seems unable to "hold firm" precisely in those places where it has to be proclaimed. The best-known example is that of the Communist milieus. The practical apostasies in nonbelieving milieus are legion but silent. They do not occur because of interaction with aggressively cantankerous doctrines. And thus they have not been flagged with caution signs. By contrast, in the Communist milieu, the breakdown of Christian lives, whether they are the lives of priests or laypeople, even though they are incomparably less frequent, have provoked severe warnings. That is because, in these cases, they were often Christians dealing with new experiences, promoting daring views on evangelization; their flight and their straying were contagious, and found reverberations, both painfully within the Church, and politically outside of the Church.

Just as Communism is able to bring countless people who are not Communists into its atmosphere, so too the Church has sought to extend security zones beyond the strictly Catholic-Communist contacts. Hence an incontestably legitimate "putting on the brakes" for evangelization. But what is baffling is that this "putting on the brakes" should have been legitimate in the first place. It is baffling that, for the sake of preserving the faith, we should be afraid of proclaiming it where it has not been proclaimed.

However, neither the Lord nor his Church is absurd: if the symptoms of a weakening faith are indisputable, it is because this faith is not faith. More precisely, it is a crippled and distorted faith, an adulterated faith that breaks down. The impact with an atheist milieu has not "destroyed" the faith; the faith that was sent in for battle with this milieu was one that was adulterated with natural beliefs and was attacked in its features that were so to speak naturalized.

For, when faith is faith, it holds firm. It holds firm, even while it suffers or is under attack. Like the Church while she is on earth, it is by nature "militant." In formerly Christian milieus, we became used to living the faith "in the barracks." Contact with atheism has led us back into battle — the battle that tests, the battle that calls for courage, in particular the courage to suffer, to suffer the very suffering of Redemption: being put to the test. But, to fight, you have to be in good health.

4. A Distorted Faith Is Not Ready for the Evangelization of Atheist Milieus

When we do not have a sense for "God's gift," the gift of his revelation, the gift of his life, we cannot have a sense for who the atheist is. When faith in God is confused with common sense, the atheist is confused with the "idiot" (I've heard such a name used). Thus, for the Christian, the atheist stands outside the sphere of the human. If he does not go so far as to diagnose the atheist with a mental defect, he nevertheless accuses him of, not an objective, but a subjective moral deformity.

Most often, the Christian "does not believe" the atheist, he does not believe in his possibility. In any event, it is only very rarely that a Christian understands what it means to be a man for whom God does not exist, a man who has not chosen things to be this way, but to whom things were shown and demonstrated to be this way. The Christian is, then, unable to get a better sense of the essential starvation this person suffers, a starvation that is often unconscious, the starvation of someone who "no longer feels his hunger," but who is dying of malnutrition in a whole dimension of his being. The Christian is unable to react to what he does not know.

Evangelization has always meant and will always mean proclaiming Good News. The Gospel is news for all of us, because it is the revelation of what man cannot know unless God tells it to him. But in atheistic milieus, this supernatural news has to be accompanied and reinforced by natural news, news that people should know but no longer know: that God exists — and that he is God.

Good news changes the level of happiness in a person's life, and this good news ought to be proclaimed by a reporter who is present, who can be heard, who speaks the language of his listeners, who speaks the language of Christ, who is the path of a real and true event, who is trustworthy, and who is credible because he shows integrity in the rest of his life.

An atrophied and adulterated faith is not a faith that is ready for evangelization. We are incapable of evangelizing to the extent that we no longer realize that we ourselves are evangelized, that we have received the good news, and that we have received it as a gift. If we think we believe something "naturally," we do not feel any obligation to proclaim it; we take it for granted that it is already known.

When we assimilate this faith to a mere "good outlook," it tends to get reduced in us to a human outlook; we are no longer able to propose it to others like people who have gratuitously been given a treasure and who want to share it. From being something indisputable, it becomes in the atheistic milieu something disputable, like a philosophical opinion. Our certainties are here and there called into question — the certainties of our faith as well as those of our outlook. And, here and there, we defend them; when the time comes for human discussion, we affirm absolutes; when the time comes for evangelization, we discuss ideas, but we do not bear witness with a life.

234

We do not proclaim the Good News because the Gospel is no longer news for us: we have grown used to it, it's old news. The living God is not an immense and overwhelming happiness; he is something we are owed, the backdrop to our lives. Happiness, then, is those changing superfluities outside of him who is permanent. We do not pause to realize what the absence of God would mean for us; thus, we do not realize what it means for others. We discuss an idea when we talk about him; we do not bear witness to a love that is received and given. We are unable to proclaim the faith to nonbelievers as a liberation from the absurdity of a world without God, because we ourselves do not perceive this absurdity.

We defend God as if he were our property; we do not proclaim him as the life of all the living, the immediate neighbor of all the living. We are not reporters of God's eternal newness, but rather polemicists defending a vision of the world that has to stay the same. Moreover, it would serve no purpose to be close enough to be heard, to speak the language of our peers, to be present and there for them, if, having fulfilled all these requirements, we ourselves had not discovered the total message that we have *received* and that we have to *pass on*.

II. The Testing and Reviving of Faith

1. Being Put to the Test

In an atheistic world, and especially in a Communist milieu, the Christian is one who is sorely tried, precisely in the measure that his faith is alive.

> *The Christian is brutally forced to take up his natural state, which is that of the Church Militant, namely, a state of war.*

He is put to the test by the aftereffects of the original temptation, tested in his mind and heart, tempted to hand over the reins of the fate of the world to human beings and leave God to rule his heaven, whether it takes the form of wanting to form the world *with* the Communists, and thus losing from view first God and then his law, or whether he wants to form the world *against* the Communists, and in the thick of the fight losing from view God's law . . . in the name of God.

He is tempted to betray the task God entrusted to man in creation,

235

whether by working with the Communists to discover in creation the destiny of humanity and its capacities for power, or by fleeing from the scientific investigation of creation as something foreign to the Christian mission or guarding against it as an area in which his faith is threatened.

He is tempted to forget that all human beings belong to God, to make God the God of certain people, whether by limiting "God's friends" to those who have a certain human outlook or who emphasize in the Gospel only what speaks in favor of the Communists, or by making the Christian God not the God the Christians proclaim but the God the Christians own, and thus one without a living connection to others. In both cases, it is a God human beings could live without.

His faith in the reality of the Incarnation of Christ, which is continued by the Church and by each member of the Church, is put to the test. He is tempted to lose the balance between the eternal life he bears within and the flowing of time that is a precondition for life, whether, in his fascination with the novelty of time, he wants to consecrate this novelty to God without making each event an "eternal event," or whether, intending to be faithful to God, he considers time "profane" or confuses eternity with permanence.

He is tried in the obedience and freedom that God wants from him, whether he makes his choices in function of a freedom that keeps in view nothing but the events, the circumstances, and the realities of the present human condition, or whether he makes his choices by withdrawing, by fleeing from the present human condition, because of a notion of man that does not evolve — that is, an ideal man that is no longer the man that God created.

He is tested in relation to the Redemption; he is tested with respect to being effective. People say to him: "What is faith good for?" He wants to give a brilliant response, to obey the imperatives of fraternal love with great panache: to feed, clothe, house, etc., but he risks losing from sight the work of redemption that is achieved not only through these acts of fraternal love, but also through self-effacement, but also through prayer, but also through the mystery of the trials that God gives us.

He is tested with respect to happiness and beatitude, tempted to work for happiness on earth, even tempted to work for a certain happiness that is not human happiness, and tempted to believe that the good will of individuals is enough for salvation.

He is tested with respect to the need for evangelizing, whether, seduced by the Communists or by others, he believes that good will is enough for salvation and that the task of forming the world has more urgency; or whether, in his passion for evangelizing, he begins to forget that evangelizing requires a proximity, a presence, an *a priori* of truthfulness, and the attitudes that Christ himself exhibits in his desire to evangelize; or even whether he begins to think that Communists or anti-Communists, whichever they may be, are un-evangelizable, and loses hope for them and thus loses his voice.

> *The Christian ought to know that, in this normal state of war, he has by virtue of office the means to see clearly and the means to fight.*

To see clearly — in other words, to be sure of whatever is certain and necessary. He ought to be convinced that the realities of the faith are beyond discussion: "You shall love the Lord with all your heart . . . more than all other things. . . . You shall love your neighbor as yourself. . . . Go . . . Preach the Gospel. . . ."

But he should be no less certain, and in the name of the faith, that everything that is not beyond discussion ought to be discussed, and everything that is not a permanent imperative needs to be chosen in freedom. He ought to know that everything that makes up our old way of looking at things, or everything that is a new outlook and draws us in, is relative and needs to be examined and revised in relation to love and evangelization that, for their part, are indisputable; that all of our other fidelities are tiny and relative whenever it is a question of fidelity to faith.

He ought to be sure of everything that is necessary. For example, prayer is necessary; this necessity gets translated into certain obligations. To the extent that we are free, we have to fulfill these obligations; but if they become impossible, we have the responsibility of finding a means of praying within our possibilities, but by all means praying, because prayer is necessary.

We have to, whether we like it or not, apprentice ourselves to the forces of grace, such as they are. In order for them to be of use to us, they have to cease being the "spiritual forces" we often take them to be. Instead, they must live in the most concrete aspect of our being. We learn that they take flesh in human aptitudes, that they correct even while they transcend them; that man redeemed by God, the new man, does not hover over the man that God created, but that the man that God created is the prime matter of redeemed

237

man; sinful man is the prime matter of the man who saves and is saved; the man who is evangelized is the prime matter of the man who evangelizes.

The realism of the faith cannot be a supernatural realism unless it is a natural realism. Faith is provoked by atheism to acquire its full dimensions: that of the human life that receives it and that of the divine life that it communicates.

An example: apprenticeship in fraternal love.

With the Gospel at our hand and temptation at our back, we have to learn once again what fraternal love is and how to live it . . . — the Gospel such as the Church presents it to us, such as she provides us with its indisputable imperatives that take precedence above all else.

Who is my neighbor? The Communists I know are human beings. Who is my neighbor? Every human being, the Communist human beings as much as any other. Without problems and without complications, I owe them — because I am Christian and because they are human beings — the love of neighbor such as Christ taught and showed to us, the love that God wanted to be inseparable from love of him. I owe them everything the Sermon on the Mount asks of me.

"You are all brothers." Among the Communists, the Christian will almost unavoidably undergo one of two possible temptations:

- either, personally attached to his Communist comrades because of the undeniable heroism that it is not rare to find among them, or more often because of the warmth, generosity, and brotherly way of acting that he meets in them, he will be tempted to lessen his love for those against whom the Communists are fighting. Another break with love: he will try to identify Christian intentions in them; thus he will drastically reduce love in the name of justice and peace; he may even, and for the same reasons, be tempted to commit some practical injustice.
- or else, as an enemy of Communism precisely because of his faith, or engaged against it in political battles, he will be tempted to refuse to call these people who serve as vehicles of Communism, who incarnate its action, by the name "brother." Sometimes, in order to do harm to their Communism, he will be tempted to harm their personal life; in order to mistreat Communism, to mistreat them; he will

at least be tempted to turn away from the concrete people named Peter, Paul, or James under the general rubric "Communists."

Whether these temptations remain dryly intellectual or whether they include, as they most often do, an emotional component that is difficult to control or master, they represent for us an extraordinary lesson about the divine dimensions of love. Often, if we find it very easy to love all human beings, it is because we have purely and simply ignored the existence of many of them.

A sinner loving other sinners

If the Christian manages to avoid all of these temptations, he will encounter others; they may seem to be opposing temptations, but in fact they are two sides of the same coin.

For one person, the temptation will be to be taken in by the Communists' "virtues"; he will think that his witness consists in matching them, in proving a Christian is capable of it. Because of his admiration for them, he will want to imitate the self-denial of some, the disinterestedness of others, the gift of self, and the striving after a human race with less suffering. *Against his will*, because it is against his heart, he will be forced to discover the prejudice, a term that is hardly appropriate for so many sincere and costly acts, a term to which only an ideological category and a faceless humanity deserve. He will also have to discover the corruption of the human heart that is inseparable from such acts: a hypertrophied heart, beating at double speed for the hopes that are genuinely human, hopes that have been stirred to a mighty pitch through propaganda, campaigns, and meetings, a hope for the poor that for us should be sacred; an atrophied heart, a whole and crucial part of it tranquilized: freedom, personal love, fidelity. This Christian will learn all over again that love cannot be admiration without being compassion. He will learn that, in our time on earth, love cannot be anything more than the love of a sinner for a sinner.

For another Christian, the temptation will be to be "disheartened" by these very corruptions, to become fundamentally antagonistic towards the ones who have been affected by these corruptions. This Christian will thus have to learn to see in his neighbor the mark of the same sin that has wounded all of us. He will have to accept, in order to receive fraternal love, to be someone who has been forgiven, not someone who is innocent. He too will have to understand that it is only through charity that we, who are sinners, love other sinners.

Of course, we should already have learned all of these things from our instruction in the faith. But on this point, as on so many others, our instruction was a cold account rendered of an uncontested fact: we were people who were saved before we even knew we had been lost. It didn't bring us joy because we didn't previously have any anxiety.

The lesson of things concerning fraternal love and all the other lessons received in an atheistic milieu make us penetrate more deeply into what we had learned. But, by the same token, we understand that, for the nonbelievers that we meet, if this teaching is separated from the proclamation of a life, from the revelation of a life, of a life in which God exists and which exists through God, it cannot be evangelization; if this teaching is reduced to itself alone, it even risks sterilizing the seed of evangelization in Christians.

Let me add, finally, that the temptations that arise from the Communist milieu present us with the obligation to understand better what it means to be part of the body of the Church, to exchange our passive discipline for a living obedience; to learn that her living substance, her flesh, is the mutual love among Christians.

2. Evangelization

To avoid all misunderstandings, let me specify in what sense I am using the word "evangelization," in case this sense happens to be inadequate or incorrect. What I mean by "evangelizing" is telling people, who don't know, who Christ is, what he said, and what he did — so that they do know.

It is not a matter merely of giving the witness of a life, but of speaking explicitly to those people who may already have heard some things about Christ, about what he did and what he said, but who have not heard or understood in a human manner, in order that they may know what we believe and what we are sure of.

It is thus not a matter of catechumens, and even less of neophytes. It is a matter of people, whether they are baptized or not, who have not yet been evangelized, who do not know what a person who believes, believes. It is thus a matter of those of whom St. Paul said, "How will they believe if we do not preach the Gospel?"

The things that characterize this evangelization are: to have as a rigorous plan of action the nothing more and nothing less of the Gospel message; to give preference to a realistic assessment of possibilities and paths of evangelization such as they present themselves in the actual conditions, circumstances, and events of life, over all other plans, strategies, and methods.

For many of us, the Lord's "Go!" consists in transforming our lack of relationships with those in our neighborhood into a genuine intimacy with genuine neighbors; to make use of the paths that the Lord prepared before inventing our own; to take as a program of action the one that plans for everyday occasions. It is an evangelization that takes place here and there, dictated by events and circumstances, demanding a very humble and docile attention, ready to be carried further and brought to term as much as to be interrupted, and entrusted to others in the hope we have in God who is faithful.

The Communist speaks — he is even generally the first to speak — whether about public or about personal matters. He talks about faith and about his faith, whether in order to attack the faith of others or to propose his own. He is not indifferent to the God in whom we believe, even if he wars against him as the most horrific lie of the spirit. Even if he is interested in God only to get rid of him for us, even if, for him, this God is not at all God, the "God" question remains for him a pressing question. If God were altogether dead and gone, there wouldn't be any reason to kill him.

An evangelization that evangelizes us.

In the Communist milieu, there is no place for any separation between the Christian life and the apostolic life, there is no place for any distrust, in practice, of apostolic activity because of a fear that it could become parasitic on the interior life. Everything is bound together by internal necessity: "Woe to me if I do not preach the Gospel," but also woe to me if I too am not evangelized in the process.

Communism is the doctrine of an action. According to its philosophy, it strives to be a living entity that is organized for action, an entity that acts. It is an anti-idealism; it accuses us of being idealists who negate life and harm it. This accusation carries with it a temptation formidable enough to unseat some of us. But if, instead, we take it as an instigation to examine and renew our faith, we will come to see to what extent faith, too, is a realism, to what extent we have turned into the theoreticians and ideologues rather than the livers and knowers of a revealed life.

241

All we can do is proclaim the faith in all its truth and all its realism, and in proclaiming it we have to be reconverted to it ourselves.

Communism recognizes dialectic as the fundamental law of all forms of life, of its development and evolution, that emerges out of a constant battle between successive life-forms. The life-forms are destroyed one after the other in order to make room for the new ones coming into being. By taking this law of life as humanity's own law, Communism seeks to submit itself to it, not only to understand its history, but to live it out. This efficacity in the world is precisely what attracts people to Communism, both those who are young and those who are no longer young. But even in this case the temptation can serve to urge us to rediscover the foundations of our faith, and perhaps even its fundamental law.

It was neither Marx nor Lenin who proposed to human beings the law of life and fruitfulness, the law of eternal life sown into a world in rebellion against God, the law of the fruitfulness of redemption: "Unless a grain of wheat falls to the ground and dies. . . ."

The Cross, of course, does not thereby turn into a counterpart to the Communist dialectic, but rather the dialectic becomes for us the piercing call of the Cross.

The Communist milieu and the conditions for evangelization.

In the first place, evangelizing means telling something to someone. In order "to tell," you have to be there. In many cases, our contacts with the Communists come about as a result of meetings that they call for the sake of a common public action or stand; these meetings are almost always the sort the Church's directives intended to proscribe. It is worth pointing out that, even if, for a particular or local reason, the Church's proscriptions should or could be relaxed here or there, such meetings would be mediocre opportunities for evangelization, and almost always difficult and ambiguous.

On the other hand, we have to emphasize the fact that the normal occasions for evangelization, the daily contacts that occur at home or work, in relationships with friends and family, the occasions that present the possibility for the simple practice of the Gospel are the best and entail no risk of disobeying the Church.

Nevertheless, the various traffic we in fact have with the Communists places us within speaking distance of them only if we not only treat them as our neighbors, but even more so if we become theirs. To be their neighbor in the first place means not avoiding them. To be their neighbor means being someone who exists, whose existence is manifest enough to be recognized; not being someone stuck inside himself. To be their neighbor means that the life they have noticed in us has a certain substance, that we carry the weight of someone who strikes them as an "authentic human being": someone who is capable of doing something well, seeing it through to the end, a person who is spontaneously aware of the same events that they themselves are interested in, events that affect people, from an individual losing his job to a public catastrophe, from the collapse of a mine to the war in Algeria.

In the face of such events, what makes us an "authentic human being" in their eyes is less our line of action or our choices, even if they diverge from theirs, as the intensity of interest driving us: the intensity of this interest, the priority that we give to others in the general shape of our life, and the things that we genuinely do for other people.

An authentic human being is one who does not hide what he thinks, who does not give in to fear, especially the fear of confronting what others deny by what he believes.

Speaking and being understood.

Even within hearing range, it is not enough for people just to listen in order for what we say to be heard and understood — in the full sense intended in the phrase "understanding a language." The first, and relatively easy, prerequisite is that we talk about everyday realities when we speak with them, in words that are not foreign to them; in this case, it's a matter of sticking with plain words that are appropriate and letting go of all the others.

But we have to realize that the transparent language of some of the simplest passages in the Gospel cannot at first be translated to the Communists. The whole Gospel comes from God and goes back to God and it is precisely the word "God" — and everything it implies — that not only becomes what is *"untranslatable"* once again in the Communist milieu, but moreover comes to mean *the opposite* of every representation of God, even the most human. In order to evangelize, this "untranslatable" word has to be delineated, gradually approached, brought to bear, and felt to be a presupposition. We have to bear witness to it by the whole way we live our life, by our choices, by our actions that imply the presence of Someone who is invisible but alive, intangible but at work.

We also have to be aware of the rigidity of the doctrinal vocabulary by which the human foundations of a "belief in God" are generally expressed. This belief has often been expressed to us in a dead language, or more specifically, in the language of people who have been dead for a long time, a language that lacks the words to express the signs of God that we find in the world today. Herein lies a whole humble work of the mind that is indispensable for evangelization, and that God leaves to us as our own task.

To evangelize is to be a reporter, to announce news to someone. News in the sense of "the latest news," in the sense of a "current event," and not a lesson of history. Evangelizing is not simply talking about something that happened, but something that is happening right now, something that is playing a role right now in the events of the world, something that concerns each of us because it concerns the world. Just as news about a new treatment for cancer would reduce the horizon of human fears, just as a new trip into space broadens the scope of human life, just as an averted war reestablishes the world's equilibrium, so too what is at stake in this news is the very meaning of life.

It is news that people may have some hesitations about, but that they would be uncomfortable denying because they know the reporter — when they know he has integrity and does not go in for silliness in everyday life, when this reporter presents himself as a witness of the event he announces, when the news he announces affects the witness's own life, news that has greater affinities to "discoveries about life," than to a philosophical dissertation.

The reporter, the Christian, is a person who, like everyone else, is committed to the exploration of the cosmos, to making use of it for the sake of humanity, passionately involving all of his intelligence and all of himself in human work, for the progress of the human race in the world.

But the reporter is a person who is bounded by Mystery, a mystery that lies beyond the grasp of reason, a mystery concerning the destiny of the world, of humanity, of each human being, the fundamental mystery of the why of life and the why of death; for the Christian, for the reporter, the "why" is a "Somebody," transcending all things because he willed all things and made all things; this Somebody revealed himself to man, explained to certain human beings the law and the purpose of life.

This Somebody is as alive as he is powerful, as powerful as he is alive;

he loves as much as he knows all the things that he made. Through Christ, this Somebody explained to man the whole science of eternal life. He remains responsible for the world and for all men, in life and in death.

Moreover, this Christian is a reporter only because, while he is in this world, he remains God's student. He has learned from God the laws of eternal life that germinate, grow, and blossom from birth until death. But, because he is Christian, he is specifically responsible for the germination, the growth, and the fruitfulness of eternal life in humanity; he must proclaim these fundamental laws of life to every living creature, he must live them himself, and live them for all those who reject them, through the willing gift of the life that is his, the gift of his life or the gift of his death. He thereby acquires an irresistible weight — such is the mystery of God's dialectic! — in the eternal destiny of humanity as a whole.

This news is proclaimed in human language, and yet Christ's own language is indispensable: this language is the one Christ speaks through us, that we speak in his name to every person we meet, to this person whom we call our neighbor.

To explain what it means to be faithful to this language of Christ will form both the introduction and conclusion of this brief text. It could serve just as well to introduce or conclude any other text that dealt with any possible form of evangelization: the language of Christ is the language of a good and brotherly heart.

III. Conclusion or Introduction: Goodness of Heart and Fraternal Evangelization

When the Holy Father proclaims to us the Gospel.

Even when they live with us, it is clear that nonbelievers are capable of completely failing to see the fundamental lines of faith in Christ and the imperatives of his love. We may sometimes want to blame ourselves for this, or more often, to blame others, but that does no good. It is also no great help to call for interior revolutions so that we might seem pure in the eyes of others and in our own.

It would be assuredly less noisy and perhaps more effective to take up a simple and peaceful reexamination of our faith; to discern its fundamental lines and the imperatives of love. Because it is sad and painful when people can no longer see these in us. But it is even more sad and painful when we cease to live them, because we have lost sight of their priority or urgency.

I will mention in this context a recent and particularly pertinent example of such a reexamination of faith. If I cite it as something that struck me personally, there are no doubt many others who would say the same.

The Holy Father had been the Holy Father for only a few weeks. Among the first public acts that the press took notice of, some were the simple putting into practice of Christian goodness, what the ancient tradition called "works of mercy." Brief speeches accompanied these acts. They served to remind us in few words of a specific point in the Christian ABC's. Other points of the ABC's were recalled in other acts and other speeches.

It became as clear as black and white that if, for many of us, goodness was in principle — and it is indeed a somewhat neglected principle! — an intrinsic part of the Christian life, what we had been calling goodness was no longer the goodness of Christ. It was scarcely even human goodness; it was being hindered by "good" reasons that were keeping us from being good, for one reason or another. By showing us the Gospel, the Holy Father reminded us, without blaring it over the loudspeakers, that wherever goodness is absent, there can be no Christian love.

The devaluation of human goodness — the devaluation of the heart.

In France, one need only see the downward fall of the word "good" in the current vocabulary in order to recognize the devaluation of goodness as a human reality. For people in general, goodness is being replaced by other values: people speak gladly of "solidarity," and especially of "effectiveness"; both of these terms will find willing supporters. The noble cause of goodness, however, has few takers these days.

And even where it is still tolerated, goodness has turned into something of a two-edged sword: they love these people at the expense of those people; they help these people and neglect or run right over those people. Instead of goodness, we have the "good" measures that society implements for society. These measures genuinely fight against suffering and help to alleviate it. But for all of that they do not replace goodness. Otherwise, the person becomes number 99 of category Z, promised aid by paragraph A of form 7.

In Christian circles, goodness has often slipped down the ladder of good mores; it is no longer inseparable from love. When the "new mentalities" take the place of the old, goodness gives way to fancier things, namely, the solidarity or effectiveness we spoke of before. We were, for good reason, warned against the sort of goodness that tends toward sentimentalism or activism, rather than love; however, because of this, we have sometimes, or maybe often, forgotten that if it is possible to have goodness without love, you can never have love without goodness.

Another devaluation that is occurring at present is that of the heart. What is more popular than the heart is anything that contradicts its freedom in practice: the unconscious or the subconscious, heredity, "depth psychology," etc. The heart is banished to the shelves of Harlequin romances, and what it becomes there scarcely resembles what it is.

If the heart is absent from the Communist teaching, it is no doubt the most crucial factor in its action. As we suggested earlier, the human heart often recovers in Communism the "functions" that it no longer has in people who have fallen into indifference or passive atheism.

The Communist dedicates himself to other people, he sacrifices himself for others. He is capable of relinquishing all personal ambition for the sake of what he sees as the good of others. For his sincere desire to help, he is capable of paying the price of his affluence, his security, and even his freedom and his very life. The nature of his atheism, which is a "pseudo-religious" atheism, preserves for him a sense of the absolute that is lacking in the atheism of the indifferent and others. He still has "ears that hear," because his heart is constantly called upon, it has not fallen into a deaf sleep.

But, as has also been said, Communism twists the heart out of shape: it hypertrophies the aspect of the heart that concerns certain goods and certain evils, certain tasks, and certain events; it exalts the hopes of the poor, not necessarily always beyond their due, but to the neglect of other hopes; it atrophies fundamental aspirations of the human heart; it tranquilizes and puts to sleep that aspect of the heart that is a rock of waiting and hope; it suffocates the personal feelings, fidelity, and love within the heart; above all, it imprisons the freedom of the heart; finally, like all other forms of atheism, Communism isolates the heart: everything in man that was made for the encounter with God becomes in atheism, and therefore in Communism, a zone of solitude. (These observations need to be nuanced according to the rich diversity of people within Communism.)

But the heart of a Communist remains a human heart, made by God and for God, capable of hearing God's call, of loving God, a human heart that is always already surrounded by God, unconsciously in contact with the God it denies.

The goodness of the heart that comes from Christ and is given by Christ allows the believing heart a foretaste of God himself. It gives the nonbelieving heart the unfamiliar taste of God and awakens it to the possibility of encountering him. It is something strange for the nonbeliever, something linked to the absolute strangeness that God represents for him. It reawakens and questions the drowsy forces of his heart — forces that are unknown to him but whose living reality he feels. It has an innate sympathy with what in the heart of the nonbeliever is at once the loneliest and the most ready to turn inwardly, secretly, toward the possibility of God.

The goodness of heart, the language of the Gospel.

The Gospel is truly proclaimed only if the Christians proclaiming it strive with all their might to have a good heart.

For, even in the midst of a world populated with good people, the goodness of a heart converted to Christ does not resemble other forms of goodness. The goodness proper to Christ does not allow place for our creative contributions until we have fulfilled its laws, which are strict and precise. It demands that we love no matter whom, all the way to the end, and no matter when it may be. It accepts no good excuse for not being good. And this "no matter who" must be for us the Peter or Paul that he is for the James or the John that we are, because this "no matter who" has to have for us the unique and irreplaceable value that he has for God.

Love for the other is brotherly and it cannot be anything else. We *are* a brother in creation and redemption with every other living person. This is a fact. Living it is another fact. This fraternity *primes* all other human relations. It does not matter in the least whether our relations with each other are flesh and blood, of affection and friendship, of society or neighborhood, we will always remain brothers in origin and in salvation. This is a fact: and now we must live it.

When we practice a love that arrogates to itself the right to mother, teach, and correct others, we slip away from the solid ground of reality: we are no longer brothers.

When love meets a nonbeliever, it becomes evangelization, but this evangelization cannot be other than fraternal. We do not come, in our generosity, offering to share something that belongs to us, namely, God. We do not come as righteous among sinners, as people who hold diplomas among the uneducated; we come to speak about our common Father, whom some people know and others don't; as people who have been forgiven, not as innocents; as people who had the fortune of being called to believe, to receive the faith, not as if it were a good that is owed us, but as something that has been deposited in us for the sake of the world: and this entails a whole manner of being.

Only a converted heart can be a brotherly heart.

The Gospel is not truly proclaimed unless the evangelization reenacts between the Christian and the others the heart-to-heart of the Christian with the Christ of the Gospel. But nothing in the world will give us the goodness of Christ except Christ himself. Nothing in the world will give us access to the heart of our neighbor except the fact of having given Christ access to ours.

Only a converted heart can be a fraternal heart, fraternally good, the translator of the good news. Christ takes it upon himself to teach us personally what is at once the condition for and the sign of the conversion of heart, which is something we can learn and receive only from him: *humility* and *meekness.*

Without humility and meekness, a fraternal heart cannot be properly Christian, possessing a Christian evangelization and goodness. This is the humility and meekness that heals in us the original pride and rebellion. Without them, we would be unable to be God's true creatures and docile children. Without them, we might perhaps be able to treat other people *like* brothers, but they would not be *our brothers,* for us and for real.

What we are but have to become: a universal people of meek and humble human beings.

This is what the "race" of Christ is, but it must nonetheless constantly come into being, and each one of us must surrender ourselves to Christ so that he may bring us into conformity with his people. Being faithful to the lineage of Christ is the very front line of our battle with the world. Often, we locate our fighting elsewhere: it is hard for us, not to fight, but to fight without grandeur. However, when a Christian takes upon himself Christ's living signature, nonbelieving hearts take notice.

To support this affirmation, allow me to refer to an experience I once had, one of the events that, had there been space, I could have used to "pepper" every paragraph in this text. I had worked for a long time with a particular Communist. He was tiresomely faithful to his convictions and loyal to his party. He had no Christian past, and no Christian memory. One day he said to me, "I once knew a Christian whom I will never forget. He was an extraordinary man: he took to heart everything that happened to other people; he never spoke about what happened to himself; he never defended himself when people tried to do him harm."

I do not know who this Christian is. But I have thanked God and I continue to thank God for him. And I ask God to make me like him, me and many others.

People of Good Will[5]

After reading the encyclical *Pacem in Terris,* many of us asked ourselves, "How can we recognize who is a person of good will? How do we keep from being fooled by appearances?"

The question is not easy. I intend here simply to lay out some of the reflections the question suggested to me.

People of good will are strewn invisibly over the earth. Good will is itself invisible. It lies within our space of inner solitude wherein God alone can penetrate and see. The person created by God is a person of good will. Sabotaged by sin and repaired by Christ, he remains a potential person of good will until he dies, a person able to say "yes" to what God proposes to him to be good, to what *seems* to him right, and *seems* to him good. Some people are required to say "yes" or refuse it in every hour of their lives; others perhaps just once, in the flash of an instant.

The visible acts of good will are not infallible indications. You can have brilliant and noble acts of good will; or tiny and common ones. In these acts, the good will seems to us evident, tangible. But, in the face of lies, deceptions, acts of oppression, acts that wound, and acts that commit evil and are evil, we are tempted either to deny the person who commits them any good will at all, or to want to know nothing about it either way, excusing the acts with a comfortable ignorance.

But in either case we would be wrong.

5. An article for *Le Journal de la paix,* February 1964.

251

We have the possibility of knowing whether the external actions of a person are good or bad, and we have the obligation of treating them accordingly. However, the best of a person's actions give only imperfect evidence of his good will; and the worst give only unclear witness against it.

By being the true neighbor of our neighbor, we are able to catch a glimpse of what is visible in good will. We are unable to love others decisively unless we know who they are, unless we know to some extent what it is they *know*. We thus come to see that, for many people, the circumstances of their lives were teachers of lies whose bad lessons were never contradicted. We come to see that some people have had their consciences educated, filled, and formed in such a way that with complete certitude they call a good thing bad and a bad thing good. We come to see that others have been trained from the beginning only to see one aspect of things, one side of the world, one slice of life, and that this habit has become in them a loss of vision.

Christ gave us his good truth, his good news, but he did not give us a monopoly on good will. When a saint passes by, lightning bolts explode across the human sky. We, on the other hand, are the flickering lights at the side of the road. The saint knows that he is our brother in weakness. He cries out to God and receives from God the strength to do the truth of God.

Realizing that we are sharers in the common human weakness allows us to have a foretaste of good will and to become, perhaps, at the heart's threshold, a sign of Christ's love.

PART FIVE

WHAT IVRY TAUGHT ME

The Atheistic Environment as a Situation Favorable for Our Own Conversion, 16 September 1964

We call attention to the title of this last public lecture that Madeleine gave, which sums up her whole testimony of hope in a single line: "The atheistic environment as a situation favorable for our own conversion."

The following is the impression she made on the person who organized the meeting:

> *"As I recall, our friend spoke about the similarities between death and faith. I can still hear her saying, 'We enter faith in the same way we enter death: alone.' Without minimizing the communal aspect of faith, she insisted:*
>
> "'You have to know how to be alone with God in order to make a community. It is like a forest that is beautiful if each tree is strong and has powerful roots — and these roots are alone.'
>
> *"Madeleine Delbrêl won over the audience, made up of some forty young men and women. A few days later, she wrote to me to tell me how much the meeting brought her back to her own youth, which is as alive as ever. And I could tell from the remarks of some of the audience that she had made a deep impression on them. They said that what struck them the most was the reality of her faith, which was*

stronger and had more integrity than the emptiness of atheism.

"And I haven't said anything about the charm that radiated from her and her words. . . ."

One of the most constant things in Madeleine's life was the horror she felt for death. It did not in the least shake her faith, but it was for her a physical repulsion, something literally unbearable. Though she never put it in these words herself, I believe that, for her, death was the deepest disorder that sin brought into the world.

In the text she composed at seventeen, *God is dead . . . long live death!,* as well as in the poems *(The Road)* she wrote in her twenties, the sense of the absurdity of death underlay everything.

Since she was a convert, the Resurrection was an even stronger source of life, but even so, she remained her whole life long deeply wounded in her flesh: it was not a fear, or a personal anxiety, but an understanding that "life itself is afflicted by death," and every death she experienced reminded her of this.

When she learned of the fatal accident of Paul Xardel, a priest from Brazil that she knew, she wrote to one of the priest's companions (two months, in fact, before her own death):

"All I can say is that I *understand* in the deepest core of my being what this trial means to you. Since I myself have absolutely no affinities for death, I was just saying last night to L., 'How strange it is that, after thirty years of living together, not a single one of our group has died. When I think about it, I feel incapable of bearing the death of a single one of them. It is hard enough for me to keep from hoping that I be the first. It's no doubt the woman in me who says that, but it's also my poor heart . . . and the strongest of men have such a heart too!'" She wrote this the 22nd of August, 1964.

On the 13th of October, in the space of less than fifteen minutes, Madeleine Delbrêl died while writing at her desk.

And so begins the spreading of her message.

"We are not the first people ever to have the mission, as Christians, to break in a 'new age.' Others before us had to tread unknown soil without being able to imitate a precursor or companion. But God will always be a father . . . if necessary, he will send us guides . . . as well as the grace to recognize them. . . ."[1]

It is our conviction that God prepared Madeleine during the thirty years before the Council in order to be, after the Council, one of the guides of the Christian vocation that is both new and old.

She reminds us of three things:

— *Remaining in the world entails certain dangers:*
"We might have the normal Christian life topple under the hypertrophy of the apostolic sense, the apostolic life wither from an exclusive focus on one particular mission, the missionary life become emptied out by an obsession with being present to the world, or being present to the world become eclipsed by the worldly vocation."[2]

— *We possess the remedy and the secret of action:*
"The first of our tasks in time is to know God as much as possible, in order to glorify him as much as possible and to compensate as much as possible for our neighbor's lack of knowledge of him.
"If we are fully convinced of this first temporal duty, I think we will be able to confront all the rest of our temporal duties without unbalancing our supernatural life: for these duties carry us implacably deeper into the first and second commandments that the Lord gave us."[3]

1. "What Ivry taught me," p. 268.
2. "In the wake of a decision from Rome," p. 153.
3. "Light and darkness," p. 193.

—*And thus there is nothing in human life that can remain foreign to us:*

"When we learn to weep with those who are weeping over the death of a child who died for no reason; over a man who was crippled for no reason; over a man who has spent twenty years in prison for no reason — then we will have learned to hope, with a heart that resembles in hope the very heart of Jesus Christ."[4]

4. "Communist hope and Christian hope," p. 229.

The Atheistic Environment as a Situation Favorable for Our Own Conversion[5]

I generally don't have any hang-ups about talking to people "with an education," as they say in Ivry. But whenever I have to deliver to such people anything that resembles a lecture, I am assailed by all sorts of anxieties. Luckily for me, my Gascony character keeps me from succumbing to shyness, which would be altogether unlike me. So here we go.

Thank you for not having given me a topic with the word "Communism" given "top billing." I never liked those kinds of topics. As a matter of fact, despite its being so much in the news lately, Communism itself is not new. If it is laden with fruits, it is still a hundred-year-old tree.

Anti-religious (more than a-religious), simplistic, dogmatic, propagandist, and noisy as it may be, apart from the countries in which it continues to rule, contact with Communism merely gives us the basic training needed to confront the more severe encounters with the contemporary forms of atheism: namely, the practically materialistic, technological, and scientific atheism.

But you have asked me about the spiritual lesson I have learned at Ivry. For this lesson, Ivry was my school of applied faith — for thirty of the sixty years of my life. In this Marxist city, my teachers and trainers were the living relationships I had with Communists, and so to address this topic I will necessarily have to speak of them. Nevertheless, I would point out that the lesson I received at Ivry goes far beyond the questions raised by Marxism.

But I have another and more serious reason to talk about them:

5. This last lecture was given to a group of students, 16 September 1964.

258

More than any other form of atheism, Communist milieus have been marked out as being particularly dangerous and even unsuitable for the life of faith. Of course, this shouldn't surprise us, given the painful and far-resounding events that have occurred in the relations between Christians and Communists — these breakdowns have made more noise by themselves than all the other silent breakdowns of faith in all other milieus or even entire regions, breakdowns in which Communism has had no role to play.

These reasonable warnings can bring to the fore a certain disconcerting paradox: the faith, which was made to be proclaimed, seems difficult to live in precisely those places where it needs to be proclaimed.

This appearance of a faith too weak to be able to endure contact with atheism has to be eliminated: faith was made to conquer the world — and where it seems, by contrast, to be the victim rather than the victor, what we are dealing with is not the faith itself, but the way we live the faith, a life that has distorted or left something essential out of the faith.

It is worthwhile clarifying the question, because it bears on the evangelization of the world we live in. There are two things we need to discern:

- whether the modern forms of atheism represent for Christians insuperable or only barely superable temptations;
- or whether, by contrast, these atheist milieus are places God intended us to be, places that provide situations that can stimulate the vigorous growth of faith within us so that it can be proclaimed to others.

According to my own experience, this second possibility is the true one; and others have had the same experience. I know that this judgment is nevertheless too subjective to work as material for a theory or a system. But, for me, it is no less certain: because it is a fact.

I have no intention of recounting my memoirs to you! . . . That would be a bit tiresome, both for you and for me! I will thus limit myself to a sort of "selected highlights." . . . In any event, the theme of this conversation will be: *"The atheistic environment: a situation favorable for our own conversion."*

Going Back to School: Memoirs of an Unprepared Student

From the moment I reached the age of reason, my parents had determined that I would become a pianist — perhaps I showed certain aptitudes . . . but nothing that would qualify as "genius." Nevertheless, my other studies had to hunt for moments that were not already claimed by the piano. I thus grew up without any real school discipline.

But I also — and this was a piece of luck! — grew up without any social compartmentalization: my family was patched together from every possible material; and *a fortiori* so was I. Because of this chaotic situation, from the time I arrived in Paris at the age of about thirteen, Intelligence with a capital "I" occupied first place in my scale of values.

Since my family was not Christian, and since we were continually uprooted because of my father's railroad job, from the age of seven to twelve I received instruction in the faith at the hands of several remarkable individuals. In Paris, however, other remarkable individuals offered me a contradictory formation. By the time I was fifteen, I was a strict atheist, and the world grew for me more absurd by the day.

As for work, I imagined I would be a "do-it-yourself-er" in a universe that was completely impervious to the intrusions of politics.

At the age of twenty, my intellectual religious search ended in a radical conversion.

I was thus a recent but relatively independent convert when, in 1933, with two companions, I arrived in Ivry in order to live the Gospel there freely.

Just in case, I had finished a degree in social work.

There were many surprises awaiting me in Ivry. In the first place, these surprises were social.

- The inequality of living conditions, the conditions of the working class at this time — before 1936 — was shocking to me. (These people had no vacations their whole lives outside of Sundays and feast days. . . .)
- These social surprises were connected with a Christian surprise.

The Christians who were living there seemed to be perfectly accustomed to what I found shocking. The three factories that paid the lowest salaries were owned and operated by Catholics who lived on the premises.

In Ivry and the surrounding region, "Christian" factories were building churches.

There was also the surprise of living in a Communist city. At the same time, I learned what a Communist city was — I, who had always been ignorant of anything about Communism other than the fact that there had been a revolution in Russia. A red flag was continuously flown over city hall. The city walls were plastered with all sorts of posters, which were changed with a remarkable frequency, announcing the most diverse local events: soviet films, ideological conferences, strategy meetings, county fairs, civil baptisms, red easters, etc.

What was also a surprise was the difference between what I saw in the Communists and what I had been told about them. In the streets, people greeted each other cheerfully by raising their fists. In the low-income housing developments, the children classified those in the enemy camps as the "Cocos" and the "Clerics" and waged arranged battles against each other. The Communist government that ran Ivry refused certain privileges or aid depending on what school the children attended, or whether they had a membership card, etc.

And once we were found out as "clerics" we became as much the target for rocks in the streets as the priests themselves. The Christians in our parish provided us with a carefully compiled list of all the Communist businesses that only traitors could patronize.

Out of a desire for the facts I once attended an election rally for Maurice Thorez, which packed the biggest theater in Ivry. "Maurice," which is the only way he was addressed among his Ivry comrades, showed up carrying an enormous spray of red roses; the crowd rose to their feet, held aloft their fists, and intoned the *Internationale*. I don't remember if it was on this night or some other similar occasion that I heard the *Marseillaise* sung and understood for the first time its original inspiration.

Finally, there was the surprise of direct contacts with Communists: my first were the "basic" contacts with the Communists in my quartier. Then, soon after, I had the daily contacts and collaborations with the council on community projects. They were the sorts of projects that any city council would organize insofar as they were indispensable for running the city. To have refused to work under such circumstances with the administrative managers of the city because they were Communists would have been tantamount to a citizen's strike.

The relationships I developed in the quartier and at work enabled me to understand *who* the Communists were and, through them, *what* Communism was.

I came to know in them generosity, disinterested work, and the self-sacrifice of those deeply involved; I came to know — and not because I was proselytized — their warm and cordial acceptance, once their walls of *a priori* mistrust fell down. The respect and affection I gave them I have never yet taken back.

It was at this point that I took up my studies in "Marxism." The way my newfound friends thought and acted provoked in me question after question concerning their ideology. Wanting to avoid giving facile responses to these questions, I searched for answers among the orthodox texts of Communism.

The Ultimate Surprise of Going Back to School

As I worked more and more with the Communists, and as I came to agree with them more and more about the scandals in the world we share and the effective measures required to eliminate such scandals, I came up with a decisive solution that seemed to work for everyone: I would leave them their atheism and hold onto our God, and together we would fight for human justice.

Before actually making this decision, I thought it would be a good idea to reread the Gospel from cover to cover. At that point, though I had never left it behind, I had started gradually to become a specialist in a few particular passages, to which I constantly returned: those in which Christ lashes out at the evil Pharisees and the rich and calls out for help for the poor; passages in which Christ seemed to be the revolutionary leader of the little ones and the oppressed. It was a sort of need to be honest that led me to undertake a complete rereading.

All the while demanding that I love my Communist friends infinitely more than I already loved them, the Gospel shed a mercilessly clear light on the fundamental disagreement that separated me from the Communists, to the point of showing it was an irreducibly different order. I was terribly bothered. . . . So bothered that I ran out and bought a pamphlet published by the Communists called *Lenin and religion,* made up entirely of citations from Lenin himself.

The pamphlet was as brief as it was effective: the Communist position with respect to religion was stated with all desirable clarity and firmness. Lenin explained by turns:

- that Communism and religion were radically incompatible;
- that the destruction of believers' faith was one of the primary tasks of Communism, necessary for the carrying through of its own mission;
- that faith could not be the "private affair" of a member of the party;
- that the question of a priest belonging to the party was a question of the priest acting in contradiction to his own conscience and not a question for the party;
- and that discussions were useless weapons against religion, what was needed was joint work with the believer accompanied by instruction.

A few passages allowed me to see precisely what level of treatment I was receiving.

All of a sudden, everything was resolved. I recalled that I was a recent convert — I was and still am someone bedazzled by God. It was and still is impossible for me to place God on one side of the balance and, on the other, all the goods of the world, whether they be for me or for the whole of humanity.

I explained things such as I saw them to my comrades . . . and since then I have reexplained them whenever the need arose. At Ivry, I agreed to work with them for circumscribed and temporally defined goals whenever these goals coincided with the Lord's commandments. And I refused every time that working with my comrades meant working directly or indirectly against God. Each time it was called for, I pulled out my references: the words of Christ. Moreover, I also refused to jump "from one activity to another" without taking the time between them to reflect and to pray — and that kept me from getting blindly caught up in the system. . . . Such has been my procedure for the last thirty years.

"Selected Highlights" from My Years at School

A practical course on the "Church militant."

We have to learn that the life of war is not just life in the barracks. We have had the opportunity to learn, on many occasions, in simple everyday life, that there is a noticeable difference between doing military service in the barracks and doing it during a time of war.

Centuries of generations in which Christians lived among Christians have transformed for us — apart from the various exceptions that the historian could no doubt lay before me — the life of the Church militant into life in the barracks. In countless milieus, regions, or professions, faith was taken to be more or less hereditary. The definition of the Christian was confused with that of the "well-meaning individual." The nonbeliever was thus a sinner with a bad will.

In these times, you could perform hundreds of fancy maneuvers, attend hundreds of higher schools of strategy, . . . without ever getting wounded, or laid up, without ever knowing the threat of death. We have lost our muscles in precisely those places where our age is striking blows to the Christian life; right where we should know how to fight, we have learned above all to argue.

It is precisely *this* life of faith, which is atrophied in essential aspects, sometimes overburdened with foreign elements, that was sent reeling in the contacts with modern atheist milieus; it is this life of faith that has given clear signs of weakness, this life of faith that made us believe and made others believe that faith — real faith — is impracticable precisely where it needs to be proclaimed.

But the true life of faith holds fast and grows strong in the atheist milieu. It knows ahead of time that it is destined to take some hard knocks, and though it doesn't go out looking for them, it is reassured when they come. It is a life that finds peace in battle and for which a soft tranquility is suspect.

We have to learn that the faith of the Church militant is by nature violent.

Conversion is a violent event. From its first pages, the Gospel calls us to *metanoia* — be converted, which means turn around; don't look at yourselves, but face me.

Baptism brought about this violent reversal. But this conversion can be something we are either fully or just barely conscious of; something fully or just barely deliberate; something fully or just barely free.

Conversion is a decisive moment in which we turn ourselves away from what we know about ourselves so that, face to face with God, God can tell us what he thinks of our life and what he wants to do with it. At this moment, God becomes something very important to us, more important than anything else, than any other life, even and especially our own.

Without this radical and overwhelming primacy of a living God, a God who calls to us, who proposes his will to our heart, which is free to answer "yes" or "no," there is no such thing as a living faith.

But if this encounter means being totally bedazzled by God, in order for it to be totally true it has to be total darkness. To have a living faith means being so blinded by it that we can be led by it; it is hard for us to accept what has been called "the dark light."

At the school of Ivry, you learn that conversion and the violence it entails lasts a whole lifetime.

We constantly tend to turn this new life, this new world, in which the "dark light" is our guide, into our old life, and into a world made by human hands: a life in which faith turns nothing on its head; a world with which faith unblinkingly comes to agreement.

Without God's vigilance, which keeps faith true by testing it, we would fall into these compromises. It is so fascinating to watch God's imagination at work in the lives of the saints . . . and to see it also at work in the lives of the people we know were simply trying to be Christians all the way. Through the extremely varied circumstances and events of each one of these lives, we see a reason that needs to obey faith in order to be itself; Christian hope compelled to transcend human hope, Christian love exploding human love. Despite the variety of forms, these lives make manifest a single life; and the same conditions needed for it to grow and be fruitful.

The trials of faith that occur in a Marxist environment seem to me no different. But, in order to keep these trials from crushing us, we have to be fully certain of the fact that these trials represent the normal condition of our life, that the forms they come in change nothing about the task they are meant to carry out in us. It seemed in the past that the cloisters had a monopoly on these trials: the teachers of mysticism presented them in their religious habits — today, they march down the street wearing everyday clothes. Maybe that's why we don't always recognize them.

And we could find enough examples of this to write a new *Interior Castles* or a new *Ways of perfection*.

The Disappearance of God and Solitude

What can be the sorest trial for us in a Communist city is the disappearance of a God who had been until then for us visible and graspable. The sign of this disappearance is a total "uselessness" of God that is vividly expressed in the life of the Communists as well as in the life of the city as a whole.

The corollary of this disappearance is the blinding epiphany of man, of his value, his power, and his collective destiny. For if the exceptional Communist milieu of Ivry — made up of national, regional, and local leaders who have all been doctrinally formed according to the level of their responsibility, as well as the basic militants entrusted with the most diverse of tasks, from the hanging of posters to administrative positions, and including the responsibilities of para-Communist movements, of educational or cultural groups, or of international meetings — if this milieu is at once a demonstration of indisputable personal virtues and effective human activity in full force, it seems as if we could do just as well without God. Nothing and no one seems to be any worse off for his absence.

The moment we cease to see such a milieu as a *trial,* it turns into a *temptation* — a temptation that is all the stronger to the extent that we are gradually able to look at things that used to be for us signs of God, *with* the eyes of our comrades and our friends.

And we see that these signs are necessarily opaque if you do not already know in advance what they mean.

At the same time, in spite of the deepest affections, we begin to feel that the faith, which makes us love others more and more, is making us strangers to them. It can happen, at this point, that we begin to accuse faith, either under our breath or out loud, of being foreign to this world. This is a profound suffering. If we do not see the necessary test that is here concealed under temptation, we would very easily fall to it. But if, on the other hand, we believe in the one who called us and who remains faithful to those he calls, if we ask him to teach us, then he will explain to us what we need to know in order to be living converts, what we may have forgotten or perhaps never really knew: that faith is a gift from God.

As a gift from God, faith, which is foreign to the world, is given to the world. To believe is to consummate between faith and the world an eternal covenant within time.

If faith creates people who are faithful, it is not a fidelity of blood, country, or honor, but a personal fidelity to the living God who calls and to whom the one who is called must respond freely and always with the whole heart of a free human being.

In order to hear this call and answer it, we need solitude. Solitude ceases to be painful and becomes instead the indispensable place wherein

God makes contact with us. Prayer reinforces the roots of solitude — it transforms the way we see all community in the Church — the trees that together are meant to make up the forest are individually given life by their solitary roots. We learn that in order to offer us faith God calls each of us by name, and that faith is not a privilege due to heredity or good behavior . . . and that it is the grace of knowing that God gives grace, the grace of being in the world committed with Christ to his mission of Redemption.

Once we have returned to the state of conversion, we learn that faith in the Son of God and the Son of Man binds us indissolubly both to the God who grants it and to man, the man of creation, humanity as a whole. For we too are able to say "all for one and one for all." Each of us has received faith on behalf of all of us.

The solitude into which we are driven by God brings us into conscious solidarity with every living human being that comes into the world, with all of the nations that Christ will gather together on the last day.

Faith and Time

The accusation of anachronism that we sometimes want to murmur against the faith can be either a harmful temptation or a trial that reinvigorates us. It gives us the opportunity to learn that the faith we possess on behalf of all human beings is the engagement of God's eternal love in time. "Faith will pass away," says St. Paul: it will endure in each of us as long as we ourselves endure. It will pass away with the world when the world itself passes away.

As often as we get accused of idealism, we begin to ask ourselves, even if we are not philosophers, whether we have made faith a philosophy without even realizing it. We ask ourselves whether faith has maintained, in our living it out in practice, the realism that belongs essentially to it, the realism of a life that can be lived only *in* the life of the person we are, in this person whom God has created and who moves, evolves, and changes. It seems that, supposedly in the name of Redemption, we sometimes tend to annihilate a little of creation: under the pretext of being Christians, we sneak away from the human condition. In these extreme instances, we treat faith the way mediums treat "spirits": the spirits may inspire them and speak to them, but they remain so to speak floating above them. Or even more commonly, we might be able to say: "I am in faith like a fish in water." But faith is given to us so that we can become it and so that it can become us.

As for ourselves, God created us at a particular moment in the history of his universe as subject to the laws of creation. These laws do not only bind us to time, but to a time that affects who we are. The faith that God gives us in 1964 is a faith for 1964. The goal of this faith is not to perpetuate the things it makes for a particular age and that ought to pass with that age. Faith is made so that the eternal love of God would be revealed to people in every age of history. It is made for every development and every tempo. The faith that so many people have carried within them as they walked the streets will also not leave the man who blasts off into space in a rocket ship. Faith would no doubt need less training for such a feat than our body would or perhaps even our courage. Faith is consecrated to eternal life, but is no less mobile and multidimensional than our human projects.

An Unexpected Guide

The new times and their guide.

We are not the first people ever to have the mission, as Christians, to break in a 'new age.' Others before us had to tread unknown soil without being able to imitate a precursor or companion. But God will always be a father; he does not test us just in order to lead us into temptation. If necessary, he will send us guides . . . as well as the grace to recognize them. . . .

With the dawning of each age, such guides come forward. Today, Paul VI is the pope of the Church *in via;* he wants to discover the image of Christ and the meeting with the world in forging ahead. To help us find this road, many guides have pointed it out to us. To recall them to mind or to mention them would take too much time. So I will speak of only one of them: John XXIII. He is inseparable from the spiritual lesson I have been talking about with you. He was the last master in this regard: and he was unexpected. He brought us back to where we needed to return: to nursery school.

"A Tiny Little Miracle"

I once read a kids' book with this title; I think that God gave to the poor kids we are — poor kids who are not true children — "a tiny little miracle." This miracle is John XXIII.

I am not trying to be funny by speaking of this huge person who was a great pope with the words, "tiny little miracle." In an age of vast human discoveries, in an age in which humanity has advanced its comprehension of the universe at an alarming speed, if we had asked for a miracle, we would have requested a marvel of cosmic proportions . . . or at least, in the Church, sudden and universal transformations. We would have asked for something staggering and immense. The wonder that we received, however, is not the one, I think, for which most of us were looking. What we got was a pope, an old pope, who came from among the poor, a man among men, a priest among priests, a bishop among bishops. This pope took on the speed of our age. He set himself to work as if he had at his disposal a life with untapped resources. He worked as one who knows he is doomed to die. He knew that Christ had redeemed time, each age and every age. He did not stand about tidying up the wings, and taking the first occasion that arose to step away from a situation that was antipathetic or incomprehensible to most of the world. He kept himself as busy as he could; he took the words of Christ literally, knowing that the palaces and administrations would be unable to keep them on their own. He lived them with his peasant realism. What he himself did not have the time to do, he left alone so that God could sort out the weeds from the grain. He let decay occur, content just not to help it along.

This pope extended open arms to the whole world and embraced it. He was everybody's neighbor; he left to Providence whatever he did not have the time to accomplish of the destiny of classes, races, and masses. He took from the modern world the voice that technology offered him in order to reach each person of whom God was father, to the four corners of the world.

He was the humble, faithful, and resounding witness of the good and fatherly God. He bore witness that he belonged to God just as each living person does. He considered himself as real as all the human beings created by God. He allowed us to understand that only if our will is disputatious will it be taken captive by Christ's mission; that this mission is free when the one who carries it out obeys the one who entrusted it to him.

But he reminded us that if Christ's Gospel is meant to be proclaimed in human tongues, it cannot be separated from the very language of Jesus Christ, and this language is goodness. He reminded us that the goodness that had lost so much of its value in the world . . . , and even among us, was with our heart the flesh of love. By the end of the very first weeks of his pontificate, many among us realized that we were Gospel illiterates. He spoke to us of the "works of mercy" as if he were speaking about a lesson from nursery school. And we didn't even remember their names anymore. But when he "put one of them into practice," the nonbelievers at their television sets, their radios, or their newspapers, marveled as if they were witness to an unknown phenomenon.

All he did was stand at the threshold of the heart of each person, not as a judge, but as a friend, ceremoniously reserving to God the discernment of good or bad will. On this fear-convulsed planet we live in, he did not wait for the slow-coming peace measures for which he worked in order to become himself a pacifist. He bequeathed to us the security of his realism, that of a peasant who knows when to reap and when to sow. He taught us that, whatever soil we may have in our world and in our age, the words of Christ are immutable laws, and they will not pass away before the heavens and the earth themselves pass away.

When he died, while so many nonbelievers wept, we at least had the consoling gratefulness that he had lived. But we still have to settle the debt analogous to the one that all those who have known saints have to settle: it remains to us to do what he taught us . . . whether we live at Ivry or anywhere else.

John XXIII showed us that, even for a pope, it is possible to live a Christian life in our world and in our age.